TINGS

foundry

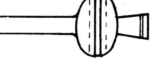

CW00558043

TAPERED

PARALLEL

**FLAT OR
RECTANGULAR**

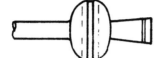

LONG FLIGHT

**TAPERED WITH
CUT-OUTS**

**PARALLEL WITH
CUT-OUTS**

ROUND

SHORT FLIGHT

HEXAGONAL

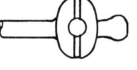

CURVED FLIGHT

**HOLES FOR PEGS
DRILLED OR
DRILLED & TAPPED**

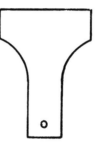

LARGE CURVED

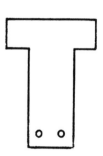

T-SHAPED

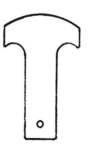

EDGE TOOL

ORNAMENTAL

SHAFTS

**BALLS &
FLIGHTS**

SPRINGS

MUSICAL HANDBELLS

A Comprehensive History
of the Bells and their Founders

Roger Smith performing at Bartholomew Fair about 1760

MUSICAL HANDBELLS

A Comprehensive History of the Bells and their Founders

William Butler

Phillimore

2000

Published by
PHILLIMORE & CO. LTD.
Shopwyke Manor Barn, Chichester, West Sussex

ISBN 1 86077 118 1

Printed and bound in Great Britain by
BOOKCRAFT LTD.
Midsomer Norton

Contents

FOREWORD

There are in the UK several thousand people, young and old, who have been captivated by the musical sound of the English handbell. The magic of the instrument is that anyone can pick up a handbell and create a tuneful sound. And two or three people can soon create a repertoire of simple tunes just by ringing two or three bells each—it's like sharing the keys of a piano and just playing the ones in front of you.

Tune ringing on handbells can be performed as a solo or in a team. Handbell sets can be as small as twelve bells and as large as 170, with music as simple as a nursery rhyme or as complex as a Rossini overture.

There are handbell ringers all over the world—UK, USA, Japan, Korea, Canada, Australasia, Singapore, Hong Kong, Finland, Estonia, France, Switzerland—and they all refer to themselves as 'English Handbell' Ringers. All nationalities acknowledge the origin of the musical handbell but I suspect that few know the development of the instrument they play.

In its heyday in the north of England, there was a large handbell set (a 'Long' set of between 140 and 170 bells) in many towns and villages of Lancashire and Yorkshire. As well as providing entertainment for the villagers, these handbell teams performed at concerts and for radio broadcasts. Competitions were held with significant prizes and people travelled great distances to see and hear these teams perform. Many of these handbell sets still exist intact and their history is well documented. In contrast, in almost every parish church where there are tower bells to call the parishioners to worship, there is also a small set of handbells. The history of these bells is usually lost in time and the only guide to the origin is the shape or a few marks on the crown. There are many occasions when news will come of 'a set of Warners' or 'some Shaw bells' that have appeared at a rally from an unknown source and with no history. How many ringers can explain to a newcomer the significance of this find or the background to these instruments that we so reverently admire?

For the first time, the information has been put together that traces the history of the handbell from early references in Nineveh through the heyday in the UK in the 1800s to the modern handbell. This has been a mammoth task for Bill, a work of much dedication but also I suspect of great reward as he uncovered new mysteries and made new revelations.

In the 20th century, bell founding in the UK has declined to the state where we have only two producers of handbells remaining. Over the past thirty years under the auspices of The Handbell Ringers of Great Britain, handbell ringing has once more grown in popularity in the UK. Alongside this growth has come the influx of handbells manufactured in the USA, which has helped to sustain the growth in demand for new bells. We should not forget, however, that all the technology of manufacture and tuning that has resulted in the modern handbell was developed in the UK over a period of 200 years.

I continually receive enquiries from around the world for a definitive work on the history of English handbells and handbell ringing. We now have the first of these works and I shall have no hesitation about directing enquirers to this volume. Handbell ringers and historians will welcome this important study of the origins of our instrument.

Alan Hartley

ALAN J. HARTLEY
Chairman, Handbell Ringers of Great Britain

Acknowledgements

When a book such as this has been compiled over the course of a quarter of a century, an enormous number of people will have been consulted. Besides the many letters I have received I have spoken with ringers at rallies and been able to examine their bells. I have given talks on the history of handbells and profited from the exchange of information afterwards. I have corresponded with ringers from most of the countries where handbells are rung to give advice or to supply information.

I have been privileged to inspect bells from several ringers' personal collections. First and foremost I should mention the Sharpe collection and the late Elizabeth Sharpe, who allowed me to examine her father's bells in the months following his death. It was this inspection which inspired this book. This collection, now owned by the Sharpe Trust, is housed in the Pitt-Rivers Museum at Oxford. I must also acknowledge the assistance given by the collections of Alan Collings, Maurice Davies, George Francis, Rev. Barry Fry, Allan Keen, Dick and Mary Lee and Jean Sanderson. The museums at Devizes, Hereford, Mary Arden House and Salisbury have also helped by allowing me to examine their collections.

I am also grateful for the help and advice given by Allan Keen on the Aldbourne Foundry, Christopher Pickford on the Rudhalls and the Bonds, and Neil Skelton for his help on the Blackbourn Foundry at Salisbury. Valerie Payne has contributed from her family researches into one of her ancestors, Henry Symondson, and Cyril Wratten has supplied many extracts from his extensive investigations into local papers. Alan Hughes gave valuable assistance with the chapter on Whitechapel, as did Colin Banton with the one on Loughborough. The references acknowledge help from many other individuals.

The extract from Larousse Encyclopedia of Music, 1977, is given with the permission of the publishers, Hamlyn Publishing Group. The majority of the photographs and drawings are my own work, but I must thank Michael Goodman of Norwich for supplying Figures 45 and 120, and Alan Hughes and his staff for producing Figure 26 from my rough draft.

I must also thank Jean Sanderson for her steady support and subtle nudging by finding me interesting handbells from time to time! Bobbie May helped me considerably by proof reading one of the 'final' drafts! Lastly, I must thank my wife Jennifer for finding me the right phrase when I was frequently lost for words and for her constant help and encouragement throughout the whole of this project.

To all these people and anyone else I have inadvertently omitted I give my heartfelt thanks; this book would have been the poorer without your help.

Author's Note

I began this book in the spring of 1976, shortly after the death of Frederick Sharpe. whom I knew well, having worked as General Secretary to the Oxford Diocesan Guild of Church Bell Ringers whilst he was Master. He had a spendid collection of old handbells and was planning to write about them some time in the future but alas, it was not to be. He died before committing any of his knowledge about them to paper. I had acquired my first set of handbells some thirty years earlier and had been interested in their history ever since. I thought I could follow on after him and publish a worthwhile book. Little did I know what I was undertaking!

During the next few years I researched what had been published and found most of it to be contradictory and speculative. In many cases, very little attention had been paid to accuracy: one writer's supposition had been treated as fact by another and so it has continued. I have made a positive effort to distinguish clearly between facts and assumptions and have included many references so that other researchers can substantiate what I have written.

During the 1970s and 1980s much of my spare time was taken up with other commitments. I followed Frederick Sharpe as Master of the Guild and this involved a great deal of travelling about the Oxford Diocese. I also compiled a Centennial History of the Guild, a massive undertaking in view of the size of the Guild and the 360 ringing towers involved. I took over as Chairman of the Central Council of Church Bellringers' Education Committee and wrote three technical books for them. Despite these obligations the research continued together with the hunt for new founders.

Retirement seemed an admirable time to complete this book, but it has still taken six years. There are gaps in my narrative and many details yet to be discovered. This offends my scientific background, but it cannot be avoided in a pioneering work. I trust readers will forgive conclusions surmised incorrectly when details are scarce and will tell me of any errors or new facts they find so that future editions will reflect more truthfully on the history of this fascinating subject.

William Butler
February 2000

Other titles by William Butler
Doubles and Minor for Beginners (1980, 1983); *The 'Waiting to Ring' Book* (1983); *Triples and Major for Beginners* (1986); *A Beginners' Guide to Change Ringing on Handbells* (1988); *100 Years of the Oxford Diocesan Guild* (1981); *Thatcham—Then and Now* (1983)

SUBSCRIBERS

Doreen Addyman
Raymond Aldington
P.E.T. Allen
Geoff D. Armitage, BA, MBHI
John Baldwin
John, Adrian and Christopher Bates
Bath and Wells Diocesan Association
David Beacham
David E. Belcham
Alan John Blair
Mary Bliss
Vivien G. Bloundele
Mary Teresa Blurton
Nigel Bullen
Roger Button Esq.
C.F.M.
Chiltern Handbell Ringers
Christchurch, Herne Bay, HR
A.E.H. Clayton
Raymond J. Clayton
Elaine Clipson
Ranald W.M. Clouston
Alan J. Collings
Bryan Cope
Vic Cox
Anthony J. Crabtree
Robert J. Crocker
A.M.C. Crowther
Heather B. Dark
Kenneth R. Davenport
Nick and Brenda Davies
George A. Dawson
Mrs. Gill Dean
John Alfred Dietz
W.H. Dobbie
Geoffrey and Joyce Dodds
Pauline L. Dover
John N. Dunn
Dr. John C. Eisel
Dr. M. Ellender
Jenny Elmes
Vaughan P. Evans
Malcolm Fairbairn
Graham and Katharine Firman
Anthony Kesseler Fortin
George Francis

D.A. Frith
Revd. Barry J. Fry
Pat and Peter Furniss
Alec Gammon
William L. Gates
Michael Goodman
Maureen Grice
Catherina Griffiths
Barbara J. Groat
Stuart Hale
Mr. Richard Hartnell
M. and P. Hatchett
James Hedgcock
Geoffrey C. Hill
Robin John Hine
D.A. Holmes
Stanley Huckle
William H. Hulme
Terry J. Jefferies
Roy H. Jones
Allan G. Keen
R.I. Kendrick
W. John Kinchin
Judith A. Kirk
James Kirkcaldy
Gordon H. Lane
Keith Lane
Brian Langworthy
Roger and Christine Lazenby
Walter A. and A. Mary Lee
Roy Lemarechal
Colin A. Lewis
David Livingston
Frank D. Mack
Mr. S.J. Marsh
George and Hilda Massey
Rachael Matsell
K. and K. Matthews
Bobbie May
Janet Menhinick
Ian and Helen Meyrick
Middlesex County Association and London
    Diocesan Guild of Church Bell Ringers
Mary Miller
Richard D. Minard
Michael P. Moreton

Wilfrid F. Moreton, M.B.E.
David and Anne Mumford
Margot Munns
Norbury Handbell Ringers
John P. Partington
Chris Pickford
Beryl Pierson
David Pobjoy
Leonard R. Porter
Miss Emma Radwell
Simon and Molly Rennie
Roy Rice
Peter Rivet
J. Robertson
Carla J. Runciman
Gwen Sampson
Keith W. Scudamore
William F. Scudamore
Miss Kay Seaman
Elisabeth Seymour
Andrew J.A. Sheldon
Mrs. V.P. Sissons
Kay and Chuck Sittig
Neil Skelton
Arnold J. Smith
Elizabeth Anne Sutherland
Margaret Taylor and Graham Button
Colin Thomas
Gwen Torrance
Philip J. Tremain
Jenny Tyack
Upton W.I. Handbell Ringers
Clarke Walters
Robert J. Walters, MNIA (Rusty)
Timothy D. Waterman
D.G. Wheeler
M.J. Whilden
Michael V. White
Marianne Wicks
Michael Wicks
Jane and John Willis
Lysbeth C. Wilson
Malcolm C. Wilson
David Wootton
Michael Wycherley

One
THE DEVELOPMENT OF
THE MODERN HANDBELL

1   Assyrian bells found at Nineveh

2   Angel ringing handbells from St John's, Stamford, Lincolnshire

3   Acolytes ringing handbells, from Bayeux Tapestry

SMALL BRONZE BELLS have been made for thousands of years. Most early civilisations had them; archaeologists excavated many on digs in the Middle East in the 19th century. Figure 1 sketches part of an Assyrian hoard found by Layard at Nineveh.[1] A principal use of these bells was on the harness of their horses, donkeys and camels, and the nomadic wandering of the tribes, the plodding of itinerant merchants and, above all, the marching of triumphal armies spread the use of bells all over the known world.

It is generally supposed that small bells were not used in music until the advent of musical handbells. However, *The Larousse Encyclopedia of Music* states:

> We should also remember that such percussion instruments as cymbals, triangles with jingle rings and various types of bells played an important part in 14th and 15th century music and musicians did not even hesitate to combine bells with a clavichord and a psaltery.[2]

These bells were not rung but suspended from a rack and struck with hammers. Many illuminated manuscripts show King David striking bells in this manner and a reproduction from the Worms Bible is portrayed in the next chapter. However, the 15th-century roof of St John's Church, Stamford, Lincolnshire, shows an angel ringing two handbells in a typical modern style! (Figure 2.) Compare this with the acolytes ringing handbells at Edward the Confessor's funeral depicted on the Bayeux Tapestry in Figure 3.

From the 16th century small bells were used for a variety of purposes, all connected with attracting attention. The town crier used his bell to gather a crowd; tradesmen used them to draw customers. During the plague a primitive type of bell of the type illustrated in Figure 4 was rung to warn householders that the plague cart approached. However, most small bells were used by the farming community to keep track of their flocks of sheep

1

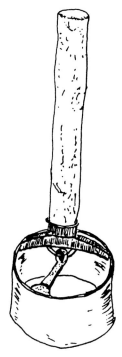

and other animals. The use of bells on sheep and other animals was once widespread. Ancient Irish literature shows that they were used from earliest times, the bells being similar to the Irish Saints' handbells. Sir Henry Dryden first pointed out that there was a fundamental difference between these early handbells and those used for sheep or cattle:

> In the former the mouth part is as wide or wider than the top part or shoulder, but in the latter the mouth is generally narrower than the shoulder. It may, indeed, be assumed that the latter shape is earlier than the former.[3]

The two types are illustrated in Figures 5 and 6.

Thousands of this second type of bell were made during the 19th century. Formed from one sixteenth inch thick metal, the clappers were generally of iron with a bulbous head, the other end being hooked over an iron crown staple. This was often formed in one piece with the canons, which were usually in the shape of a flattened letter M. Large bells of this type were used on cows and other cattle; the smaller were reserved for sheep and goats. One is illustrated in Figure 7. Rev. H.T. Ellacombe describes how the Potter family made these bells at Market Lavington, Wiltshire in the mid-19th century:

> Sheet iron is bent into the form, then riveted together. The intended bell is then bound round with narrow strips of thin brass; some borax is added as a flux, and the whole being enveloped in loam or clay, is submitted to the heat of a furnace, by which the brass is melted and gets intermixed with the heated iron, so rendering it sonorous. Otherwise they were plated with brass, the iron being first dipped in tin, as plated articles are now produced.[4]

4 Home made plague bell used in London 1666

These bells were plentiful in south-eastern England. As you go further north and west their use became less and less common until it was almost absent in Scotland.

Some Sussex sheep bells were made of smelted, or charcoal iron.[5] The largest of these, sometimes called a cluck, was put on the impetuous sheep that ranged far and wide over the downs. Smaller bells, termed cluckets, were reserved for the more placid members of the flock! A shepherd could tell where particular sheep were by the sound of their bells. They also acted as a warning: an agitated jangling might indicate that a sheep was being worried by a dog. Sheep stealers were deterred by them as any disturbance of the flock at night could warn the shepherd. Variations in the shape of these bells may be found. There are square canister types, similar to the cluckets but squarer in section. Rounded canister types also exist. These were formed by curving a flat sheet of metal into an open ended cylinder and riveting it together. A flat or curved top was then made and the two parts brazed together. The bell was finished by brazing another piece of metal in the form of a circle to the crown, thus making the canons.

A few miles from Devizes is the village of Great Cheverell. Amongst the population of 500 in the early 19th century was a family called Potter living at Winsmore's Mill. It is more than probable that

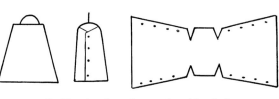

5   Template for early type riveted handbell

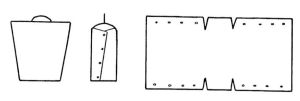

6   Template for riveted cattle bell

7 Nineteenth-century cattle bell

they were related to the family of the same name who lived at Market Lavington a few miles away, and whose manufacturing methods have been described. At Great Cheverell they made edge tools till the beginning of the 20th century,[6] but between 1827 and 1880 they specialised in sheep bells. The last of them to follow this occupation was James Potter, who was also described as a farmer.[7] He ran the bell founding business from the forge adjoining his house at 42 High Street.

It is likely that his successor was William Lancaster, who built up this business to a remarkable degree at his blacksmith's shop in Townsend. His bells were beautifully shaped, fastened by leather thongs cut from old harness to wooden yokes, lovingly carved from gorse wood. Until his death in 1919 he sent these bells all over the country, supplying them in eight different sizes. An example of a trade card issued by him can be seen in Figure 8.

An interesting legend concerning small bells from this part of the country is the tale of the phantom bell of Wilcot, a small village only eight miles from Great Cheverell. This ghostly bell became known nationally in the reign of James I: people made pilgrimages to hear it and it is said that even the King sent a delegate to make a report. The story started one night in 1624. One of the ringers was making his way home after a particularly boisterous evening at the inn when he conceived the idea of having a late night ring at the church. He called in at the vicarage and demanded the key; the vicar naturally refused and the drunk went away muttering threats of vengeance. He went to see a noted Devizes wizard, named Cantle, and told him the story. Cantle is supposed to have said, 'Does the vicar not like ringing? He shall have enough of it!' From

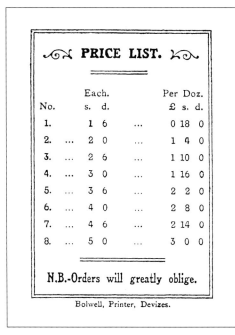

8 Both sides of William Lancaster's trade card

9 Hemispherical sheep bell by Robert Wells

10 Ancient crotal found in barrow at Headington Hill, Oxford

11 Crotal by Robert Wells

that time on a small bell sounded continuously in the vicar's bedroom. It could not be heard outside the house and the sound was lost if the listener put his head outside the window. Cantle was arrested and lodged in Salisbury Jail. He said that the bell would not stop ringing until he died … and it didn't!

Another sort of bell used extensively, especially for sheep, was the bronze hemispherical bell, illustrated at Figure 9. These were generally cast by established bell founders: James Burrough of Devizes is said to be a mid-18th-century manufacturer of them.[8] A prolific founder of these bells was Robert Wells, of Aldbourne, whom we will discuss in greater detail later on. These bells all contained cast-in iron crown staples and iron clappers. Gossett reports that these bells were still being made in quantity in 1909, and sold by weight at one shilling per pound.[9]

The crotal, or rumbler, was also used. This was cast as a complete sphere with a single opening, consisting of a slot joining two holes, a metal ball being placed inside before casting. Some of these are of very ancient origin. Figure 10 illustrates one found in a barrow on Headington Hill, Oxford. Examples may be found in all the early civilisations.[10] Moses was instructed to prepare robes for Aaron with bells of gold around the hem.[11] The cope of Lanfranc, the 11th Archbishop of Canterbury, was decorated with 51 bells.[12] Douglas Hughes has written an interesting account of how these bells are cast.[13] From 1763 to 1799 Robert Wells, or his son Robert, cast many of these, varying in diameter between one and six inches. They may be identified by the initials R W on them. An example is shown at Figure 11. Another 18th-century example, possibly by Thomas Swain, is in the Wiltshire County Museum, Devizes, and is illustrated at Figure 12.

Small crotals were used on bridles. Morris quotes the use of them on the horses of pilgrims visiting the shrine of St Thomas à Becket at Canterbury.[14] Others were worn between the ears of the horse. Hip bells were fastened to the back band of the harness on draught horses so that they lay on the hips of the horse. They are extremely rare now.

Traditionally shaped bells were also used for sheep and other animals. Figures 13 and 14 are typical examples. Many, made of brass, were cast by the thousand in the Birmingham area during the 19th century and exported to South Africa and South America.[15] Dozens of small foundries produced these bells: an account of some of them is included in a later chapter. They were not tuned, although Rev. W.L. Bowles, writing in 1828, describes how a Shaftesbury eccentric, Lawson Huddleston, would travel around the countryside, tuning all the sheep bells to an exact musical scale.[16]

Small traditional bells were hung on the hames, the metal collar to which the traces are fixed. An Assyrian sculpture in the British Museum shows two horses drawing a chariot with bells attached thus.[17] Neck bells similar to those given to sheep and oxen were sometimes given to horses. It was possibly to this type of bell that the prophet Zachariah was referring when he said that 'Holiness unto the Lord' should be upon the bells of the horses.[18] Figure 15 is a drawing taken from Ellacombe which illustrates a bell inscribed 'Campana Thomae'; this was found in the Thames and is thought to have been worn by the horse of a pilgrim going to Canterbury.[19]

12 Crotal by Thomas Swain

13 Sheep bell of traditional shape

14 Animal neck bell

15 Bell probably used on a pilgrim's horse

Bells of this type were gathered together into sets to form what are known as box, or latten bells. Strictly speaking, latten refers to an alloy of copper, tin, zinc and lead, the metal formerly used for monumental brasses. However, country folk gave the name latten to these sets of bells as they thought they were made of a similar sort of metal. These sets were a great feature of the old-time horse teams and were developed by the Cors at their Aldbourne Foundry at the end of the 17th century. Bells had been used for many years before that time on horse- and ox-drawn wagons: the Cors' contribution was to take a number of these bells and tune them so they formed a pleasant cadence as the team swayed its way along the narrow country lanes. Approaching carters would hear this and could halt where the lane was wider to let them pass. Daniel Defoe notes in his journal during a tour of England between 1724 and 1727 that they could be heard as the wagons loaded with wheat and grain were brought to market.[20] At fairs and festivals they would prove a popular attraction: James Bridgman, a later founder, travelled around the Berkshire and Wiltshire fairs in the mid-19th century with a stall at which he sold all types of bells that he had made at his Aldbourne foundry.

Each wagon set comprised four units, or boxes, one for each horse. Three of the boxes would contain four bells, the other taking the three largest bells. The box was generally constructed with an iron frame with two spikes which passed down into the harness. The top would be covered with a leather fringe, sometimes plain, but more often ornamented. Two of these are illustrated at Figure 16, together with a set of large crotals. Figure 17 shows an alternative method of support. An excellent description of the use of these bells is given by Thomas Hardy:

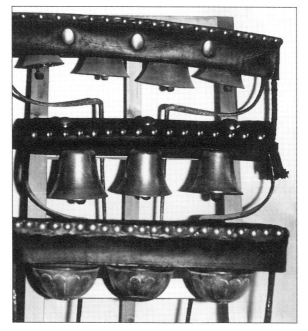

16 Two sets of Latten bells and one of crotals

17   Latten bell set by Robert Wells

18   Set of ox bells by Robert Wells in the Hereford Museum

A load of timber was to be sent away before dawn that morning to a builder whose works were in a town many miles off. The trunks were chained down to a heavy timber carriage with enormous red wheels, and four of the most powerful of Melbury's horses were harnessed in front to draw them.

The horses wore their bells that day. There were sixteen to the team, carried on a frame above each animal's shoulders, and tuned to scale, so as to form two octaves, running from the highest note on the right or offside of the leader to the lowest on the left or nearside of the shaft horse. Melbury was the last to retain horse bells in that neighbourhood; for living at Little Hintock, where the lanes yet remained as narrow as before the days of turnpike roads these sound signals were as useful to him and his neighbours as they had been in former times. Much backing was saved in the course of a year by the warning notes they cast ahead; moreover, the tones of all the teams in the district being known to the carters of each, they could tell a long way off on a dark night whether they were about to encounter friends or strangers.[21]

Similar sets of bells were used on ox teams, but these became very rare after oxen were no longer employed on the roads. They may be found occasionally collected together in a frame as in the set by Robert Wells illustrated in Figure 18, now in the Hereford Museum. A set of this tremendous weight was probably affixed to the wagon.

The modern handbell has been developed from these musical latten bells. In the early part of the 18th century ringers observed these bells and took them to practise their change ringing in the warmth of the hostelry rather than in draughty towers. From there it was a short step to their use for carols and traditional country tunes and the birth of the musical handbell.

Two
THE FIRST HANDBELLS

BEFORE I DISCUSS how handbells were made, I ought to explain how large bells were manufactured prior to the 19th century. A core was made of loam, similar in shape to the interior of the bell, then a false bell of clay or wax was formed over it. An outer mould was then built around this and the whole baked. If wax were being used, it ran out and was recovered: this was termed 'the lost wax process'. If clay were being used for the pseudo-bell, the mould was separated and the clay bell broken up and removed. The two parts of the mould were then re-assembled and molten bronze poured into the vacant space.

Theophilus, an 11th-century monk, describes a process broadly similar to this in an early treatise, *De Diversis Artibus*.[1] Two centuries later Walter de Odyngton, a monk at Evesham, explained the principle of casting bells of different notes.[2] He pointed out that by making a bell thicker, its note would be higher. He accomplished this by weighing different amounts of wax and coating it over a core of fixed size. This produced bells of roughly the same exterior dimensions, but varying thicknesses of construction.

19 Illustration from Worms Bible

The Worms Bible of 1148 shows a man playing with two hammers on an octave of small bells and it is noticeable that all the bells appear to be the same size.[3] Figure 19 reproduces part of this illustration.

The problem with casting church bells of constant diameter and varying thickness is that the higher notes of the thicker bells overpowers the lower notes of the thinner bells. Founders tried altering the note by changing the diameter at the mouth, keeping the thickness at the soundbow constant. This had the opposite effect; now the deeper notes of the bigger bells drowned the smaller bells. Experiments showed that a combination of the two produced the best results, so with bells of average weight, the ratio of diameter to the thickness is usually fifteen to one. With lighter bells of three to four hundredweight the ratio decreases to thirteen or fourteen to one and for even smaller church bells it is approximately ten to one.

If musical handbells were cast to these ratios, the bass bells would be much too heavy for tune ringing. Large handbells of this type are useful for attracting attention. In 1605 Robert Dowe presented one for an unusual purpose to St Sepulchre without Newgate, Holborn Viaduct. He left instructions that 'twelve solemn tolls with double strokes' should be rung on it at 10 o'clock on the night before an execution outside the window of the condemned cell at Newgate.

20 Robert Dowe's handbell

After this, the ringer was to call on the prisoners to repent, telling them that, when the passing bell rang for them on St Sepulchre's tenor the following day, all godly people listening would pray for them.[4] In 1888 the Charity Commissioners altered the terms of the original gift to use the money for helping deserving prisoners.[5] The redundant handbell, illustrated here as Figure 20, may still be seen in the church.

To produce sets of wagon, or latten bells the founder needed to revive a technique that church bell founders had discarded years before. This involved designing bells to a standard thickness, but with different diameters.

Bronze casting is an ancient skill; man has practised it for nearly five thousand years. In the Middle Ages, casting in sand developed into a fine art. Bell founders discovered that small bells could be cast in loam sand, using a pattern bell. The process was quick compared with the traditional method of casting a bell, and, more important, once a pattern had been made, all the bells cast from one of its moulds would have similar characteristics. The materials were to hand. Naturally occurring clay bonded sands are common in England and the early handbell founders certainly had access to them. Experiments showed that the sand had to contain five to fifteen per cent of clay to bind it together. These days foundrymen use a variety of loam sands dependent on the type of casting they are making; for instance, they might make up a synthetic mixture by adding ten per cent of a mineral clay, such as bentonite, to washed sand.[6]

Pattern bells had to be prepared. It is interesting to speculate how the first ones were made and of what material they were constructed. Later founders used bronze; in the late 19th century James Shaw used white metal patterns.[7] Some members of the White family used an existing handbell as a pattern, moving it slightly in the sand mould to allow extra metal for tuning. Early sets

21 Moulding box and pattern bells

of latten bells were not tuned, but remained maiden bells.[8] As customers became more discerning, bells had to be tuned and patterns needed to be oversize in order to remove metal. Often the founder placed his name or initials on these patterns to identify his bells. Eighteenth-century founders usually placed their initials in relief on the inside waist of the bell; it is possible that this was done by marking the pattern bell, but much more likely by impressing the initials or founder's mark in the sand of the core. However, as it became more common to tune a bell by removing metal from inside as well as the outside, later founders inscribed their initials on the crown of the pattern. When bells started to be numbered, these too were inscribed on the top of the pattern.

When the sand and pattern were ready, the latter was placed mouth down on a flat surface and a casting frame, rather like a bottomless box, put around it. Modern founders now use an iron box as in Figure 21. The pattern was covered with a separating media or parting powder—talc, mica or bone flour— and then sieved sand was pushed firmly around the lower part of the pattern, forming the exterior shape of the lip, waist and shoulder of the bell. The sand was smoothed off and a second frame accurately positioned over the first section using the guide pins. More parting powder was sprinkled over the upper part of the bell and a peg of wood was placed on top of the argent, the part of the bell to which the strap is attached, and more sand rammed around. The peg would later be removed to provide the channel for the molten metal. When all was firm, the sand would be smoothed off level to the top of the box.

The two sections of the box now had to be carefully turned upside down as in Figure 22. Another box frame was added and aligned by the guide pins. Dry dusting powder was sprinkled over the exposed sand and the inner part of the pattern to aid the later parting of the boxes and the removal of the patterns.

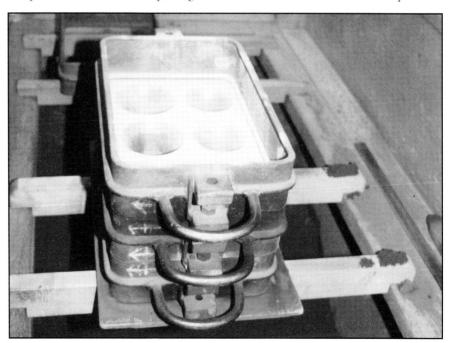

22 Moulding box turned upside down showing inside of pattern bells

23 Removing pattern bells

More sand was carefully sieved into the box, tamped down and levelled off. The three sections of the box were then turned upside down, yet again, and the top part carefully removed to expose the crowns of the patterns. The second section could now be lifted off, totally exposing the pattern bell, which could now be gently separated from the core or inner mould by a smart tap as in Figure 23.

At this point, 18th-century founders inserted an iron loop, or crown staple into the sand. Part of this staple would protrude above the sand core, and would be cast into the crown of the bell. The cast-in staple was used to suspend the iron clapper for latten sets: if the bells were to be used as handbells the staple would be broken off. The peg could now be taken out of the upper box and the three boxes very carefully reassembled. This was a very sensitive operation: bells are very thin castings and all the foregoing work could be ruined by an unsteady hand! All was ready now for pouring the metal.

Bell metal is an alloy of copper and tin. Whitechapel handbells usually contain about twenty per cent of tin, the remainder being copper. Taylors tend to use a higher proportion of tin, usually twenty-three per cent.[9] The more tin added to the alloy, the brighter and more intense the sound, but there is a penalty: the bell becomes more brittle and liable to crack. In the 18th and 19th centuries founders used alloys with a lower proportion of tin: this is one reason why their handbells sound less bright. The quantity of tin added to the alloy can alter the note. Elphick reports that bells of the same size and thickness sound differently according to the proportions of the two metals.[10] More tin will raise the pitch. Some founders have increased the tin content for smaller bells to increase the intensity of sound.

24   A primitive lathe operated back and forth by a lath

The founder melted the copper in his furnace and then, just before he poured the metal into the prepared sand moulds, added the tin. The two metals have vastly different melting points. Copper melts at over one thousand degrees Centigrade and tin at less than two hundred and fifty. If the founder added the tin too soon it would evaporate and the resulting castings would be low in tin. As we have seen, this would alter the characteristics of the bell.

Imperfections in castings are often caused by poor control of the molten metal. With very thin castings like handbells it is preferable to keep the metal as hot as possible. However, raising the temperature too high can make the surface of the cast bell too rough or 'pebbly'. Allowing the oxides, which form a slag on the surface of the molten metal, to pass into the mould can cause holes to develop. Pouring too quickly can wash some of the sand from the surface of the mould: these can result in irregular shaped depressions on the casting.[11] All these faults may be seen in 18th-century handbells and also in some 19th-century founders' work too!

When cool, the bell would be broken out of the sand and the riser, the metal stem through which the mould was filled, would be cut off. The first latten, horse and handbells were left as cast; as time progressed they were roughly finished with a file. Many examples may be seen of these. When ringers demanded bells for practising change and tune ringing, improvements in pitch and tone were required and it became necessary to tune these rough-cast bells more accurately. Early in the 18th century lathe tuning was introduced.

Lathes have been known from ancient times. The first probably consisted of two dead centres fixed between two tree trunks an appropriate distance apart. A cord would be wrapped around the work, and an assistant would pull this and rotate backwards and forwards the piece being turned. The turner would sit on the ground and hold the cutting tool. In later times the cord would be attached to a lath or thin stick fixed above the work-piece, looped around the work and culminate in a noose into which the turner placed his foot. The work was then rotated by treading down, the lath acting as a return spring. The word lathe is thought to be derived from this process.[12] An illustration of a lathe of this type with a lath attached above and below may be seen in Figure 24.

The French developed the wood-turning lathe in the Middle Ages, and by the 17th century foot-operated treadle lathes, able to rotate work continuously, were fairly common. An example is shown in Figure 25. The Industrial Revolution in England in the 18th and 19th centuries demanded greater precision in machine tools and the lathe was adapted for use in removing unwanted metal.[13]

25   An early continuously rotating treadle lathe

From about 1740 they were put to good use by the handbell founders who could now tune their bells more efficiently. Removing metal made their bells thinner and so brought them down to pitch.

Robert Wells was one of the earliest founders to tune his bells on a lathe. Many examples of his work exist; his bells are quite common. He would start off by turning the largest bell in each set till it had a reasonable finish and then tune the remainder of the bells in the set to this bell. For instance, if the largest bell were cast as a 22,[14] it would normally be considered to be a C. However, by this process it might finish up half a tone either side of C, i.e. anywhere between B and C sharp. This is the reason why duplicate bells from separate sets often differ considerably.

Most old sets are pitched differently from modern handbells. The tuning fork is said to have been invented by the trumpeter, John Shore, in 1711.[15] However, they were not used in tuning bells until the introduction of Simpson tuning in the late 19th century.[16] Bell tuners like Henry W. Haley and his son William, for instance, were celebrated for the acuity of their hearing and perfect pitch, but they broadly set their own pitch.

The situation was very confused anyway, for pitch varied from country to country. Taking the note A, Philharmonic Pitch in England was 424 cycles per second in 1813; over the next fifty years it was gradually raised to 455 cycles per second, mainly by the makers of wind instruments who were seeking a more brilliant effect.[17] In France, Continental Pitch was set at 435 cycles per second in 1885. At an International Conference in May 1939 the pitch of A was fixed as 440 cycles per second,[18] and this is now the standard to which modern handbells are tuned.

Besides the strike note, handbells sound partials or overtones, some of which are pleasant and others less so. Old sets of handbells used for tune ringing sometimes demonstrate this! Modern handbells are tuned to have an overtone of one-twelfth. If you take a new bell size 22C, its pitch will be the same as middle C on the piano, i.e. 256 cycles per second. If you strike it and then lightly touch it at the lip, the strike note will be dampened and you will hear the harmonic. This will be 11G, 12 diatonic notes higher, resonating at 782 cycles per second. Many old handbells that are pleasing to listen to probably have this harmonic occurring naturally due to the shape of the bell.

After the bell had been tuned, the inside of the crown was drilled to take the clapper staple and a hole made in the argent so the leather strap handle could be riveted on. Handbells have a peg argent which is slightly tapered. Elphick[19] suggests that the first handbell founders to cast bells with these were the Cors of Aldbourne; I shall discuss this family in detail in the next chapter. The argent nearly always sits on a raised disc of metal slightly larger than the argent on the crown of the bell: I usually refer to this as the button. On the inside of the crown some manufacturers placed a concave depression around the iron loop, or crown staple, which held the clapper. These buttons and depressions are often characteristic of a particular group of founders. Figure 26 illustrates the various types.

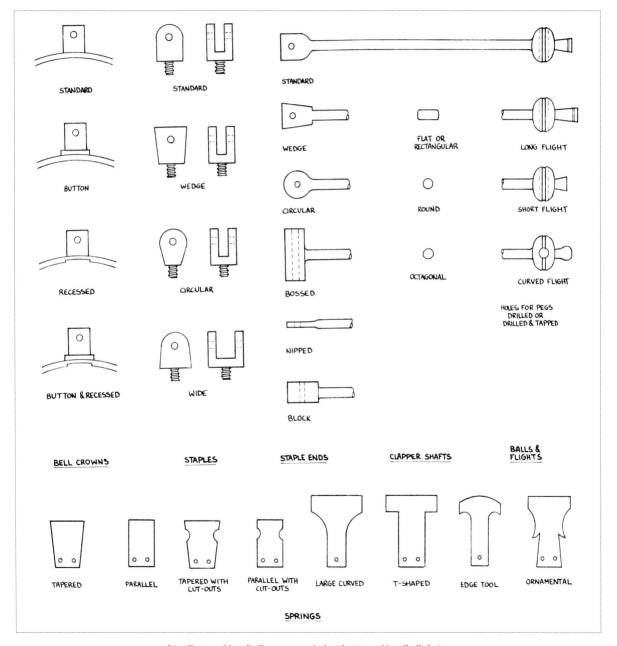

26 Types of handbell crowns and classification of handbell fittings

As I mentioned in an earlier paragraph, most 18th- and many early 19th-century handbells were made with cast-in iron loops, or crown staples. Before being drilled for a handbell clapper assembly these would have been broken off. All the bells made by Robert Wells I have seen have remnants of these loops, even those that were intended for musical handbells.

Modern clapper assemblies are screwed into the crown of the bell. The first clapper staples did not have a screw thread, but were pushed into a drilled hole and pegged by a pin through the argent. Many of these old staples have been maltreated and broken by being twisted. Before dismantling an old handbell it is advisable to check this point first by removing the strap handle.

The clappers of musical handbells move in one plane only. It was soon realised that, if the clapper were held off the bell after it had struck, the bell would vibrate freely and give a clearer sound. To accomplish this thin pieces of sheet metal were attached to each side of the staple to act as buffers and restrict the movement of the clapper. Many types of these springs have been used and their shape is often typical of the founder. Figure 26 also classifies many of the types of fittings found.

Circular leather caps were not fitted on the first handbells, but were generally in vogue by the end of the 18th century. Each cap has a rectangular hole cut in it to pass over the argent and then the leather strap is riveted to the argent. Ornamental designs are usually stamped on the leather work: these are often individual to the founder and can be used to identify him. The White family had a tradition that each member of the family made his own ornaments.[20] Later chapters give details of the leather stamps of founders.

Three

THE COR FOUNDRY

ALDBOURNE IS A pleasant village, nestling in a fold of the Wiltshire downs. Today's narrow streets differ little from those of the early years of the 18th century when there was a flourishing bell foundry situated here. To find the origins of the foundry it is necessary to go back even further, to 1642, the time of the Civil War. At that time a gunsmith called William Cor lived here with his wife Mary. No doubt his business thrived during that stormy period when King and Parliament struggled for supremacy. It is not known whose side he was on, although much of the surrounding area was for Parliament, but it is known that he outlived the conflict, surviving until 1668. It is interesting to note that *Tintinnalogia*, written by Richard Duckworth from nearby Oxford and the first book on the art of ringing, was published in the same year. William Cor's will shows he was survived by five sons, Robert, William, John, Oliver, and Allen.[1]

A copy of William's family tree, compiled from various sources, is given at Figure 27. The name Cor may be spelt in several different ways. On tower and handbells the family spelt it as COR; on documents referring to members of the family it is usually given as CORR. Indeed, when they signed their names they used the latter version. Sometimes a variant such as CURR is found. I intend to follow the practice adopted by them on their bells and use COR throughout this book.

Little is known about the eldest son, Robert, apart from the fact he too worked with metals. According to his father's will, he kept William's 'great vice' in his workshop; this was bequeathed to Oliver. As the eldest, Robert had probably followed his father in the trade of gunsmith. He may have been single or a widower, for the will did not mention his wife, although it did for those of William's three youngest sons. Robert survived his father by only three years. It is clear from the will that the second son, William I, had left home and was not expected to return, for arrangements were made for his legacy to be distributed amongst his brothers if he did not come back and collect it. I shall have more to say about this brother in the next chapter.

The next two sons, John and Oliver, are known from contemporary documentary evidence to be bellfounders, although no church bells of either of them are known to exist. John's will, dated 19

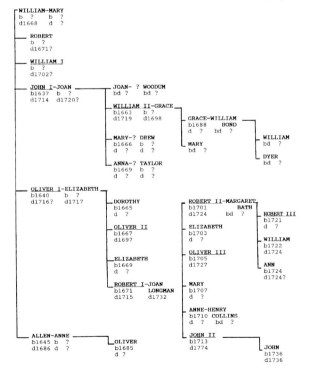

27 The Cor family tree

October 1714, describes him as a bellfounder.[2] There is not much more known about him, apart from the fact he probably had little schooling, for he did not sign his will, only making his mark. However, it was the custom in those days to leave the drawing up of a will to the last possible moment and it is possible that he may have been too weak or ill to sign. The information available on his brother Oliver is more extensive. His father bequeathed him a pair of foundry bellows and an iron anvil, as well as the vice that was in his brother Robert's workshop. These indicate that he too was working with metals at that time. Another source, a private Act of Parliament,[3] describes how Oliver Cor of Aldbourne, Bell Founder, made a Settlement, dated 25 March 1699, on his son Robert, who was about to marry. Yet another reference to him was found by Lukis in the churchwardens' accounts at Marlborough, when he charged £39 for work on St Peter's bells in 1698.[4]

Allen, the youngest, is referred to as Allin in the inventory of his goods taken after his death in April 1686.[5] This indicates that he had a six-roomed house, with a workshop in an outhouse containing a furnace valued at two pounds ten shillings. The total value of all his goods and property was £42. The Letters of Administration granted to his wife, Ann, show he was a gunsmith.[6]

Returning to John and Oliver, what else is known about these men? Nothing extra has yet been discovered about John. Oliver may have been better educated: his signature appears in a number of documents in the Aldbourne records. A tracing of it, taken from a deed of 1703, appears in Figure 28.[7] He served as a churchwarden for two years, from 1688 to 1689, a post normally held by the more influential members of the village. He had money and property, both perhaps acquired by marriage. Towards middle age he moved away from Aldbourne and traded as a merchant in London. He died some time before his wife Elizabeth, who was described as a widow when she was buried at Aldbourne in 1717. I shall call these brothers John I and Oliver I to distinguish them from later members of the family. As may be seen from the family tree, John I married and had three children. His eldest child and only son, William II, also became a bellfounder. Oliver I had four children, one of whom, Robert I, succeeded to the bellfounding business of his father. There is no documentary evidence to suggest his elder brother, Oliver II, was connected with the foundry, although I strongly suspect he cast handbells: he died in 1697, aged thirty. Although this is a book primarily about handbells, I shall need to refer constantly to the church bells each founder produced, because tower bells are often dated, whilst handbells rarely are. Beginning with Robert I, church bells by him have been identified from 1694 onwards.[8] William II and Robert I cast a bell together in 1696,[9] whilst the first church bell attributed to William II alone is at Faccombe, Hampshire, dated 1699.[10] This bell has both churchwardens' names on it, one of whom was Thomas Lake. I shall refer to him again later in this chapter.

According to their names on the bells, William II and Robert I individually cast nine bells each and 81 together. Of the latter, 35 are in Wiltshire, 19 in Oxfordshire, 14 in Hampshire, six in Gloucestershire, five in Warwickshire and one each in Berkshire and Dorset. It is surprising that so few exist in Berkshire, for the county border is only eight miles away. It was not the competition:

28   Oliver Cor's signature

Samuel Knight, the Reading founder, had moved to Holborn, London, to widen his sphere of operations. One problem, however, that faced the Cors wherever they traded was the isolation of Aldbourne. Until the Turnpike Act of 1814, the only road in and out of the village was a rough track to Hungerford.

William II married some time before 1688, for in that year the baptism of his elder daughter was recorded; she was called Grace after her mother. They had one other child, a daughter called Mary. Apart from his bells, small and large, little else is known about William II, although the churchwardens' accounts for Aldbourne record that he looked after the clock and chimes from 1712 to 1719, receiving from them the sum of £3 per year.[11] His wife died in 1698 and William II himself in 1719. His will is signed with a fair hand; a tracing of his signature is given at Figure 29.[12] The inventory of his goods taken after his death shows he had £10 in his purse, a considerable sum, and that his stock in trade and the debts owed to him totalled £250. It makes no mention of a workshop; it seems he had no premises of his own and worked out of his cousin's shop. William divided all his estate between his two daughters, with the strict proviso that they should look after his widowed mother for the rest of her life.

29 William II Cor's signature

William II's cousin Robert I was eight years his junior. He owned several properties in the village, one of which had been ceded to him by his father as a marriage gift. He ran a profitable wooden button making business.[13] He also followed in his father's footsteps by becoming vicar's warden from 1706 to 1711. In 1699 he married Joan Longman from Binley, near St Mary Bourne, Hants, and her father-in-law Oliver I gave her £200 as a wedding gift. Expressed in equivalent purchasing power today this would be worth more than £25,000.[14] Joan's father, Robert Longman, was a man of property in St Mary Bourne. He was churchwarden in 1699 when Robert I cast two bells for the parish,[15] and this is obviously when Robert and Joan met. Over the next 14 years Robert I and Joan had six children, the three boys, Robert II, Oliver III and John II all following their father and grandfather in becoming bellfounders.

An interesting fact, which has only recently come to light, is that Robert I and Joan owned the foundry as a partnership. An inventory of Cor property taken in 1735 records:

> Joan and Robert Corr did carry on the joynt trade of a Bell ffoundry by way of partnership … [16]

This inventory also valued her work clothes in the Cor Bell House at £2, showing she was an active partner in the business. She may have attended to the casting of small bells such as horse bells, handbells and crotals or rumblers.

Their business prospered and, with more work, Robert I found it necessary to resite the bell foundry. In 1713 he purchased from Elizabeth Bond a large property known as the Court House, together with the land surrounding it and 'the pigeon house thereon standing'.[17] Elizabeth Bond, who had been left the manor of Aldbourne by her husband, George, had earlier sold East Leake Farm to Robert I's father, Oliver I, then described as 'a merchant of London', at a peppercorn rent for 200 years, provided he paid £67 a year to the crown.[18]

However, difficult times were approaching for the family. Robert I died in 1715 at the comparatively early age of forty-four. All his children were under age. The eldest, Robert II, was only 14, so Robert's will appointed two trustees to see to their education and take care of their finances until they reached the age of twenty-one. One of the trustees was John Longman, Joan's brother, and the other was Thomas Lake, described as a 'kinsman', the churchwarden of Faccombe, mentioned earlier. Both of them lived more than twenty miles away. It seems odd that Robert's cousin William II, who lived only a few minutes away, was not chosen as a trustee.

Why was William not chosen? His name appears on church bells with Robert's and it has always been assumed they were partners. Indeed, it is usually suggested that William was the senior partner, for not only was he older but his name invariably appeared first on a bell. However, William is not mentioned in Robert's will, either as a partner, a beneficiary, or as a trustee of his children. One possible reason for not choosing him as a trustee was his age: at 52 he might not expect to see them reach their majority.

John Longman, Joan's brother, had inherited his father's properties about 1706, for the records show he then took over paying the tithes on them. He also succeeded him as churchwarden at St Mary Bourne. He was granted administration of Robert I's estate, but it is not clear whether he did very much. Robert II was the new owner and, although only 14, managed the foundry with his mother's and uncle's assistance. A half interest in the tools of the business was left to 10-year-old Oliver III, together with the Court House, where the foundry was situated, and various other properties in Aldbourne. Three church bells from the firm bear dates between 1716 and 1719 and the names of William and Robert Cor.[19]

In 1719, whilst still only 18, Robert II married Margaret Bath of Ashbury, a village about eight miles away. She bore him two sons, Robert III, born in 1721, and William a year later. The latter died in 1724, aged two years, followed by his father, who was only 23 years old. He died intestate and his wife administered his estate. The foundry was managed by his mother Joan, with the assistance of Robert II's 19-year-old brother, Oliver III. In the next three years Oliver III cast 11 bells. He too died very young, aged only 22. He died intestate and unmarried, so the tools, Court House and other property passed to Robert III. Once again Joan tried to cope with the business, this time assisted by her youngest son John II. The strain was too much for her and she died intestate in 1732.

The affairs of the family were now in a precarious state. Robert I's eldest daughter Elizabeth was granted administration of her mother's estate and also tried to replace her as manager of the foundry. Difficulties abounded; her father's money had all been spent and her mother's was nearly all exhausted, and the legacies left by her father had still not been paid. She quarrelled with her brother John II who was actually running the foundry and eventually the family split into factions and would not work together.

John II was only 15 years old when he cast his first church bell, for Chieveley, Berkshire in 1728.[20] During the next 13 years he cast 17 more, two of which, for Durley, Hampshire in 1730, bore the initials, 'J and R Cor'.[21] This is surprising because Robert III was only nine years old at the time. It is possible that Margaret insisted that her son's name should be cast on these bells to demonstrate his ownership of the foundry.

Margaret, Robert II's widow, who had been left with the infant Robert III, took a new husband, Edward Westall, in 1732. She had spent most of her own money in discharging foundry debts incurred by her late husband, so she and her new husband decided to try to obtain some compensation for her financial losses by bringing an action against the Cors and John Longman, whom they alleged had failed to administer Robert I's estate properly. No doubt to the relief of all concerned, the matter was settled amicably. The private Act of Parliament mentioned earlier was passed to enable Robert III, the actual owner of the foundry and other property, to sell six dwellings in Aldbourne. This realised the sum of £1,080, which paid off all the outstanding claims, including the debts incurred by members of the family in running the estate and businesses. Margaret Westall had her dower paid and all the costs and expenses of the action she had brought were met. The residue was divided between Elizabeth, Ann and Mary Cor, the three daughters of Robert I. Robert III, who was now 17 years old, had equal shares with his uncle John II in the tools and foundry equipment and the Court House in which the foundry was situated became their property as tenants-in-common.

One of the last bells cast by John II is dated 1741 and is at Great Bedwyn, Wiltshire. Two others, at Houghton, Hampshire, are by 'R Cor' and dated 1742. H.B. Walters, writing in 1929, considers this date to be an error for 1724 and considers the bells to be the work of Robert II.[22] However, it seems unlikely to me that a founder would transpose two figures in the date on two separate bells. The churchwardens' initials are cast on one of the bells and some time in the future an enterprising campanologist will settle the matter one way or another by checking if they match the wardens elected in 1742! It would be nice to consider these bells Robert III's individual contribution to the art of bellfounding, made when he was just 20 years old.

The Cors did no more bellfounding. John II retired and died in 1774. Robert III concentrated on the other business developed by his family, wooden button making.[23] He vacated the Court House, bought by his grandfather in 1713, which had originally been a hunting lodge for John of Gaunt, Duke of Lancaster, and moved to the Curr Farm House.[24]

Turning now to the handbells produced by the Cors, William II has, in the past, been credited with being the first to cast these. This may be true. However, a careful examination of a large number of Cor handbells has brought to light some interesting new facts which permit a different interpretation. Their handbells have rounded shoulders and flared lips. They are not tuned as such: occasionally there are file marks in a horizontal direction around the waist and skirt parallel to the lip as may be seen in Figure 30, but they are generally left as sand-cast.

30 Horizontal file marks on an Oliver III and Robert II Cor bell

31 One type of Aldbourne dabchick

32 Another type of dabchick

33 William Cor's trade mark

34 A second trade mark of William Cor

The argent sits on a small raised pad of metal about an inch in diameter on the crown, and inside the bell there is a depression in an equivalent position. Their bells always have a cast-in crown staple, often quite substantial. The majority of their bells contain the name or initials of the founder cast in relief on the waist inside the bell. In many cases this is accompanied by their trade mark, a bird, also cast in relief. This has been variously described as a swan, a pheasant or a duck. However, it is more likely to be a dabchick, for this was used as a nickname for Aldbournites for many generations.[25]

The story of how this nickname arose is worth recording. One day, a strange bird is said to have appeared on the village pond. No-one knew what it was, so they brought out the oldest inhabitant, placed him in a barrow and wheeled him round the pond. After asking to be wheeled round twice more he pronounced the bird to be a dabchick. Villagers from Ramsbury, who saw many of the birds on the River Kennet, mocked the locals with cries of 'Dabchicks!' and the name stuck.[26] It is interesting to speculate which came first, the nickname or Cor's trademark. A dabchick is, by the way, another name for the little grebe, a type of short winged, almost tailless, diving bird.

Dabchicks are rarely used without a name or initials. However, some have been found: Figure 31 shows one on a bell in the Collings collection. Figure 32 is taken from a bell in the Sharpe collection. On this bell no initials are visible at first sight; they are tucked up on either side of the cast-in staple in the crown! The bird in Figures 32 to 34 perches on a circle or letter O; this has often led to bells being credited to Oliver. Some writers have indicated that a crescent is used:[27] I am sure these crescents are caused by poorly executed impressions of the circle with part of it missing. The photograph of the William Cor bell from the Fry collection in Figure 41 shows this clearly. Figure 42 illustrates a similar bell from the Collings collection on which the founder's fingerprint may be seen!

The different varieties of dabchicks found and their irregular placing on bells indicates that dabchicks were not cast on the pattern bells. They were probably formed by impressing a sheet metal or wooden die into the sand moulds once the patterns were removed. Lost, worn or damaged dies would need replacing, hence the different varieties.

Modern founders have found it useful to engrave their name or initials on the crown of their pattern bells; this enables all their castings to carry their name in the same place. The Cors would have found it difficult to do this because their initials are placed in relief inside the bell; the impressed letters would be damaged in removing the pattern from the sand mould. Robert Cor was remarkably consistent in placing his letters, which leads me to suggest he had a block made up with his name. It is significant that, when bells are credited to both William and Robert, the latter's initials are regular whilst the relative position of the W is not. I have not seen enough examples of Oliver and Robert Cor's bells to determine if the same is true of their bells.

I have traced four types of lettering on the small bells cast by members of the Cor family. Type I is a sans serif alphabet of small capitals, four millimetres high, used exclusively by William. I have seen only one example of this, illustrated at Figure 40: he used only the letters, W C. Type II is a similar sans

35 Mark used by Oliver III and Robert II Cor

36 Trade mark of Robert I or II Cor

37 Used on handbells cast by William and Robert I Cor

38 Mark used by Oliver I or II and Robert I Cor

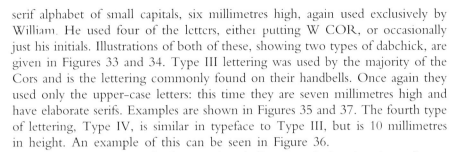

serif alphabet of small capitals, six millimetres high, again used exclusively by William. He used four of the letters, either putting W COR, or occasionally just his initials. Illustrations of both of these, showing two types of dabchick, are given in Figures 33 and 34. Type III lettering was used by the majority of the Cors and is the lettering commonly found on their handbells. Once again they used only the upper-case letters: this time they are seven millimetres high and have elaborate serifs. Examples are shown in Figures 35 and 37. The fourth type of lettering, Type IV, is similar in typeface to Type III, but is 10 millimetres in height. An example of this can be seen in Figure 36.

I now want to consider how various bells are marked and perhaps allocate them to individual founders. I have seen Cor bells marked in 10 different ways. Four of these only have lettering; one has a dabchick only and six have a dabchick and lettering. The group with lettering only are marked:

COR   OR COR   I COR   W C

Those which include both lettering and a dabchick are:

W C   W COR   WR COR   R COR   OR COR   W C I L

I think it unlikely that, once they had started to use the dabchick as a trade mark, they would have not used it consistently. Hence I think we can place the bells with lettering only in an earlier group than those with the trademark. Figure 36 shows some marks on bells in Mary Arden House Museum which have Type IV lettering with a dabchick impressed over part of the name.

We can speculate that the bell marked just 'COR' in Figure 39 is an early one; possibly dating from the last quarter of the 17th century and made by John I or Oliver I. Bells marked OR COR, as in Figure 38, would be either from Oliver I and his son Robert I, or from Oliver II and his younger brother, Robert I. The bell marked I COR in Figures 45 and 47 would belong to John I, pre-dating the handbells of his son, William.

I am inclined to place the bell marked W C in Type I lettering as shown in Figure 40 in a class of its own and will refer to it in the next chapter. William Cor's bells marked with his name or initials in Type II lettering would date from his taking over his father's work and thus pre-date his bells made in conjunction with his cousin Robert I. (Figures 41 and 42.) The bell marked WC IL in Figure 48 is an interesting one. It has a dabchick, but the bird is facing right instead of left. The lettering is very similar to Type IV. Allan Keen,[28] who found this handbell near to Aldbourne, suggests that I L could refer

39 One of the earliest Cor trade marks

40 A rare William II Cor mark

41 William II Cor mark showing damaged ring

42 A William II Cor bell showing the founder's fingerprint

43 Photograph of an Oliver III and Robert II Cor mark

44 Photograph showing leather 'springs'

45 Photograph of a John I Cor mark

to John Longman, Robert I's executor, and that he made this bell in conjunction with William II around 1715.

The other bells with Type IV lettering are by Robert Cor and I suggest that, if the previous assumption is correct, then these bells are by Robert II continuing the use of the lettering. This is supported by the fact that the only bells I have seen with this lettering are fitted with contemporary fittings of a later style.

All the Cor bells were cast with an iron crown staple or loop, from which the clappers were suspended. These were also of iron, with a hook at the staple end. When used as musical wagon bells, the clapper balls were of iron, sometimes shaped like a three-pointed star.[29] If the bells were to be used as handbells, hard wooden balls were screwed onto the clapper shank.[30]

When horse bells were first adapted for use in tune or change ringing some means had to be found to control the swing of these clappers. What may have been an initial attempt at achieving this can be found on a set of 12 Cor bells at the Mary Arden House and Country Museum. A piece of leather has been fitted over the cast-in crown staple by cutting a slot to fit over the loop. The

46 Cor handbells showing 18th-century halfpennies as washers

47 Rubbing of John I Cor mark

48 Rare mark of William II Cor and John Longman

clapper can now be hooked in, and the leather restrains its wild swinging and partially restricts its movement to one plane. The photograph in Figure 44 illustrates this. This set of bells originally came from Shipston-on-Stour and was regularly used up to the 1930s. Eight of the bells bear Robert Cor's name; the remaining four are by him and William. The bells are in an unrestored condition; some of the straps are riveted to the argent using 18th-century copper half-pennies as washers. (Figure 46.)

Sharpe records that later bells by the Cors used for handbell ringing are found with two cast-in metal plates to form a staple, enabling a more modern type clapper assembly to be used.[31] *The Ringing World* for 1990 records a set of 16 bells by WR COR in Norfolk, two complete octaves and one semitone, the tenor being approximately 15C.[32] About half the bells have the dabchick and name as in Figure 37; in some cases this has been partly filed away when tuned. The bells have clapper staples which are pushed into a hole in the bell and pegged. The clappers are of modern shape, without springs but with hardwood pegs as strikers. I'm sure these clappers and staples were fitted later and are not contemporary with the actual bells.

Four
SUCCESSORS TO THE CORS

49 Rubbing of a William Rose mark

BEFORE I CONTINUE with the work of the Aldbourne founders I must make a diversion to deal with the bell with the initials W C in Type I lettering, illustrated in Figure 40. This bell has been roughly tuned in a similar manner to another large group of bells. Several sets, a number of individual handbells and some horse or house bells have been found with the initials W R cast inside in lettering 10 millimetres high. (Figure 49.) In his collection, Sharpe queries whether these were by William Rudder of Birmingham. Despite extensive research I have not been able to substantiate this. The name is not known to campanologists and the Birmingham Trade Directories have not proved helpful.[1] One partnership 'Handasyd & Rudder' manufactured plumbers' brass ware, but no bell founders or handbell founders were discovered.

These bells usually have wide lips and rounded shoulders, similar to Cor bells. All those I have seen have been roughly filed in a diagonal manner around the outside of the bell as shown in Figure 50, together with more smoothing around the inside of the lip. All have cast-in iron staples; on the handbells these have been broken off. On one set of six the clapper assemblies are all made of iron and screwed rather than pegged into the bell. The clapper shafts are square with the edges chamfered, with the clapper balls shaped rather like two truncated cones joined at their widest part. Straight wooden pegs are used as strikers. The flights are blunt points. Long steel springs with curved T-shaped ends reach up to the balls of the clappers. One of these clappers is illustrated at Figure 51. Only one of the bells is numbered: a tiny '9' is inscribed on the crown of a bell whose note is equivalent to 12F sharp. This number is illustrated in Figure 52.

Another set of eight handbells' at Seaton, Devon, has been cast without argents, and has square holes cut through the crown of each bell. The bells have numbers inscribed on the crown; these numbers are a different size from the previous set, that for '12' has the 2 the wrong way round, as shown in Figure 52. The note of this bell is flat of 16B. Like the previous set, the bells are filed on the outside diagonally. The clapper staples have long squared shafts that pass through the holes in the crowns into wooden handles and locked into place with nuts.[2]

50 Diagonal file marks on a William Rose handbell

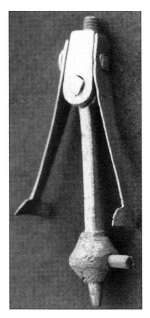

51 Early clapper of William Rose

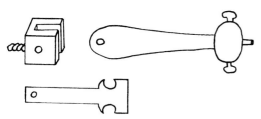

52 Differing numbers from three sets of William Rose handbells

54 Dabchick from a William Rose bell

The stems of the clappers are square, with round balls and peg flights. Long steel springs reach almost to the balls.

A third set of W R handbells has recently been discovered in an antique shop in the Hereford area. Eight of the bells have W R cast inside, the other two are plain. All the bells have been extensively polished on the exterior, but it is possible to see traces of the typical diagonal filing. They are all recessed around the crown staple hole which has been drilled and tapped. A few of the bells have numbers: these are only four to five millimetres in height, similar to the first set mentioned above. The number '6' is shown in Figure 52.

The fittings of this set are more modern than those mentioned earlier, although they are still made of iron. The staple is rectangular and the clapper is flat in section with a poorly formed ball. The flights are variable: some are tapered whilst others are of a normal shape. The long curved springs are made of sheet iron and are ornamented with cut out circles. The leather caps are small and thin compared with modern bells, but some of this may be shrinkage due to the leather drying out. The handles and caps are not marked with any stamps. Sketches of some of these fittings are illustrated in Figure 53.

House and horse bells often have twin lines five millimetres up from the lip on the exterior and some also have these twin lines at the crown. They retain their cast-in iron loops as staples and have a hooked iron clapper with an iron ball.

A most intriguing example of this founder's work forms part of the collection owned by Dr. Alan Collings. It has W R in the standard lettering on the inside of the bell, but facing it is one of the Aldbourne dabchicks! Two filled-in circles, eight millimetres in diameter, are positioned underneath the bird, one at the front and one at the back. (Figure 54.) The name William Rose has been put forward as the founder of these bells. It is a fairly common name and can be found in most of the villages around Aldbourne, although not in Aldbourne itself. After examining most of the options I consider it most likely that they were the work of William Rose of Lambourn. Members of this family were blacksmiths at Lambourn from the 17th century onwards and William was one of their common Christian names. Children were christened with this name in 1607, 1641, 1684, 1702, 1738, 1743, 1777 and 1779. In 1736 William Rose, the Lambourn blacksmith, was paid £45 to put a girdle of iron around the church tower to prevent it splitting.

The fact which sways me towards this Rose family, rather than any of those in the other villages surrounding Aldbourne, is that the Cors had connections with Lambourn, less than five miles away over the downs. In 1616 for example a John Curr married a local girl, Joanne Batt. It is possible this John Curr was a brother to William Cor, the gunsmith of Aldbourne who died in 1668 and whose sons started the Aldbourne foundry. Secondly, a William Cor was buried at Lambourn in 1702. The entry is given in this manner:

4 November 1702   William Curr of this Towne.[3]

53 Fittings from a later set of William Rose handbells

I have not found records of any other Cors in either the births, marriages or deaths in the Lambourn registers. I suggest these facts may be interpreted in the following way:

When William Cor, the gunsmith of Aldbourne, died in 1668 his will implied that his second son, also called William, had left home and seemed unlikely to return and collect his legacy.[4] This may have been over a disagreement; we shall never know, but I suggest that he finally finished up in Lambourn. When he died the addition 'of this Towne' after his name indicated that he was a long-standing resident, although not born at Lambourn. The date 1702 fits in with the dates of the deaths of his brothers, who all died between 1686 and 1714. Finally, the handbell bearing a dabchick indicates an Aldbourne connection.

The small bell with the initials W C in Type I lettering has been finished by filing in a diagonal manner similar to the handbells with the initials W R and not like those of the Aldbourne Cors, who, when they did finish their bells, normally filed them round the bell parallel to the lip. I conjecture that this bell may be by this William Cor of Lambourn, the brother of John I and Robert I. These two men were both bell founders as was shown in Chapter 3. It seems plausible that a third brother also made small bells.

On the basis of the above reasoning, I am going to postulate that a modest foundry for casting small bells existed in the 18th century at Lambourn. In the course of time they may have taken over some of the Cor patterns, or used one of their bells as a pattern. These were used by one of the blacksmiths, William Rose, to make the bells marked with the initials W R. Further research on this founder is required.

55   Rumbler bell by Edward Read

I ended Chapter 3 with John Cor having ceased founding at Aldbourne in 1741 and his nephew Robert III turned to the alternative family business of button making. For a short while no bells were cast in Aldbourne. The next bells to be made in the village were the work of a man called John Stares. Allan Keen, in his researches on the Aldbourne Bell Foundry, has discovered that in 1743 the Court House, at one time the property of Robert I, was sold by John II and William Brown to John Stares.[5] Stares was not an Aldbourne man; the deed of sale describes him as a warrener from Liddington, about five miles away. Little else is known about him. His known church bells number 16 and were cast in either 1744 or 1746. Ten remain, one in Berkshire and one in Wiltshire, and the rest in the county of Hampshire. I have not been able to identify positively any handbells by him, although some uninscribed 18th-century bells could be his work. However, crotals with his initials have been recorded:[6] one is in the Devizes Museum.

56   Mark of Edward Plumer

Edward Read may also have cast handbells at Aldbourne after the Cors had retired. Between the years 1751 and 1753 he cast nine bells for churches in

57 Photograph of Edward Plumer's mark

Berkshire and Hampshire, but only seven remain. In 1743 he was involved in a mortgage on the Court House, so he may have worked with John Stares.[7] Like others in Aldbourne, he had a second business as a fustian weaver and he appears to have followed this trade solely after 1753. He was steward of the manor for three years and in his final year appeared to get into some financial difficulties. He sold some land and property in 1759, but this did not seem to alleviate his problem, as he was declared bankrupt in 1762.[8] As with Stares, no handbells of his have been identified, although crotals with his initials are known. The photograph in Figure 55 shows one from the Keen collection.

E. Plumer, too, may have had connections with the Aldbourne foundry. No-one of that surname appears to have lived in Aldbourne in the 18th century, although the name does appear in the Lambourn registers in the seventeenth. However, the name Edward Plomer does occur in the 18th-century registers of Ramsbury, an adjacent village:

| 1701 | 6 Oct | Mary Plomer, child of Edward Plomer |
| 1713 | 4 Jul | Edward Plomer, child of Edward Plomer |

I have examined three examples of his bells, all exactly the same size, and all taken from separate collections. He cast his name E PLUMER in relief inside the bell in capital letters five millimetres high. (Figures 56 and 57.) One example has the name twice, on opposite sides of the bell. The bells appear to be of later manufacture than those of Cor and Rose; the button under the argent is much larger and the exteriors have been turned and polished. I have recently been informed of a quarter set of horse team bells by him.[9]

Handbells of an early appearance have been found with the initials W G inside. One is included in the Sharpe collection and has very rounded shoulders, reminiscent of bells by the Cors. The name of William Gwynn of Aldbourne has been put forward as their founder. He was born in 1749 and may have been related to an earlier family of the same name from the neighbouring village of Ramsbury. The surname also occurs later in Lambourn. A 1790 pamphlet about Aldbourne gives his trade as a fustian weaver; the Enclosure Act of 1806 states that he had a willow weaving shop in West Street.[10] He must have been wealthy: when in 1787 the ringers decided to augment the old six bells at St Michael's Church, he jointly gave the second bell. Its inscription is:

THE GIFT OF JOS PIZZIE & WM GWYNN OF ALDBOURN ROBERT WELLS FECIT 1787

MUSIC AND RINGING WE LIKE SO WELL;

AND FOR THAT REASON WE GAVE THIS BELL.

As the inscription shows, he was a keen ringer and he took part in the first peal on the bells, rung on 3 May 1791. Two other local bellfounders took part, Edne Witts and James Wells. At 55, Edne was probably the oldest member of the group, whilst at 19, James would have been the youngest. We know little

58 Rubbing of William Gwynn's mark (small initials)

59 Rubbing of William Gwynn's mark (large initials)

60 Photograph of William Gwynn's large initials

61 Rubbing of William Gwynn's incised initials

62 Photograph of incised initials of William Gwynn

more about William Gwynn. The parish registers note he was buried on 19 December 1813, aged 64.

He may have taken possession of the Cor patterns, or more likely used one of their bells as a guide. In addition to the bell owned by the Sharpe Trust, I have noted several other examples of his work. A bell of his in the Sanderson Collection has the usual button under the argent and no depression around the staple hole. It is 80 millimetres in diameter and has a school-bell type wooden handle. The clapper has an octagonal stem, a regular type ball and a normal flared flight. The springs are of iron with T-shaped ends. His initials on this bell are larger than on the Sharpe example: illustrations of both can be found at Figures 58 and 59. A photograph of the larger may be seen in Figure 60.

In a farmhouse in Pembrokeshire I discovered a bell with his initials inside which had no button under the argent. It had a flattish crown with smooth curved shoulders and at right angles to the argent was a trace of a mark. In other details it conformed to the other bells of his I have seen. I recently obtained another bell by him. It is a small school bell, 100 millimetres in diameter, with an iron crown staple and an iron clapper. It has, however, the initials W G engraved on the crown! I consider it to be a 19th-century bell, so perhaps one of Gwynn's descendants cast it. A rubbing from the initials is depicted in Figure 61 and photographs in Figures 62 and 63.

Before I leave William Gwynn it is worth noting that a large number of rumbler bells or crotals have been discovered with his initials. One from the Keen Collection can be seen at Figure 64. Note the similarity of the lettering to that on the bells. *The Searcher* suggests that casting rumblers must have been a family concern for a century or more.[11] It notes that the larger W G rumblers are very similar to those of Robert Wells, apart from the hanging loops which are square in shape, whilst those of Wells are circular.

Another Aldbourne founder was Edne Witts. He was born about 1737 and was descended from either Thomas or Edward de Wit, who became residents in the village about the middle of the 17th century.[12] Their name indicates that they may have been 17th-century refugees escaping from the wave of religious persecution taking place in Europe at that time. Edward de Wit introduced the art of fustian weaving into the village. Fustian is a coarse, twilled cotton fabric, originally made with a linen warp and a cotton weft, and includes material such as moleskin, velveteen and corduroy. The dictionary suggests the word fustian came from El-Fustat (Old Cairo) where the cloth may first have been made. Edward built up a good, profitable business; in 1666 he issued his own trade tokens, which had a weaver's shuttle on the reverse.

Edne too worked as a fustian weaver, but, like others in Aldbourne, added founding as a sideline. Some crotals bear his initials and handbells with his name inside can be found. The lettering he used is illustrated in Figures 65 and 66. Two small tower bells of his are known: one at Aldbourne Market House, cast in 1760, and the other, dated 1774, at Culham, some 18 miles from Aldbourne.[13] Gifford suggests that he may have been a moulder for Wells, but this is unlikely.[14] His wife Elizabeth was some ten years older and bore him at least three children. The eldest, Richard, died a baby in 1761. A second son, named Edne

64 Rumbler bell by William Gwynn

after his father, was born in 1764 and survived until he was twenty-three. A daughter, Elizabeth, was born in 1776 and lived until 1830.

As mentioned above, Edne was a member of the local band of ringers and took part in the first peal on Aldbourne bells on 3 May 1791. He rang the third bell, whilst a relative, Broome Witts, conducted it from the sixth. A photograph of the peal board is shown in Figure 67. Edne survived his wife by nine years, dying in 1808, aged 71. He was buried in Aldbourne churchyard, although his memorial stone has now disappeared.

Handbells by Witts are not common. In the Oxford Diocesan Guild Library is a copy of *The Church Bells of Wiltshire* by H.B. Walters. Annotated in the margin of page 312 in Frederick Sharpe's distinctive handwriting is:

> A set of 10 hand bells by E. Witts at Aldbourne Manor House—W A Brown.

This note is probably fifty years old and the bells may now have come on to the market.

Dr. A. Collings recently purchased a set of 13 bells by Witts for his collection. They are obviously a set, although only five are marked with E WITTS on the inside. There are no other markings on the bells. All have high domed crowns with a button beneath the argent and a

63 Photograph of William Gwynn school bell

E WITTS

65 Rubbing of Edne Witts' name

similarly sized recess inside the bell. One most unusual feature of the set is the fixing of the crown staples. A rod, attached to the iron crown staple, passes through a hole drilled the length of the argent and is fastened with a nut on top. This means that the leather strap handle cannot be fixed in the normal way. A hole is drilled either side of this independent crown staple and the handle fixed with two rivets. The brass clappers have octagonal stems and very short flights. The clapper balls are small with flattened sides and holes drilled for the wooden striker balls. The staple ends of the clappers vary from bell to bell, but are all held to the staples with iron pins.

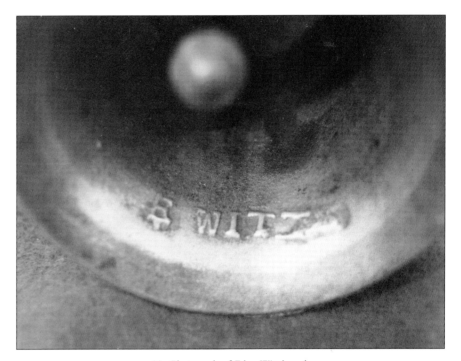

66 Photograph of Edne Witts' mark

Five

THE WELLS

THE MAJOR FORCE in handbell manufacture in the 18th century was the business of the Wells of Aldbourne. Surprisingly, very little has been published about this foundry. H.B. Walters, writing in 1929, gave some information extracted from the parish registers of Aldbourne and from this he built up a family tree which has been extensively quoted by subsequent authors.[1] Allan Keen has extracted considerably more information: what follows owes a great deal to his work.[2]

On 28 December 1713, William Wells, a blacksmith of Ramsbury, was married in Aldbourne church to Mary Reeves, also of Ramsbury. Why did they get married at Aldbourne? Keen suggests that they may have had some connection with the village: it is possible that Mary was a servant there. William may also have served his apprenticeship as a blacksmith in the village; seven years later he bought Smith's Forge, situated in the centre of Aldbourne, from John Looker.[3] They had four children and the youngest of the four, their only son, was Robert, born in 1725. There is no record of which trade Robert initially followed; as an

67 Peal board from Aldbourne, dated 3 May 1791

68 Tower of St Michael, Aldbourne, Wilts, home of many handbell founders

69   Photograph showing double stamping of R WELLS

only son he may have become a blacksmith like his father. However, during his formative years he would have noted the bellfounding work of the Cors decreasing and it is possible he saw an opportunity to take over, and build up, their small bell work. I think it most likely he made small bells many years before he started casting church bells, probably shortly after the demise of the Cor foundry in 1742. Robert married Sarah Brown, a local girl, on 4 November 1755 at Aldbourne church.[4] They had eight children of whom the two boys, Robert and James, later became bell founders.

Walters gives Robert's first church bell as at Hemington, Somerset, cast in 1760.[5] This is an error. It seems odd that this error has been perpetuated by subsequent writers for nearly fifty years. Ellacombe was 84 when he published the *Church Bells of Somerset* and he had obtained all his information by letter from incumbents, vergers and churchwardens.[6] It is not surprising that the book is notoriously inaccurate but, even so, surely some doubt must have been raised, for no bell by Wells is mentioned at Hemington. What is now considered to be his first year as a church bell founder is 1763, when he cast the 17-hundredweight tenor at East Garston, Berks.[7] It is interesting to note that the fifth, the next smaller bell, was cast by Edward Read in 1753. Almost certainly Robert Wells saw this bell cast in the village 10 years earlier. Another bell cast by Robert in 1763 was the priest's bell at Stanford-in-the-Vale, Oxon.[8] This is much smaller and may possibly have been cast earlier than the East Garston bell. About eighty of his bells remained when Walters did his survey in 1929.[9]

His foundry was said to be in Bell Court, a house at the south-west corner of the village green.[10] Another author suggests that he also used the Court House 'and other foundries in the village'.[11] His work must have suffered a severe blow when, on the night of 12 September 1760, a terrible fire razed the village, destroying 72 houses and barns full of corn, fustian, and other material ready for weaving.[12] The loss was astronomical; the value of the property and goods ruined was put at more than £20,000.

Robert must have struggled to get his business together after this. Besides his trade in small bells he was also a fustian weaver and his losses must have been considerable. It may have been the fire which decided him to branch out and take up casting larger bells.

He must have been one of the first bellfounders to make good use of advertising. Lukis gives a transcript of an advertisement which appeared in the *Marlborough Journal* of 6 June 1772;[13] Wratten records that he placed the same advertisement in the paper earlier in the year on Saturday 11 April and 12 May:

At the BELLFOUNDERY [*sic*] at Aldbourne, Wilts, CHURCH BELLS are caſt in a more elegant, and as muſical a Manner, as in any Part of the Kingdom, the

Founder having made the Theory of Sounds, as well as the Nature of Metal his chief Study; alfo hangs the fame, finding all Materials in the moſt complete and concife Manner. And alfo, Hand-Bells prepared ftrictly in Tune, in any Key; Horfe Bells, Clock and Room Bells, the neateſt of their feveral Kinds: Likewife Mill Braffes caſt, and fold at the loweſt Prices.
> All orders will be punctually obferved by
>   ROB. WELLS, Founder.
He gives Ready Money and the beſt Prices for Bell Metal.[14]

Advertisements in a similar vein had appeared in 1767 in the *Reading Mercury* and *Oxford Gazette*. This one appeared in *Jackson's Oxford Journal* for Saturday 31 December 1768:

At the BELL FOUNDRY, at Aldbourne, Wilts, Church Bells are caſt in a more elegant and as muſical a Manner as in any Part of the Kingdom, (the Founder having made the Theory of Sounds, as well as the Nature of Metal, his chief Study:) Alfo hangs the fame, finding all Materials, in the moſt complete and concife Manner: And alfo Hand Bells and Muſical Clock Bells prepared ftrictly in Tune, in any Key: Horfe Bells of all Kinds, Muſical Sheep Bells, Room and Gate Bells, &. the neateſt of their feveral Kinds: Likewife different Kinds of Water and Beer Cocks, &. on the beſt Constructions. Mill Braffes caſt and fold at the loweſt Prices; and all Orders will be punctually ferved, by
>   ROBERT WELLS, Founder.
N.B. He gives Ready Money and the Beſt Prices for Bell Metal.[15]

Another disastrous fire swept the village on 24 August 1777. A strong west wind drove the conflagration from one end of the village to the other, encompassing a barn and cottages in West Street and also the properties on the green. Being August, there was little water in the village pond and the fire raged, destroying many houses, 26 barns and much farm machinery.[16] The Wells were not spared: Robert's mother Mary, who had been a widow for nine years, lost goods to the value of nearly £75, whilst Robert himself lost property and goods worth £234.[17] An appeal was launched to help those worst affected; losses of over £10,000 were estimated over and above the insurance. Robert was treasurer and he made this plaintive plea to the inhabitants of Reading, Hungerford, Lambourn, Wantage and Abingdon:

Let us therefore, fellow Christians, neighbours and Countrymen, throw ourselves at your Feet and humbly beg your Aid.[18]

His last church bell was cast for East Hagbourne, Oxfordshire in 1781 in conjunction with his eldest son, Robert II.[19] He died on 23 June later that year and was buried in the churchyard at the south-east corner of the church. A memorial stone to him still exists, although the lettering is now very worn.

Before I discuss his handbells I want to look at the work of his sons, Robert II and James. Robert II was Robert and Sarah Wells' eldest child, born in 1756, whilst James was their youngest, born in 1771. After his father died, Robert II succeeded to the foundry and for his first church bell cast the fifth at Shalbourne in 1782.[20] During the next 11 years he sent more than 70 church bells to Berkshire, Wiltshire, Oxfordshire, Warwickshire, Hampshire, Dorset and Somerset towers. About the middle of 1793 he took into partnership his younger brother, James, and their names appear together on bells until 1798. During these five years they cast about a dozen bells.

Robert II was a churchwarden at Aldbourne in 1786 and the following year he cast two trebles to augment the six bells into eight. He donated the treble himself, as can be seen by the inscription, whilst two of the ringers, Joshua Pizzie and William Gwynn, gave the second bell.[21] It is reputed that these bells were set upside down outside the *Blue Boar* and filled with beer, free for all to drink, before they were hung in the tower.[22] All three donors were fustian manufacturers according to a leaflet issued in 1790.[23] In 1798 Robert II retired from the foundry leaving James in sole charge, and shortly afterwards left Aldbourne and moved with his wife to Newbury, Berkshire. He lived here until his death in May 1822, aged 66, after which his body was returned to Aldbourne and buried in the churchyard. A tombstone at the south-east end of the church, now used as a pavement, marked his last resting place.

James was a more prolific church bell founder than the previous members of his family. He had Smith's Forge, bought by his grandfather 80 years earlier, which now had two furnaces. He cast bells there in the garden.[24] In the period up to 1810 he cast nearly 100 bells for churches as far afield as Ireland.[25] He became a wealthy man. In addition to the bell foundry, which now occupied three sites in Aldbourne, he owned other property in the village and agricultural land outside it. He dealt in corn and fustian.[26] Under the parliamentary enclosure of Aldbourne in 1809, as one of the principal residential proprietors, he gained considerably more land.[27]

It was very shortly after receiving this land that his fortunes seemed to change. In 1810 he needed cash and had to mortgage his property for £5,000.[28] The bellfoundry business declined and he cast fewer and fewer bells; his last complete ring was one of five bells for Deane, Hampshire in 1821.[29] After this he appeared to cast only single bells. It is interesting to speculate on the cause of this drop in business. Julyan, writing for *The Field* in 1942, suggested the cause was the improvement in roads and transport.[30] When the Aldbourne foundry was established pack horses and wagons were the main means of transport and one manufacturing centre was as good as another. As new roads were built and lines of communication improved, out-of-the-way villages like Aldbourne found their prices undercut by the businesses in the major centres. The Industrial Revolution, the canals and the railways all hastened the end. James went out of business in 1825 and was declared bankrupt on 28 June. At a public auction of his property on 24 August the bell foundry was purchased by Thomas Mears of Whitechapel.[31] Like his brother Robert, James decided to move to Newbury and in 1830 was living in Bartholemew Place.[32] He died later that year, aged 59, and was buried at Aldbourne. His memorial stone may be seen at the south-east corner of the church alongside those of his father and brother.

In nearly eighty years of casting, the Wells manufactured an immense number of horse, animal and house bells, besides many sets of handbells. In addition they cast cup bells and crotals, sometimes called rumblers. As their work is so common I have been able to substantiate an assumption I made earlier. Chapter 2 discussed whether they prepared their patterns with their names cast inside, or if they impressed them into the core after the pattern was removed. The photograph in Figure 69 clearly shows that two attempts were made to impress

RWELLS

70 Different rubbings from same pattern (See Figure 71)

RW

71 Different rubbings from same pattern (See Figure 70)

Robert Wells' name into the sand. Figures 70 and 71 show rubbings taken from two of his bells. Both bells are the same size and profile and have identical numbers on the crown. However, one is marked with his name and the other with his initials. I have other handbells of similar sizes which have the same inscription but cast on different parts of the interior waist. This method of impressing the letters into the sand has led to some erroneous conclusions being drawn in the past. Letters are sometimes poorly imprinted, conveying the wrong information. Becky Mayer, in a short monograph for the American Bell Association,[33] discusses a Wells handbell which appears to have the note marked inside. The bell is a 12F and the founder appears to have cast his initials followed by the letter F. As may be seen, from the rubbing shown in Figure 72, the bottom stroke of the E of Wells has been omitted as well as the final three letters of his name. Another example, also from the USA,[34] is shown in Figure 73. This is a rubbing from a post bell which has been mis-stamped in a similar fashion. A photograph of another example is shown in Figure 74. Figure 75 is a photograph of a massive latten set of 10 bells by Wells in the Hereford Museum. Part of one of these bells is illustrated in Figure 76 and shows his initials as R V.

RWF RWF

72 Mis-stamping resulting in R WF

73 R WF from a post bell

74 Photograph of R WF

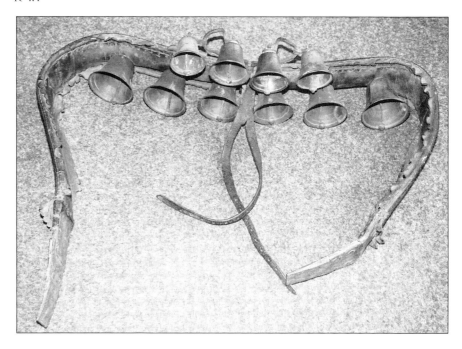

75 Ten bell latten set of Wells bells

76 Wells bell marked as R V

R WELLS

77 R Wells lettering, Type I

Three sizes of letters were used by both Roberts. It would be very convenient if Robert I had always printed his name in full, whilst Robert II used only his initials! However, I do not think this is so. Examples of the three types are shown in Figures 77 to 79. I have seen very few examples of handbells produced by James Wells; on those I have seen he used only his initials, as shown in Figures 80 and 81.

Robert I was the first to number handbells. The English notation system was devised by him and there has been much discussion on how he planned it. One theory is that he took the size of his smallest bell, which had the note of C, and called it number 1, or 1C. He then numbered all the other diatonic notes down the scale. His range covered three octaves, so his largest bell, which also was a C, became 22C. Another theory suggests he numbered his range of bells upwards starting from his largest one. He called this bell 22C because it was 22 inches in circumference and had the approximate note of C. Whichever theory is correct, there is no doubt that Robert conceived the system to cover the range of bells he cast. When later founders produced bells an octave lower they extended the numbers down to 29C and later to

RW

78 R Wells lettering, Type II

R WELLS

79 R Wells lettering, Type III

JW

80 J Wells lettering

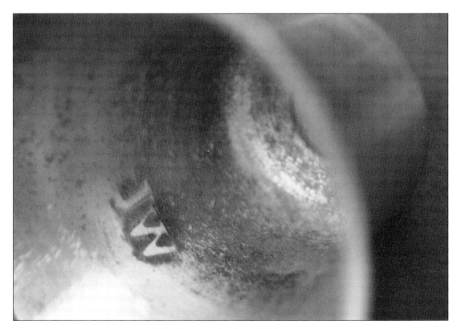

81 Photograph of J Wells lettering

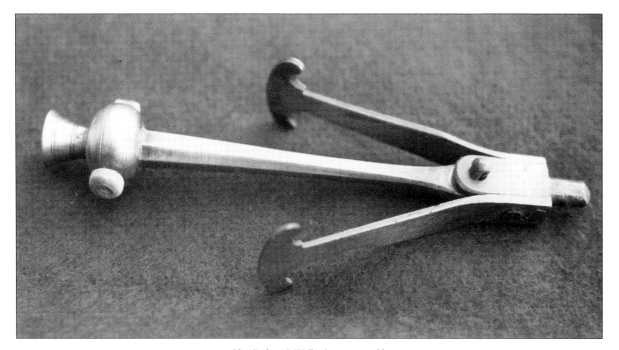

82 Comparison of Wells numbers

32G. With smaller bells they had a problem. They solved this by taking the numbers after 1C into the nought series, giving 07D, 06E, and so on. Some founders subsequently produced a double zero series, 007D, 006E, etc.

These numbers were deeply engraved in the crown of each pattern; it would then be reproduced on each bell cast. It is interesting to look at the numbers and compare the fonts of the figures he used. They vary in size as you would expect,

83   Robert I Wells clapper assembly

but at least four types of the numeral 1 are used as can be seen from the illustrations of the numbers 21, 19 and 11 in Figure 82 and the 12 in Figure 84. This could indicate that he widened the range of the bells he produced over a prolonged period. The position of the numbers on the crown varies with the size of the bell. On bells larger than 12F the number is placed at a right angle to the end of the argent, whilst on smaller bells it is placed parallel to it.

All the Wells bells I have seen have had circular depressions on the interior around the staple hole and they have all had cast-in iron staples. Bells to be used in latten sets were equipped with iron wire clappers and balls. When bells were intended for use as handbells the cast-in staples have been broken off and the bells drilled to take the clapper staple. Robert I pegged his staples in with a pin through the argent; successive members of the family drilled and tapped the bells and added screw threads to the staples.

Early clapper assemblies were of brass with the clapper stems octagonal in section. The ball was neatly turned, but rather flattened, whilst the flight gracefully swelled from the top of the ball. In most cases the ball and the flight were of equal length. The staple end was rounded and held into the staple with an

84   Photograph of Robert Wells post bell

85   Photograph of Robert Wells rumbler bell

iron rivet. The springs were shaped in the manner of a lawn edging tool, and reached up two thirds the length of the clapper. They were positively held to the staple with two iron rivets even in the smaller assemblies. The strikers were hardwood buttons pushed into drilled holes in the balls.

Later clapper assemblies were screwed into the bells rather than pegged, and springs with squared ends fitted. These were often held with one rivet, with the edge of the spring being hammered around the staple to hold it firmly. I have seen only a few contemporary straps and caps, but my records indicate that these have been without markings. Photographs of one of these fittings and a Wells post bell are illustrated in Figures 83 and 84.

The Wells also produced a wide range of crotals, one of which is illustrated in Figure 85. These were produced in sizes from 1 to 30, the largest being 5¼ inches in diameter. According to Brears, these rumblers are absolutely identical to those of the York founder, Edward Seller, but with Seller's initials replaced by R W.[35] As Seller's patterns were being sold off in 1763, it is quite likely that Wells bought and used them. For more details on the work of Edward Seller, see Chapter 15.

Six

OTHER 18TH-CENTURY FOUNDERS

86 Rubbings of Edward Hemins' mark

A NUMBER OF handbells can be attributed to the 18th century by their shape and in this chapter I shall take a brief look at these. In some cases I shall only be able to discuss the bells that have been found and unable to identify their founders. On the other hand, it is known from documentary evidence that some founders cast handbells, but at present we have not been able to identify any of their bells!

One man whose small bells have been resolved through his tower bell work is Edward Hemins. In the latter part of the 17th century a gunsmith and clockmaker named Edward Hemins lived in Bicester, Oxfordshire. He made a number of clocks for the locality, one of which was for Islip in 1707. He had three sons, Edward, Benjamin and Joseph. Edward, the eldest, was born in 1698 and succeeded his father in his business. No guns of his are known, but his tower and grandfather clocks earned him a good reputation.

Like some other clockmakers, Edward decided it would be profitable to make the bells on which his clocks struck and so, sometime in his late 20s, he began to cast his own bells. He probably started with small bells for his grandfather clocks; as a gunsmith he was used to working with metals and the bronze used for casting bells is very similar to gunmetal. House and shop bells would have followed, with possibly handbells for the local ringers to practise upon. His small bells are similar in shape to those being produced by the Aldbourne founders at that time and are marked with a fleur de lys and his initials in relief on a small shield on the inside waist of the bell. They are quite rare: I have one in my own collection and the only other one I have seen is in the Sharpe Collection. Rubbings from both bells are illustrated at Figure 86, and a photograph of one is at Figure 87.

It is not known where he obtained his experience as a church bell founder. Frederick Sharpe comments that some of his church bells have inscriptions similar in character to those of the Bagleys, who had a foundry at Chacombe, Northamptonshire, some 18 miles away.[1] His first church bells were cast in 1728 and are all in Buckinghamshire. They include a ring of five for Wootton Underwood and a small priest's bell for Preston Bissett. On all these he records his address as Bissiter; later he called the town Bister. The bells are good, clean castings, with clear cut lettering. Over the next 16 years he cast bells for 25 churches in the three counties of

87 Photograph of Edward Hemins' mark

Buckinghamshire, Oxfordshire and Northamptonshire. His last casting was probably the current fifth bell at neighbouring Ambrosden, which bears the date 28 May 1743.[2] He died in 1744, and was buried on 8 April.

He was survived by his wife, Elizabeth, and four children, Martha, Edward, John and Richard. His will, dated 17 April 1739, was proved a year after his death. In it he made provision for his wife and then passed the gunsmith's business to his brother Benjamin:

> all my working tools instruments yt are made use of & belonging to ye trade of a gunsmith' together with 'all the gunns barrels locks & stocks which I shall leave.[3]

He appointed his two brothers and two local worthies, John Walker, a maltster, and Richard Wells, a draper, to be his executors and administrators. They were enjoined to sell:

> my workhouse or shop call'd or known by the name of the Foundering Shop situate & being in Bisiter aforesd with ye appurts thereto belonging.[4]

They were to add the money raised from the sale to the rest of his estate and, after paying his debts and funeral expenses, were to divide the remainder in equal shares between his mother and his four children.

At the time of his death he had several jobs in hand and in order to complete this work his executors put this 'obituary' notice in the *Reading Mercury* of 4 June 1744:

> Whereas the ingenious Edward Hemmins, Clockmaker in Bicester, Oxon, is lately deceas'd, and has left several very curious Pieces of Work, some of which are unfinished; This is therefore to acquaint any Person that is a very good Hand, and can come well recommended, that he may meet with good Encouragement by applying to his Executors, John Walker, Richard Walls [sic], and Joseph Hemmins, who live in the same town. N.B. They will be secure from being pres'd during their being employ'd by the above Persons.[5]

The sale of the foundry brought to an end the work of the Bicester Bell Foundry. His brother Joseph later moved to Banbury and worked as a clockmaker; one of his clocks is at South Newington. Edward's children do not appear to have continued in the business.

A few years before Edward Hemins died, James Burrough was working in Devizes. Little is known about him or his foundry, although the latter is said to have been at The Ark, Long Street, Devizes.[6] Some two dozen of his church bells have been found in Wiltshire and one each in the counties of Berkshire and Hampshire. These church bells are all inscribed with dates between 1738 and 1755.[7] Chapter 1 intimates that he produced hemispherical bells; Ingram suggests he also made handbells and illustrates some from the Devizes Museum.[8] These bells are, however, of 19th-century manufacture and are clearly the work of James Bridgman of Aldbourne. Chapter 9 discusses his work. A metal detector magazine suggests that rumbler bells by him may also be found.[9] He may have cast these, together with house and handbells, but I am extremely doubtful: I have not positively identified any over the last 40 years of searching. He died about 1755 and is said to have been succeeded by a man named Hope.[10]

John Kingston was another Wiltshire founder. Thomas Bayley started the Bridgwater foundry in 1743 and, after it had passed through several hands,

88 Rubbing of John Kingston's mark

89 Rubbing of Noah Bloomfield's mark

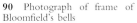

90 Photograph of frame of Bloomfield's bells

John Kingston owned it in 1790.[11] A few church bells by him exist, including one at Mere, Wiltshire, which he cast in 1828. His house bells are not uncommon: those I have seen have his initials in lettering either six or eight millimetres high, separated by a star: I ★ K. These are inscribed on the crown together with the weight of the bell. The two examples I have are labelled '11 oz' and '3 lb'. A rubbing from one of these is illustrated in Figure 88. Sets of his handbells do exist but are rare. I have seen one set only and that was about twenty years ago; unfortunately I was unable to record any details.

A number of handbells broadly similar in shape to Aldbourne castings have been found with N B cast in relief inside. The bells have been finished by hand filing, and have no numbers. A rubbing of the initials is shown in Figure 89. Sharpe has one in his collection, and attributes it either to Noah Blomfield of Mendlesham, or to Nicholas Blondel of Guernsey, a clockmaker, who cast a single bell for St Sampson, Guernsey, in 1759.[12] Recent evidence has come to light which enables me to disregard the Guernsey connection. Unknown to Fred Sharpe there exists at Mary Arden House, Wilmcote, Warwickshire, a wagon frame containing some of these handbells. A photograph of this may be seen in Figure 90. Other single bells have also been traced which suggests they were cast in England rather than Guernsey. However, the clinching argument comes from documentary evidence which shows they are the work of Noah Bloomfield of Mendlesham, Suffolk. Families by the name of Blomfield or Bloomfield were living at Mendlesham in Suffolk in the 16th century. The International Genealogical Index shows Ham and Ezekiel Blomfield were each raising a family in the early 18th century and it is likely that Noah was the son of one of these. He married about 1759 and had at least five children, including Noah (1760), Sophia (1767), Bathsheba (1771) and Jonah (1772).

He was casting handbells in 1766, for in December of that year he provided a ring of 10 handbells as a prize for some competition ringing in Framlingham, as this advertisement from the *Ipswich Journal* shows:

> ON MONDAY the 29th of December next will be given Gratis, at JAMES CHURCHYARD's at the Sign of the WHITE HART in FRAMLINGHAM, a new Peal of TEN HAND BELLS, to be rung for at the Steeple, by not less than three Companies, and to ring 1008 of Bob-Major, cleanest and best, as will be determined by proper Judges, are entitled to the Bells: to enter their Names by 12 o'Clock the same Day, and Dinner to be on the Table exactly at One. These Hand-Bells were cast by Mr. Noah Bloomfield of Mendlesham, who gives a Part in them, - - - Their value is not less than three Guineas. All Gentlemen who please to favour me with their Company, shall be kindly entertained, by their humble Servant, JAMES CHURCHYARD.[13]

91 Mark of 'RR' (Robert Romley ?)

If Noah relied only on the manufacture and supply of cattle and other small bells, his business must have fallen off considerably over the next few years, because towards the end of 1778 his creditors declared him bankrupt:

> ALL Persons indebted to the estate and ectects of NOAH BLOOMFIELD of Mendlesham, a bankrupt, are desired forthwith to pay the same to Mr. Samuel Alexander or Mr. Isaac Paske, of Needham-Market, the assignees of the said bankrupt's estate and effects.[14]

Little else is known about him. I have not been able to trace the year he died. In 1801 he may have had another daughter called Evangelist, although this was probably his granddaughter as his eldest son was also called Noah. Another descendant may have resided at Stonham Aspall, some five miles away. When their front seven bells were recast by Thomas Mears in 1826 some of the ringers' names were recorded on the bells. On the seventh bell are the names of Jon Roper and John Blomfield.

In the latter part of the 18th century a handbell founder by the name of John Jarrett lived in Worcestershire. Although I have not seen any of his bells, I have records of three sets. The first of these is an octave, the largest bell being size 18G. All the bells are roughly tuned, being hand filed to pitch, with the tenor inscribed around the waist:

J JARRETT
Founder
St John's Road
WORCESTER 15

Another set of 12, owned at one time by the donor of the Bewdley Folk Museum, had the tenor similarly inscribed, but this time he gave his address as Ombersley, Worcestershire.

Finally, Mr. John Hinton of Worcester owns a unique set of 15 Jarrett bells. They are mounted without handles in a coffin shaped box and played by tapping with two hammers.[16] This set has been in his family for over 150 years and five generations of Hintons have given public performances on them.

A few bells possess the initials of the founder, but it has not yet proved possible to identify who cast them. The first of these is from my own collection and has R R in 11mm lettering, cast in relief inside the lip. On the exterior the bell has twin parallel lines at the soundbow and crown and two more just below the argent. (Figures 91 to 93.) This bell may be the work of Robert Romley, a London clock bell manufacturer in the last part of the 18th century.

Several interesting bells of this period are included in the Sharpe Collection. One has a long waist and a slightly later shape with I T in 7mm lettering inside. (Figure 94.) An article in *The Searcher* attributes these initials to the founder John Thornton.[17] He was a Suffolk founder who

92 Photograph of 'RR' mark

93 Exterior of 'RR' bell

94 Mark of 'IT' (John Thornton ?)

95 Mark of 'IC'

96 Photograph of mark of 'HH'

succeeded Henry Pleasant at Sudbury, and cast a number of church bells in East Anglia in the first quarter of the 18th century.[18] Twelve of these were in Suffolk, seven in Cambridgeshire, three in Norfolk and 13 in Essex. Some of them have now been recast.[19]

Another handbell has I C in 9mm lettering inside the lip. Another unidentified pair of initials are H H which were on a handbell submitted to me from East Anglia. A further bell, this time in the Davies Collection, has the initials I G above those of S K inside. Rubbings or photographs of these initials are given in Figures 95 to 97.

Thomas Osborn was a well-known founder in East Anglia in the 18th century. L'Estrange notes that his baptism is recorded in the Downham Market registers on 19 October 1741.[20] His father was a joiner and he took up a similar trade as a carpenter, but later in his life became a foreman at Joseph Eayre's bell foundry at St Neots. After a spell as partner to Eayre's successor, Edward Arnold, he set up on his own account at Downham Market and cast many bells between 1779 and 1806. The following advertisement appeared in the *Norwich Mercury* for 17 December 1796:

CHURCHWARDENS and others having any quantity of old Bells to dispose of, may hear of a purchaser by applying to Thomas Osborn, Bell Founder and Bell Hanger, at Downham, in Norfolk, who will give the best price.—Letters (post paid) will be answered.
Mill Brass Musical hand Bells on reasonable terms.

Whether Osborn cast handbells himself or obtained them from another source is open to conjecture. I am inclined to think he did produce them. He was an experienced founder capable of casting good quality church bells; the manufacture of handbells would not present him with any problems. Another pointer towards his regular supply of them at that time may be an advertisement in the *Ipswich Journal* regarding his restoration of the bells at Wickham Skeith, Suffolk.[22] A ring of 12 handbells was opened (i.e. a new set) when he added two trebles and restored the original four church bells in 1780. He could have cast these handbells, although it is possible they were a set obtained from the effects of the bankrupt Noah Bloomfield of Mendlesham, only three miles away. However, he could not have used this source when he returned to Wickham Skeith nearly twenty years later and recast the fifth, supplying this time 10 handbells.[23] I have not identified any of his handbells.

Osborn was succeeded by his grandson, William Dobson, about six months before his death on 6 December 1806. An excellent account of this was given

97 Mark of IG/SK

by David Cubitt in *The Ringing World* for 1976.[24] He quotes an advertisement in the *Bury and Norwich Post* for 1806 which concludes:

> N.B. Mill Brasses of a superior quality, on the most reasonable terms.

Unlike the 1796 advertisement, handbells are not mentioned. In 1807 Dobson published a list of work carried out by him and his grandfather since the opening of the foundry in 1779, and again, handbells are not mentioned, although the list concludes with:

> N.B. Turret-clock, Ship and Dinner Bells, also Mill Brasses of superior quality, on the most reasonable terms.[25]

Dobson's greatest ring of church bells was the 12 he cast in 1813 for St Nicholas, Liverpool, to replace the bells broken when the steeple collapsed before morning service on Sunday, 11 February 1810. When this new ring was opened on 4 June 1814 the churchwardens presented a silver cup valued at 20 guineas for the best ringing[26] whilst Dobson gave a set of handbells for the second best performance.[27] These handbells were made by Henry Symondson, of Tottenham Court Road, London (see Chapter 8). I therefore conclude that it is questionable whether William Dobson made handbells.

He closed the foundry in 1832 and sold the business to Thomas Mears at Whitechapel. He moved to London and worked in a lawyer's office for some time before his death in 1842.[28]

Seven

HANDBELLS FROM WHITECHAPEL

IN 1970 THE Whitechapel Bell Foundry celebrated 400 years of casting church bells, reckoning that its first master founder was Robert Mot in 1570. More recent research indicates a direct line can be traced back to Robert Chamberlain, who was casting in Aldgate in 1420.[1] The foundry has the reputation of being the oldest established manufacturing business in England. It moved to its current premises in 1738, when Thomas Lester took over the grounds and some of the buildings of a 70-year-old coaching hostelry, *The Artichoke Inn*, on the south side of the Whitechapel Road. Since that time they have sent church bells and handbells all over the world. In previous chapters I have detailed some of the church bell work of the handbell founders I have been discussing in order to date their handbells. The large output of the Whitechapel Bell Foundry over many years is well documented, so I shall concentrate mainly on their handbells and other small bells.

A fire in the first half of the 19th century destroyed part of the foundry and, as a result, most of the documentary records prior to 1837 are missing. The first Whitechapel founder whose handbells can positively be identified is Thomas Mears, who marked them internally with his initials. However, I attribute some handbells to one of his predecessors, Thomas Lester. He was foreman to Richard Phelps, who, when he died in 1738, gave Thomas his bellfounding business at Whitechapel, together with his implements and tools.[2] He also left him the lease on the foundry premises but Thomas took out a lease on the site of *The Artichoke Inn*.

Thomas recast the bells of Hexham Abbey in 1742. It is probable that at the same time he provided them with a set of handbells for the ringers to practise upon. There are two 18th-century handbells kept in the ringing chamber, obviously the remnants of an earlier set. They have no markings and have not been tuned. There is a depression around the staple hole, which has been drilled but not tapped. They differ from the Cor bells of the same period by the shoulders being less rounded and the lips less flared; they are, in fact, very similar to Whitechapel bells from a later period. (Figure 98.)

98   Thomas Lester handbell from Hexham Abbey

99 Iron spring by Thomas Lester

The fittings indicate their early age. The clapper staples, which are pegged into the bell with an iron pin, are made of brass and are small and insubstantial. The long iron springs are held with a single rivet to the staple and curve upwards to spade-like ends. (Figures 99 and 100.) The octagonal stemmed clapper has a plain ball with a very short flight and the wide flattened staple-end is connected to the staple with an iron split pin. The leather caps are plain, with no markings, as are the leather straps. The latter are fastened to the argent with an iron rivet passing through two octagonal brass washers. The Hexham handbells have not been turned, but there is a tradition at Whitechapel that one of the lathes in the handbell shop dates from Thomas Lester's time. This massive mahogany lathe is illustrated in Figure 101.

In 1752, like his predecessor Richard Phelps, Thomas Lester took his foreman, Thomas Pack, into partnership. Seventeen years later, shortly before he died, he also made his nephew, William Chapman, a partner. He died in June 1769 and the firm became Pack and Chapman, leasing the foundry property from Sarah Oliver, Lester's granddaughter. A broadsheet issued shortly after Lester's death states that 1,102 bells were cast by the foundry during his working life but does not mention musical handbells. I have no knowledge of any handbells by Pack and Chapman.

Whilst William Chapman was recasting Great Dunstan at Canterbury in 1762 he noticed a young man taking a great interest in the work and he offered to take him back to London and train him as a bellfounder.[3] This was William Mears, who later became Chapman's partner and subsequently sole owner of

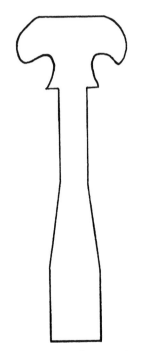

100   Drawing of Lester spring

101   Eighteenth-century lathe at Whitechapel

102   House bell with T M incised on crown

103   Handbell with T M incised on crown

104   Bell with T M incised on
crown from Sharpe Collection

the firm. This was a turbulent period at the foundry. The ownership of the foundry premises had passed via Sarah Oliver to Robert Patrick, a cheesemonger, who for four years set up and, with considerable help from other bellfounders, cast bells at Whitechapel.[4] William Mears was twice declared bankrupt. On the second occasion, in 1789, he fled the country and his financial affairs were passed to a receiver. In March 1791 the latter sent this invoice to the parish of Ashdon, Essex, for work carried out by William Mears:

5 March 1788   To a Peal of 6 Hand Bells £1 1 6
               Box and Book[5]   1 2[5]

I have not discovered if these handbells still exist.

Thomas Mears I took over the foundry in 1790; his father, William Mears, died the next year. There is no mention of handbells in a newspaper advertisement of April 1790, although some old handbells in the tower at Hayes, Middlesex may have been supplied by him when he cast them a ring of six church bells in 1798. The bells have no identifying marks apart from twin parallel lines engraved inside the bell at the soundbow, with a further pair at the waist. I am inclined to think they are the work of a later Whitechapel founder.

Thomas I took his son, Thomas II, into partnership in 1805 and a few years later they issued a broadsheet detailing the work carried out by the foundry since 1738. This amounted to 200 rings of five or more bells, totalling more than 1,800 bells. The broadsheet concludes:

ALSO CASTS SHIP, PLANTATION, TERRET, CLOCK, HAND & HOUSE BELLS, MUSICAL HANDBELLS, MILL BRASSES &c &c

A house bell I have in my collection has T M engraved on the crown and may be Thomas I's work: an illustration of this mark is given in Figure 102. Another bell I photographed some years ago was marked differently: see Figure 103. Finally, the Sharpe Collection has a bell with T M on the crown: a rubbing of this is shown in Figure 104. Thomas died in 1810 and Thomas Mears II took charge of the foundry.

Thomas II was a good business man. Under his leadership the foundry flourished, sending bells all over the country. He bought the foundry property from the descendants of Sarah Oliver in 1818 and seven years later purchased the bellfounding side of the business of John Briant of Hertford.[6] The latter made good business sense: whilst Briant had been operating, Mears had sent

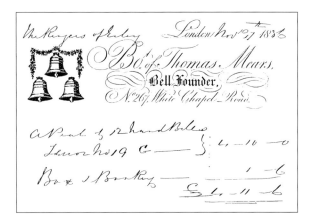

105   Thomas Mears II invoice to Eling, Hampshire

106   Mark of Thomas Mears II

107   Interior of Thomas Mears II bell showing initials

108   Interior of Thomas Mears II bell showing MEARS plate

109   Interior of Thomas Mears II bell showing initials but no lines

only 18 bells to Hertfordshire, whilst Briant had supplied ninety-six.[7] Chapter 8 will discuss John Briant's work and handbells. As recorded in Chapter 5, he also took over James Wells' foundry at Aldbourne in 1825. This was a significant purchase for his handbell department. They not only acquired the extensive range of Wells' patterns for handbells and crotals, they were also joined by James Bridgman, James Wells' experienced assistant, together with Wells' coachman, a man called Kimber, who helped with the foundry work.[8]

Thomas II took over two other foundries: the great Rudhall foundry at Gloucester in 1830 and William Dobson's foundry at Downham Market in 1833. It is unlikely that either of these takeovers improved or increased the Mears production of handbells.

At the opening of the new ring of 12 bells in the Waterloo Tower at Quex Park on 4 August 1819, Thomas presented a boxed set of handbells to John Powell Powell. He had cast all the bells and supplied the timber frame for a cost of £824; no doubt the trifling cost of the handbells, about £4 10s., had been included in this cost![9] Preserved in the ringing chamber of Eling, Hampshire is an invoice of his for 12 handbells in a box: total cost £4 11s. 6d. This billhead is illustrated in Figure 105.

The introduction of the Wells handbell patterns greatly improved the quality and range of Thomas II's handbells. He was facing stiff competition from the other London handbell manufacturers: William Dunn and Henry Symondson were building up a good reputation for their work. He replaced his patterns with those of Wells and added engraved twin parallel lines at the lip and waist inside the bell. In some cases he added his initials T.M with a full stop between the letters. I also have an example where he impressed an oval plate with MEARS, LONDON into the sand of the core before casting. Examples of these may be seen in Figures 106 to 109. He retained the Wells' system of numbering and also continued Wells' plan of casting an iron crown staple in all bells, breaking them out when making musical handbells. These bells were then drilled but not generally tapped with a screw thread, the clapper staples being pegged into the argent. The clapper staples were small and not very substantial and held the octagonal stemmed clappers by means of a steel pin. The ball of the clapper was drilled for wooden ball strikers; long flights finished the clapper assembly. Long brass springs with spade-shaped ends reached more than halfway up the clapper shaft.

Thomas II died in 1844 and two of his sons, Charles and George, carried on the business under the name "C & G MEARS". Charles died in 1855, but the firm traded under the same name for a few more years. George continued the firm with his younger brother John until 1864, when he took Robert Stainbank in as a partner, the firm trading as "Mears and Stainbank". Robert Stainbank immediately got rid of John Mears and the following year he bought out George, who took early retirement and moved to Landport, Portsmouth, where he died in 1873, aged 53.[10]

110   Leather stamps of George Mears

I have notes of a bell from the Sharpe Collection, size 18G, which has been engraved on the upper waist:

C & G MEARS
FOUNDERS
LONDON
1853

Apart from the size 18 on the crown, the bell had no other distinguishing marks. The clapper assembly had a small staple, with an octagonal stemmed clapper held to it by a split pin peg. The ball had a long flight and held wooden balls as strikers. The tapered brass spring had semicircular cut outs and was fastened to the staple by two rivets, one above the other. The strap had the note stamped on the bend on the top rather than in the usual position. The leather cap was stamped alternately with two symbols, one rather like the Ace of Clubs and the other two concentric circles. Examples of these can be seen in Figure 110. A photograph of a C & G Mears bell similarly engraved may be seen in Figure 111.

Some old handbells at Cranleigh, Surrey were probably supplied when their third bell was recast by George Mears in 1862. The 19F, 12F and 7B have engraved double lines on the interior of the bell at lip and waist, whilst the 20E has MEARS at right angles to the argent with 20 opposite. The clapper stems are octagonal, tapering from the ball and large flight to the flattened, circular staple end. The staples are small, but screwed into the bell. George Mears introduced tapping the bell so clapper staples could be screwed in about 1860: in this he emulated the other London founders who had initiated this several decades earlier. The springs and leather caps are similar to those on the 1853 bell mentioned previously. In *The Church Bells of Herefordshire*, Sharpe illustrates one of George Mears' 1854 billheads for a set of 12 handbells packed in a box, for £4 12s. 6d., only 1s. more than Thomas Mears charged Eling nearly twenty years earlier.[11]

At this point I ought to mention the Oliver family. Three generations of them worked on handbells at Whitechapel and a former generation was also employed by the firm. Charles Oliver was Thomas Mears II's bell-hanger and he installed the frame and bells at Quex Park in 1819. George Oliver was born in 1837 and worked in the foundry from 1860 until 1918, the year before he died. In addition to his work in the handbell shop he was also an inventor. He devised a campanaphone using hemispherical bells which he produced at a workshop in Canal Street and exported to France. He also engraved on ivory. The Whitechapel handbells he produced can all be identified because he marked them with a small scratched cross inside the bell. His son, Ethelbert, known as Bert, was born in 1873 and worked in the handbell shop from 1890

111   An engraved C & G Mears bell of 1852

112   Cap with Bert Oliver's personal leather stamp

until 1929, the year he died. He carried on the tradition of marking the handbells he produced by stamping the caps with a wavy line rather like an elongated letter S. (Figure 112.) His son, Ernest, was born in 1915 and he accepted a job in the handbell shop in 1929, working there till he retired in 1985. His retirement ended a one and a quarter centuries' association with his family and handbells at Whitechapel.

Returning to Robert Stainbank, he revitalised the foundry, which had become somewhat neglected. Besides his church bell work he kept up the production of handbells as may be seen from a 24-page booklet published about 1875 which he reprinted from *Cassell's Magazine of Art* of 1854. This contains 10 full-page woodcuts illustrating the foundry and foundry techniques. Two of the pictures refer to the production of small bells, described in the text as 'hand and house tintinnabulums'![12] The illustrations are reproduced in Figures 113 and 114. It is interesting to observe the paper hats worn by some of the workmen. The management at that time issued every man each Monday morning with half a sheet of brown paper to make them!

Stainbank increased the range of handbells on offer. When Henry Hubbard produced the third edition of his *Elements of Campanalogia* in 1868 he added at the end an advertisement for Mears and Stainbank which stated:

> Musical Hand-Bells in Sets, from One to Seven and a half Octaves.

House bells with M & S incised on the crown date from about this period. However, I think they were made not by Mears and Stainbank but by Martineau and Smith of Birmingham and will deal with them in Chapter 14.

Stainbank died on 27 January 1883 and was succeeded by his son-in-law, Alfred Lawson. Working at the foundry at that time was Arthur Hughes, a civil engineer, who had been taken on in 1881 by Robert Stainbank to oversee some projected Government casting work. Lawson decided not to continue with this venture and Arthur Hughes was put in charge of the foundry when William Wariskett, the general manager, retired after Stainbank's death.[13] In 1885 Alfred Lawson bought the goodwill of the Redenhall Foundry of Moore, Holmes and Mackenzie, and three years later he purchased that of T.C. Lewis, an organ builder and bellfounder of Brixham. He set about modernising the foundry, introducing a travelling crane, drying ovens and iron cope cases. He also published a catalogue in 1885, outlining all the export

113   1854 woodcut depicting drawing the crucible

114   1854 woodcut depicting casting small bells

115   Leather cap of the 1880s

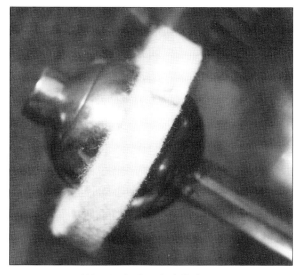

116   Head of a split ball clapper

117   Curved T-shaped spring

work the foundry had undertaken in addition to the work for the home market. Unfortunately, musical handbells received only a one-line mention on the very last page![14] A leather cap from this period is shown in Figure 115.

In the latter years of the 19th century Mears gained a good reputation for their handbells, sending a number of long sets to the north of England where the competition for the honours at the annual Handbell Contest at Belle Vue, Manchester, was intense. It has been said that, whilst their reputation for handbells grew, that for their tower bells declined. Mears pioneered the development of split ball clappers for handbells. These were initially proposed for the bass octave of bells, but it was possible at one time to get them for the bottom four octaves. The main reason for their introduction was that it gave the bass ringer quicker response and enabled more effective bass runs. The much heavier clapper ball also gave greater control over the volume of sound produced. Normal shaped springs were found to be of limited use as metal fatigue quickly caused them to snap, so T-shaped curved springs bound round with leather or felt were introduced.[15] (Figures 116 and 117.)

Alfred Lawson died in 1904 and Arthur Hughes took over the foundry. A photograph of him is given at Figure 118. He and his wife, Emma, had three sons, Albert Arthur, Robert Arthur and Leonard Arthur, all of whom worked at the foundry during the next two decades. The foundry was offered two more businesses. In 1906 William Shaw proposed that Arthur Hughes should purchase the Bradford Foundry of James Shaw & Son; this had declined from its former 19th-century eminence after a disastrous fire in 1901. Arthur recalled the firm purchasing the goodwill of the Redenhall Foundry and the Brixham Foundry, neither of which had gained them anything financially, so he declined William Shaw's offer. Similarly, he rejected a later offer to take over Gillett and Johnston.

About 1911 the firm issued a new catalogue. This time, besides a list of the church bells they had cast, it included a small section on handbells. Page 43 noted they issued a separate price list for these. Also included in the preface is the following testimonial:

118 Arthur Hughes

A set of 172 Bells which we recently supplied, was reported upon by the Musical Judges at the Manchester Contest:- 'Bells well in tune, nicely modulated, and of exquisite tone; eminent musicians say they are the most musical and mellow Peal of Bells they have ever heard.'[16]

Arthur Hughes died on 2 August 1916 and the foundry was managed by Albert and Leonard whilst Robert was serving with the Rifle Brigade in France.[17] Later Leonard dropped out and Albert and Robert became the active partners. This continued until 1928 when Albert ran the firm on his own. He married Annie Smith in 1910, and their three children were Kathleen, William and Douglas. A third catalogue was issued in 1920, largely reprinting the 1911 one, including the testimonial given above, which by now was not 'recent'! Another difference was, that as well as stating on page 41 that separate handbell lists were issued, they actually gave one 12 pages later!

William joined the firm in 1935 and became a partner in 1945. There was very little handbell business in the period between the wars and the handbell staff was reduced to one man with a boy helping part-time. Albert considered ending handbell production altogether, but his wife Annie, who was a solo handbell performer of considerable skill, persuaded him to continue making them. This was a wise decision, because, when the foundry was released from war work and started making bells again, the expertise was still available to make handbells. Within a few years the clamour for English handbells began with the USA boom, when the American Guild of English Handbell Ringers was established.

Douglas, William's younger brother, joined the firm in 1945 after leaving the Forces. He became a partner in 1950 and took charge of the handbell shop.[18] Many of the modifications made to the handbell fittings listed below were due to him. The success or failure of a set of handbells depends on the accuracy of the tuner. During the 19th century Mears were fortunate in the men they employed in this capacity. However, in the second half of the 20th century science enabled them to introduce strobe tuning, which permitted tuning to a very high standard by the less gifted. This was installed in the handbell shop on 30 June 1956.

Round clapper stems were brought in around 1930. Clapper balls were drilled and threaded to take the leather pegs in the latter part of the 19th century, but the practice was discontinued sometime before the Second World War, perhaps as a cost-cutting measure. In 1955 they resumed threading them. The leather pegs were handmade up till September 1963; after that they were made

119 Stamps for leather caps used at Whitechapel (1)

120 Stamps for leather caps used at Whitechapel (2)

in a jig. From 1961 the smaller bells had nylon and polythene pegs fitted; nylon staple pins were introduced the following year. Half hard brass springs were introduced in 1947. Up to 1950 they were tapered; in that year parallel sided straight brass springs with D-shaped notches replaced them. In the late 1950s the notches were left out. In 1952 all the clapper staples were redesigned: only eight sizes are used now. Up till then they were cast and hand-filed: now they are machined from bar on a capstan lathe. The caps are currently stamped with a rose and oak leaf ornament which was first used in June 1954. Figures 119 and 120 illustrate leather stamps used at Whitechapel over the years. Since July 1961 both sharps and flats have been marked on the straps: A sharp and B flat, for example. Prior to this only one or the other was

121 Mark from a post-1964 MEARS bell

marked. When stiffened handles were first used they were blocked with an extra piece of leather which was stitched in. Between 1950 and 1969 the extra leather was glued in. Since then it has been fastened with screw nails. During the autumn of 1964 the argents on the handbells were lengthened and the opportunity was taken to re-engrave the patterns with the MEARS opposite the size number and parallel to the argent. Prior to that it was at right angles to it. An example of a rubbing from a post-1964 bell is depicted at Figure 121.

A well-designed handbell brochure aimed mainly at the American market was issued in the early 1960s by Albert Hughes.[19] Its 16 pages contained largely full-page photographs of the manufacture, tuning and fitting of Whitechapel handbells, including their packing for shipment overseas. Two of the illustrations showing the casting of small bells in the mid-19th century (those shown in Figures 113 and 114) were reproduced from the 1875 booklet.

Albert Hughes died on 11 August 1964 and the foundry passed to his sons, William and Douglas.[20] The photograph in Figure 122 shows Albert with them. Albert had guided the foundry through a difficult period, especially during the war when the foundry was damaged many times in air raids. The export of many sets of handbells to America during the 1950s earned valuable dollars in the years of post-war austerity and eased the country's balance of payments.

In 1968 the firm became a limited company trading as The Whitechapel Bell Foundry Limited; William and Douglas Hughes became the first directors of the new company. Two years later, to celebrate the firm's quatercentenary, the tenor bell of all the sets of handbells made between 12 February 1970 and 10 February 1971 was engraved 1570-1970. Leather-handled post bells, rather like a town crier's bell, which had been a feature of the firm for many years, were discontinued after 1970.

William's son, Alan Hughes, joined the staff of the foundry in 1966 and became a director in 1972. The 1970s was a growth era for Whitechapel handbells; they had earned a deserved reputation for the best handbells in the world and everybody wanted them. The demand from England had increased dramatically with the resurgence of interest after the formation in 1967 of The

122 William, Albert and
Douglas Hughes

Handbell Ringers of Great Britain and the demand from America continued
unabated. At one period the waiting list was so long it could take three years
for an order to be fulfilled. With inflation at an all-time high in Britain it was
a difficult time for both the foundry and its customers. Appendix VII compares
the relative cost of handbells over the years to the cost of living.

In the 1990s the standard range of five octaves of bells was increased by
making available a top octave, from 007D to 0001C. This had always been
obtainable: many of the big Northern teams had used these in the late 19th
century. However, this was the first time the octave had been a standard item.
At the same time the standard range was extended by casting bells down to
32G. New patterns were introduced for all the bells apart from the top octave
in the second half of the 1990s; constant packing of the old patterns in and out
of the moulding sand had eroded the metal and made the resultant bells too thin
to tune! These latest patterns no longer have MEARS engraved upon them.
Finally, bells are no longer cast through a riser from the argent but via the lip.
This gives better castings.

William died on 30 October 1993 aged 81. Until shortly before his death
he had worked six days a week in the foundry, reserving Saturday mornings for
taking parties round the works.[21] Douglas died on 29 March 1997 aged 79,
leaving Alan as the sole master founder. Alan's wife, Kathryn, joined the company after William's death and became a director after Douglas died. Production
of handbells continues as before and Whitechapel exports sets all over the
world.

Eight
THE SYMONDSONS

123 A Henry Symondson handbell

THE STORY of the Symondsons and their handbells may be considered to begin with a Hertfordshire founder, John Briant. It is said that he came from Exning, a Suffolk village a few miles from Newmarket, although his baptism in 1749 is not recorded in the parish registers.[1] His father wanted him to go to university and take Holy Orders, but he preferred to work with his hands and turned to clockmaking and bellfounding. Andrews suggests that he may have served as an apprentice to the Bagleys at Chacombe, Northamptonshire, or to Joseph Eayres or his successors at St Neots, but no record of this has been found.[2]

His obituary states that he was a plain, blunt-spoken man, generous in nature and broadminded in religious matters.[3] A good example of his attitude is given by his reply when asked why he did not get a carriage for himself:

> I don't want a carriage; I'm satisfied with the station of life that God has placed me in. I've enjoyed more real pleasure in my favourite pursuits than the wealth of India could afford.[4]

Both his marriages were short-lived. His first wife, Mary Hanley, whom he married in 1786, died seven years later. They had two daughters; the elder of these, Mary, married Solomon Shaw of St Albans in 1810, whilst her sister died in infancy. He remarried in 1802 to Ann Fyson. This marriage lasted less than three years: Ann died in 1805, preceded by her infant son, John. Their daughter Catherine survived both parents.

In 1781 he set up as a bellfounder and clockmaker in Parliament Row, Hertford. He was fortunate to obtain the patronage of James Cecil, 6th Earl of Salisbury. Through this and his good reputation for excellent craftsmanship, his business flourished. During the next 45 years he cast over 420 church bells, dispatching 20 complete rings to a dozen counties. His largest bell was the old tenor at St Michael, Coventry, which weighed over 31 hundredweight.

Henry Symondson was for some years his foreman and tuner. When he retuned Benington bells in 1838 he discussed Briant's work with Leonard Proctor, a well-known ringer of the time, and said of him:

> that 'no man took so much pains and trouble as his master in turning out superior bells in perfect tune' and that 'oftentimes he would rather lose by a job than have the reflection that he had sent out a bad bell.'[5]

124 Rubbing of Henry Symondson's initials

Briant's expertise as a founder was sought even in his retirement. The Dean and Chapter of Lincoln Cathedral, through their Clerk of Works, Edward Bentham, wrote to him in 1828 regarding repairs to the badly cracked Great Tom of Lincoln. Briant strongly opposed cutting out the crack to make the bell usable again. The experiment was tried and Briant was proved right when it resulted in a costly failure.[6] He was also highly regarded as a clockmaker. There is no definitive list of his turret clocks but more than 30 are known. Among these were clocks for King's College, Cambridge, Shire Hall, Hertford, and Blenheim Palace.[7] He also made grandfather clocks.

There is only one known contemporary reference to his work as a handbell founder. This occurs in the peal book of the Hertford College Youths:

> Rec 27th Demr, 1821 of Messrs Worsley and Biggin,
> two Pound ten on Acct. for a Peal of 10 Hand Bells
>
> £2 10s. 0d.   John Briant.
>   2   0s. 0d.
>
> Recd. full 8th Apr. 1822.   John Briant.[8]

The Hertford College Youths was divided into several groups. First there were the active church bell ringers, known as the 'steeple' ringers. To qualify for membership they had to ring over 1,000 changes on the church bells, so they may have used these handbells for practising in comfort! Another section was made up of influential townspeople who were only interested in the society's social functions. A third group were the handbell ringers, whom Trollope, in his account of the Hertford College Youths, describes as 'the tune ringers'.[9] This group probably would have made most use of the handbells, which may have been lost in the fire that destroyed All Saints, Hertford in 1891.

Briant may also have made a set for the Saffron Walden company. In 1798 he cast them a new ring of eight church bells which were first rung in December 1799. At that time a founder often included a set of handbells for the ringers to practise upon when supplying them with a new ring. The company certainly had some handbells, for in 1833 they replaced their existing set with another from Thomas Mears:

> sold Ashdon Ringers 14 hand bells and box to put them in for the sum of £2
> Paid Mr Mears for hand bells as per Bill £7-8-0[10]

Briant was a practical ringing member of the Hertford College Youths. In 1782 he rang the tenor to a peal of Oxford Treble Bob Major at St Andrew, Hertford. This was shortly after he had added four smaller bells to the existing four to make a ring of eight.[11] He was elected steward of the society in 1781 and a year later joined the Society of College Youths, a London society founded in 1637.[12] He retired from bellfounding in 1825, selling the business to Thomas Mears II. He was in straitened circumstances; his philosophical views and kindly nature made him averse to forcing payment of his bills. Many parishes took advantage of this and did not pay and he finished his life as a pauper. His patron obtained a place for him in Marlborough Almshouses, St Albans, where he died on 27 February 1829. At his funeral Henry Symondson fulfilled his employer's last request by placing a gross of iron screws in his coffin, an old custom said to date back to the time of the Ancient Egyptians.[13]

I have not seen any bells that can be credited to Briant. W.G. Bull, in a letter to *The Bell News* in 1900, claimed to have 94 ancient handbells by various manufacturers.[14] Amongst these were some with J B inscribed on the crown. I cannot attribute these to any other founder, so they may be Briant's work.

Although a great deal has been discovered about Henry Symondson, much of his early history remains uncertain. At the time of the 1841 census he stated he was 60 years old and born in Middlesex. This would put his year of birth as 1781. However, records show he joined the Society of Cumberland Youths in 1793.[15] A 12-year-old would not have been elected a member at that period, so he must have been four or five years older. He married Mary Thompson in 1800 at St Leonard's, Shoreditch, and in the next 19 years Mary had eight children, all of whom were baptised at St Giles-in-the-Fields.[16] This indicates that the family home was always in the vicinity of Tottenham Court Road from where he carried out his business of making sets of handbells.[17] Jennings implies his production of handbells was a secondary occupation to his work in orchestras and the theatre as an accomplished violinist: I have not been able to follow up this line of enquiry.[18]

It would be interesting to know where he gained his experience as a tuner. It is possible that he originally found employment with one of the two Warner firms who were brass and bell founding at this time; both were within easy walking distance of Tottenham Court Road.[19] But when did he start to work for John Briant? His presence at Briant's funeral indicates a close association with him, but was this during Briant's last years as a founder, or at some earlier time?

The Hertford foundry closed when Thomas Mears bought the bell founding business in 1825. Briant's foreman in the clock making department, James Skerman, continued to make turret clocks, only now on his own account.[20] Later his son, William, joined the firm and ran it until his death in 1874. One theory is that, in a manner similar to Skerman's carrying on the clock making, Briant passed on to Symondson his handbell business, including the patterns. I have associated Briant's handbells with those with I B inscribed on the crown of the bell; Symondson's handbells have H S inscribed on them in a similar position. A comparison of the profiles of the bells might help to substantiate this theory, but I have not traced any handbells by Briant.

I consider it more likely that Symondson was running a handbell business of his own before he worked for Briant. Parry, in *The Story of Handbells*, suggests that Briant instructed Symondson as his tuner to prepare patterns for handbells.[21] This implies that he was with Briant for many years; Andrews, in his biography of Briant, does not substantiate this.[22] If he worked at the Hertford foundry for only the last few years of its life then, instead of John Briant casting his own handbells, Symondson may have produced them for him.

A handbell is in existence engraved with the address '267 Tottenham Court Road'.[23] The parish records show that Symondson, described as a bell founder, was living here in 1814 when two of his children were baptised at St Giles-in-the-Fields. In 1817, when the next child was baptised, he was described as a brass founder and had moved to 8 Bosiers Court, St Marylebone.[24] The earliest known dated handbell by Symondson is fixed over the entrance door in the ringing chamber of St Michael and All Angels, Ashton-under-Lyne. It is an unusually thick bell with a traditional clapper assembly screwed in, although the bell does not appear ever to have been rung. No strap or cap is fitted and the bell is fixed to a bracket by a clamp around the argent. Nothing is inscribed on the crown of the bell, but the waist is engraved:

<table>
<tr><td>Symondson
Brafs Founder
No 1 Tottenham Court Road
London</td><td>on reverse</td><td>This Peal was Won
at Liverpool,
by the College youths
of Ashton under Line
June 4 1814[25]</td></tr>
</table>

John Day wrote an account of this ringing match for *The Bell News* in 1895, although he makes no mention of the Ashton-under-Lyne ringers or the hand-bells.[26] He describes how a new ring of 12 bells, cast by William Dobson of Downham Market, Norfolk, for St Nicholas, Liverpool, was opened on 4 June 1814. To ensure good ringing the authorities arranged to give two prizes for the best touches or peals: a silver cup, value 20 guineas, or 20 guineas in cash. Ringers were present from Sheffield, Birmingham and other places, but there was no complete 12-bell band. According to Day, a composite band from these two cities rang a peal of Grandsire Cinques and was awarded both prizes, the Birmingham ringers taking the cup and the Sheffield ringers the money. John Day wrote some eighty years after the event, working from hearsay, and his interpretation was not entirely correct. The local paper, the *Liverpool Mercury*, reported that a set of 12 handbells was also presented; the one left at St Michael's is obviously the tenor of that ring.[27] This gives us some conclusive evidence for Symondson producing sets of handbells in 1814, some 10 years before he is generally regarded to have left John Briant and set up on his own.

Another dateable set of Symondson's bells is at Holy Trinity, Cuckfield, Sussex. In 1815 the ringers augmented their tower bells to a ring of eight and purchased, at the same time, two octaves of handbells from Henry Symondson, tenor size 21D. Thirteen of these bells remain in the tower, mounted on a tapping frame, with a plaque recording their origin. This was added in 1881 when a new set of Warner's bells was purchased.

Henry was a competent ringer and we can gain some idea of his activities by the peals he rang. As mentioned already, he joined the Society of Cumberland Youths in 1793, but later that year left them to join the Junior Society.[28] It may seem strange to modern ringers that he changed his allegiance to his society so quickly. However, it must be remembered that the peal ringing fraternity of the 18th-century London ringing societies was small and exclusive and the opportunity to progress was very limited. This accounts for the constant changing from one society to another that was characteristic of the period.

Several of his early peals are worthy of mention. He rang in a peal of 5,453 Grandsire Caters at St-Mary-le-Bow on 2 January 1794, only the second time that a peal had been rung on these bells by only 10 men.[29] He then went back to the old Society of Cumberland Youths for a couple of years and rang several peals, including one of 10,080 Plain Bob Major at Edmonton. In 1797 he was with the Junior Society again, ringing a splendid peal of 6,003 Stedman Caters on the difficult bells at Christ Church, Spitalfields. This was the longest peal in the method at the time, although the composition by John Noonan was found to be false many years later.[30] Also that year he rang a 6,160 Plain Bob Major at King Edward the Confessor's Chapel at Romford. One further notable peal was the first true peal of Stedman Triples, which was rung at St Giles-in-the-Fields on 22 May 1799.[31] John Noonan again composed and conducted this; the

Osborn MSS records that Noonan said he used as much paper in working this out as would have papered the inside of St Giles' Church![32]

Henry had five sons, two of whom, Phillip and James, joined him in the handbell business. His eldest son, who was also called Henry, inherited his father's acute hearing. He became a piano tuner, responding to the great surge in the demand for this instrument in the early years of the 19th century.[33] Henry also had some practical skill as a ringer and with his father and 10 others formed the Junior Society of College Youths in 1820. On 28 May they rang the first peal for this society, one of Grandsire Caters at Fulham with Henry senior conducting. Later in the year they followed this up with another at Bishop's Stortford. Trollope comments on the status of the men who formed this society, suggesting that they were of the 'same class of men as the Junior Cumberlands, and in almost every way inferior to the real College Youths'.[34]

Henry's third son, Phillip, was born in 1809, and later joined his father in the handbell business in Tottenham Court Road. He too became a competent ringer and rang in a number of peals for the newly formed St James' Society, eventually joining the Society of Cumberland Youths in 1835. The following year his father produced a set of 42 handbells for Charles Ashmore, landlord of the *Ram Inn*, Mansfield, Nottinghamshire, the tenor of which was inscribed on the waist:

SYMONDSON
Bell Founder
Tottenham Court Road
LONDON

Handbells were a great attraction in public houses at that time and the Symondsons were kept busy catering for the demand. Many landlords bought them and regular meetings of ringers were held for practising method ringing, lapping and tune ringing. The latter brought in more custom, as may be seen from this account of the ringers at the *Ram Inn*:

> The hand-bell ringers became deservedly popular and I am told that patrons of the Inn would throw pennies into the hearth, which in time became slightly worn away in a hollow. At one time it was the custom to pay 4d to go into the bell-room. In their palmy days the ringers played regularly on Mondays, (after Service) to an admiring audience and their own profit. Their fame spread far and wide, and they were in great request at local celebrations. On one famous occasion the band went over to Palterton Wakes for the day, on Monday, but were so popular with the dancing music they played, that the inhabitants insisted on their remaining the whole week at this dizzy festival, which they did. Being mostly frame-work knitters, they could take their own time, though what their wives said on their return has never been recorded.[35]

At some period Henry took Phillip into partnership. One reference gives a set with the tenor engraved "Symonson & Son" as being purchased in 1830.[36] This set was recast in 1877. In the Francis Collection is a brass house bell with a wire clapper and P S & H S engraved on the crown. In my collection I have a single bell, size 22C, with H★S on the crown and "Symondson & Son" engraved on the waist. Another octave, still in existence in 1967, had the tenor engraved round the waist:

Symondson
and Son, Founders
N-1- Tottingham [*sic*]
Court Road
London
Penge Union.[37]

Although both Henry and Phillip record their occupations as bell founders, they did not cast their own handbells. A brass and bronze founder, William Pontifex, of the firm Messrs Pontifex and Wood, of Shoe Lane, produced their blanks for them and they tuned and finished the bells.[38] Henry engraved his initials on the crown of his patterns at a right angle to the argent with a four-pointed star between the letters. (Figure 123.) Generally the number of the bell was placed opposite the initials above 12F; on bells smaller than 11G the initials were parallel to the argent. Henry and Phillip were the first handbell makers to pay strict attention to getting the bells into tune; their sets were much sought after in the first half of the 19th century.

In 1838 Henry improved and tuned the church bells at Benington, Hertfordshire, for Leonard Proctor, also making him a set of 32 handbells.[39] Trade was obviously good, for he obtained the use of additional premises at the back of a house in Clipstone Street, Fitzroy Square, a short distance away. He also had a sign made in the shape of a large handbell which he hung, mouth upwards, outside 1 Tottenham Court Road.

A 39-inch diameter bell, originally at St Mary, Redbourn, Hertfordshire, but recast by Taylors in 1953, had this inscription:

TAYLOR & SYMONDSON BELLFOUNDERS OXFORD LONDON & LOUGHBORO' 1839[40]

Some writers have interpreted this as Henry entering into a partnership with John Taylor and working with him at his newly established foundry at Loughborough.[41] John W. Taylor, writing in *The Bell News* in 1900, indicated that this was not the case; it was merely a bell made by mutual arrangement. No doubt Henry obtained the order for the bell from his Hertfordshire connections and invited John Taylor to do the actual casting.

A list of Handbell Founders, compiled by Robert W Leavett and Jean Sanderson and published in *Reverberations* in Spring 1988, credits handbells

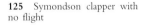

125 Symondson clapper with no flight

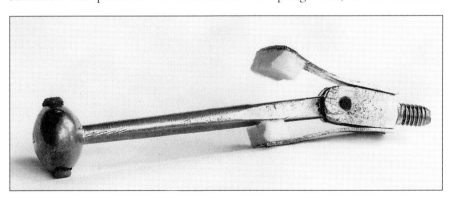

126 Characteristic shape of Symondson spring

127 Early Symondson leather stamp

128 Drawing of later Symondson leather stamp

jointly to Henry Symondson and John Taylor from 1825 to 1839. I consider this most unlikely; I'm sure Jennings in his researches into the Taylor archives for his book *Master of my Art* would have found references to them. I regard the attributing of handbells jointly to Briant and Symondson as also doubtful.

Some of Henry's fittings differed from those of other founders of the time. On one set that I have seen the flights of the clappers have been left off. The brass ball was finished off smoothly, no doubt so that the bells could be placed mouth downwards on a table or the floor without straining the springs. The majority of his springs had an easily recognisable 'notched' appearance. The ornaments used on his early leather caps appear to be a series of bell-shaped flower heads; on a later set, which has the largest bell 22C engraved 'Symondson & Son', the ornaments are two adjacent circles between two trefoils. Illustrations of these and other fittings are shown in Figures 125 to 128.

Little more is known of Henry Symondson senior. His name appears in the three annual Post Office Directories for 1840-2, but after that he is no longer mentioned. He is presumed to have died about 1843, although no death certificate has been traced. Phillip now ran the business. The 1843 Post Office Directory shows that Phillip and his youngest brother James occupied both addresses. James was about 24 years old at this time and had worked with his father for some years, for the 1841 Census lists his occupation as a bell maker. The following year James is not mentioned, although Phillip continued to produce sets of handbells from Tottenham Court Road for the next three years.

Around the year 1846 Phillip left Tottenham Court Road and moved to 32 Wellesley Street, Somerstown, a road that was demolished some twenty years later when St Pancras Station was built.[42] Later that year he moved the business again, this time to 30 Clerkenwell Close, where he went into partnership with James Platt.[43] They appear to have used the Symondson patterns independently, for the Waltham Abbey Ringers own a set of handbells with H S on the crown of the bells, the tenor being inscribed round the waist:[44]

James Platt		Society of Ringers
Bellfounder	*on reverse*	of Waltham Abbey
30 Clerkenwell Close		1846
London		

Another set had the tenor engraved 'Phillip Symondson, Bell Founder, 30 Clerkenwell Close, London'.[45] I have a single bell, size 21D, inscribed similarly. This address was actually James Platt's home, where he lived with his wife Elizabeth and their family.[46] Although he describes himself as a bellfounder on this set of handbells, he was actually a watchmaker. The census return records this trade, in which he was joined by his son, James, and John Evans, an apprentice. He did, however, produce a number of other sets of handbells: examples have been found with J P on the crown instead of H S.[47] These almost certainly date from a later period.

James Platt was born about 1799 in Clerkenwell and probably became acquainted with the Symondsons through ringing. He rang in the first peal for the St James Society in 1827 and averaged two or three peals of Grandsire

129   Roman numeral on Symondson bell

Triples or Caters a year for the next 25 years, including three for the College Youths. In one of his peals, rung for the St James Society at Staines in 1830, Phillip Symondson took part, as did also William Dunn, another London handbell founder.[48] In 1850 Phillip produced a set of 51 handbells in the key of G for the Sheffield Society of Hallamshire Youths. The newspaper account records that the bells were considered perfect and reflected great credit on the founder. They were 'opened' at a dinner held at *The Spread Eagle*, Fargate, with a performance of Jullien's 'Drum Polka'.[49]

During 1853 the newspaper *Bell's Life in London* records the opening of several sets of bells by Phillip. The Duke of Norfolk presented a set of 49 bells in the key of C to the Glossop Society of Bell Ringers and they played some of the most popular tunes of the day to a crowded audience in the Town Hall. Two sets of his went to Birmingham. One ring of 12 for change ringing went to the St Martin's Guild, who later in the year also received a chromatic ring of 40 in the key of C, 'considered to be the finest peal ever sent to Birmingham'.[50]

An unusual Symondson handbell may date from this period. Normally, the number of each bell is inscribed in Arabic numerals, thus: 15. A set of 12 in Norfolk, tenor 19F sharp, has one bell marked in Roman numerals, XV, as may be seen from the photograph in Figure 129.[51] It would be interesting to know why this was done and which of the Symondsons did it.

130 A handbell by James Symondson

In 1848 Henry Symondson junior died of consumption aged forty-five. Five years later James Symondson followed him to an early grave; he was only thirty-three. At some period he had made some handbells on his own account; I have a typical Symondson 16B with J★S on the crown parallel to the argent. A photograph and rubbing are shown in Figures 130 and 131. A few years after this Phillip became mentally ill, was certified insane and confined to St Pancras Workhouse. He died here in 1863 aged 54, bringing to an end a firm that had helped to revolutionise the production of handbells.

When Henry Symondson started, most sets were small and tuned rather haphazardly. Church bell ringers used them to practise upon, although they were also a source of village and public house entertainment. The middle years of the 19th century saw the growth of sets of handbells into musical instruments used for concert performances. Some credit for this must go to the Symondsons for their meticulous care and attention to detail.[52]

131 Rubbing of James Symondson's intitials

Nine
AN ALDBOURNE DIVERSION

132 Aldbourne peal board

133 Bridgman's initials on a Wells bell (1)

134 Bridgman's initials on a Wells bell (2)

IN CHAPTER 5 we saw how the Aldbourne Foundry declined after the Napoleonic Wars and how James Wells eventually became bankrupt and sold out to Thomas Mears. One of his assistants was a man in his 40s called James Bridgman, who was a capable bell hanger and also experienced in small bell production. James was a local man, born about 1782 at Aldbourne.[1] In 1803 he married Mary Brind, also from an established Aldbourne family, and they had four children, although his only son John died when he was four. We know very little about his early years apart from the fact he learnt to ring and became a member of the local band. He evidently achieved some skill, for he took part in a peal of Grandsire Triples on 21 January 1806, the second peal rung by the local band. A photograph of this peal board is shown in Figure 132.

He found himself out of a job in 1825 with the demise of James Wells' business, so when he was offered a position at Whitechapel he promptly accepted.[2] Another who transferred to Whitechapel with him was James Wells' coachman, a man called Kimber, who no doubt also assisted with bell hanging or foundry work. Two of Kimber's sons subsequently worked for Whitechapel: Richard, who was a blacksmith's labourer, and his younger brother, William Thomas, who was a bell moulder. The latter was a skilled craftsman with the brush, pen and chisel and many of his delicate, exact drawings are preserved at the foundry, providing a valuable source of reference.[3]

James, Mary and their two daughters, both under 10, found the East End of London vastly different from the wide open spaces of the Wiltshire Downs. James stuck it for three years and then returned in 1828 to the village of his birth, where he set up as a handbell founder and a bellhanger. His premises were in High Town, probably in a cottage of that name.[4] It is said that he stole away from Whitechapel at the dead of night, carrying away with him the Aldbourne handbell patterns. This is a good example of hearsay evidence, for the story was passed to me by Fred Sharpe, who was told it by Albert Hughes, who received it from Dr. A.D. Tyssen, who heard it direct from John Mears after it happened! He did use some of Robert Wells' patterns; a comparison between the bells of both founders clearly shows this. One Bridgman bell recorded in *The Ringing World* has the letters I B superimposed over the partially erased initials R W on the inside waist.[5] A bell in the Collings Collection marked similarly, size 7D, is shown in

135 Bridgman's initials on a Wells bell (3)

Figure 133. I have examined two other bells showing both sets of initials; these are illustrated in Figures 134 and 135. These bells show parallel lines similar to a Thomas Mears bell; this is not usual in Bridgman's bells.

I have inspected scores of bells by Bridgman, but have seen very few examples where his initials are duplicated with those of Wells. As I observed in Chapter 5 I consider that Wells impressed his name or initials into the sand core before reassembling the mould and that they were not present on his patterns. In this case, how did Wells' initials get into Bridgman's bells? I suspect that Bridgman used one of Robert Wells' handbells as a pattern and the act of removing it from the mould scattered Wells' initials. It is interesting to note that no bells have been found with I B superimposed over James Wells' initials. All his bells had cast-in staples which were removed for handbells. These were then drilled and tapped for the clapper staples. The clapper was similar to Wells' except that he used small leather pegs rather like the wooden ones used by Wells. I have no records of his leather stamps for caps or straps. A rubbing from one of his bells is shown in Figure 136.

Once back at Aldbourne, Bridgman picked up the threads of village life again. He did not become so deeply involved in the ringing, for he did not take part in either of the two local peals for the accession of Queen Victoria, both rung in March 1837.[6] His name appears in the churchwardens' accounts on a number of occasions, mainly in connection with repairs to the bells.[7] In 1843 he provided two church bells for St Martin's, Salisbury to augment the ring of four to six.[8] He charged £63 for this work. The bells were cast by Thomas Mears II, which suggests that Bridgman was acting as an agent for him. This would indicate that he had either received Mears' blessing to take the handbell patterns some years earlier, or they had subsequently made their peace!

I·B

136 Rubbing of Bridgman's initials

In the slack periods between bell hanging jobs he cast many small bells and crotals, or rumblers. One of these is illustrated at Figure 137. These included sets of handbells as well as clock, house, sheep and latten bells. The latter were usually made up four to a set and then hung in a wood and leather housing.[9] During the 1830s and 1840s he was a regular attender at the local fairs and markets with a display of these, doing a good trade with the farmers.[10]

In 1851 he was rehanging some bells when his foot slipped off the frame and he fell through an open hatchway to the ground, injuring his spine.

137 Crotal by James Bridgman

138 Examples of Henry Bond's mark

He never recovered properly from this and had to give up work. His wife, Mary, died in 1854, aged 71, and James himself followed her to the grave in 1858, aged 76.[11] His successor was Henry Bond, who was reputed to have worked for him at some time. According to the Census returns, Henry Bond was born at Chadlington, Oxfordshire, in 1829.[12] However, the parish registers show he was actually born on 13 January 1827, the illegitimate son of William Green and Elizabeth Bond.[13] In 1853 he married Emma Faulkner, a 17-year-old girl from Burford, and they had two sons and four daughters.

At the time of Bridgman's accident he was working as a bell hanger from the home of his uncle, Thomas Bond, who was a gamekeeper and bailiff on an estate at Westcote, Gloucestershire, some 25 miles from Aldbourne. Henry may have spent some time at Aldbourne during the following years, for he acquired Bridgman's tools and handbell patterns from Elizabeth Bridgman and added production of handbells to his Westcote business.

In the first half of the 1860s he transferred the business five miles down the road to Burford. He established his foundry in Sheep Street, where Lloyds Bank now stands, although he moved to new premises across the road to Ends in 1878.[14] Unlike Bridgman, he cast church bells as well as small bells, as this trade card issued in the 1890s shows:

> … (successor to J.Bridgman) Bell Founder and Church Bell Hanger, Sheep Street, Burford, Oxon., Begs to inform the public that he has taken to the business of Mr. J.Bridgman, of Aldbourne, Wilts, with all the original patterns, and intends carrying it on at the above address, where he hopes to meet with their patronage and support. Orders for Church Bells, Turret Bells, House Bells, Clock Bells, and Bells of every description, executed promptly, and on moderate terms. Bell Ropes of the best quality supplied. Sets of hammers fixed for one man to chime the bells.[15]

Bell hangers have to know how to ring a church bell. When Henry moved to Burford he joined the local band at the church and rang with them. It is possible he learned to ring whilst at Aldbourne, although their bells were not in good order at that time.

He inscribed his initials on the crown of his patterns and they are reproduced on the crown of his handbells and other small bells. The height of the lettering varies according to the size of the bell: two examples are shown in Figure 138.

Henry had two sons, both of whom followed him into the business. The elder, also called Henry, was born in 1855 whilst his father was at Westcote, although he spent most of his childhood years at Burford. He served an apprenticeship, possibly with William Blews of Birmingham, and also spent some time working for James Barwell. He must have been involved in the work at the foundry before this time, however, for the second bell at Burford, dated 1868, has an inscription indicating that it was made by Bond and Son.[16] In about 1885 he returned to Burford to live.[17] At the time of the 1891 census he was living with his wife Mary Ann a few doors away from his father in Sheep Street. Mary Ann was a widow and her two children lived with them. They had no children of their own and were not married long, for she died in February 1893.

When his father died in 1905, Henry II became the owner of the business and spent the rest of his life working in and around Burford. He was a millwright and engineer besides being a bell founder and bell hanger, and he found much of his time was taken up with agricultural engineering and odd jobbing. In 1922 he moved the foundry premises to Witney Street, where it was to remain for the next 25 years. He, too, was a member of the local band of ringers at Burford and rang a few peals, mainly Grandsire Triples, in his home area. A contemporary account describes him as a heavy-looking, unwieldy man who had a heart of gold.[18] He aimed to give good workmanship and service; the money he was paid was a secondary consideration. The local farmers and others for whom he undertook work tended to exploit him, either failing to pay their bills at all or keeping him waiting for months.

As he grew older he was dogged by poor health, work was more difficult and he had to live more frugally. Inflation after the war reduced his standard of living even further. He applied for his old age pension when he was 70, but the application was refused. After more applications and representations by local worthies it was finally granted in 1928, but he died later that year, aged seventy-three.

His brother, Thomas, succeeded to the foundry. Born in 1879 he was 24 years younger than Henry and worked for most of his life in and around the medieval building on the banks of the River Windrush. The pattern and carpenter's shops adjoined the street, and the assembly shop, furnace and main foundry building were in the large garden. He started ringing in his mid teens and became a better ringer than either his father or brother. At that time the Rev. F.E. Robinson, Master of the Oxford Diocesan Guild, was in his prime as a peal ringer, endeavouring to become the first man to ring a thousand peals. Thomas rang in about two dozen of these, mostly Stedman Triples, which took place in the towers around Burford.

Thomas was a bellfounder and bell hanger but, like Henry, had to spend much of his time on repairs to agricultural and water-mill machinery.[19] He did not set himself the high standard of castings achieved by his father: Elphick comments that the lettering and moulding wires of his Sussex bell are poor.[20] Perhaps this was inevitable in a one-man business. Frederick Sharpe, who used to visit him at work, describes how Thomas would light the bell-furnace fire and then cast a fishing line into the river at the bottom of the garden, hoping to catch a trout! He would then alternate between the furnace and the fishing line until the metal was ready.[21]

On the outbreak of the Second World War the foundry was shut. The handbell patterns passed down from the old Aldbourne founders had remained in sporadic use until then. Thomas died on 13 March 1947 and the last one-man bell foundry in England closed. He left four daughters although he had traded as 'Bond and Son'. In his *Church Bells of Oxfordshire*, Sharpe gives some views of the foundry taken in 1941.[22] In two of them the handbell patterns are clearly visible. Some of the Bond patterns, tools and brochures were preserved and are now in the Tolsey Museum, Burford.

Ten

WILLIAM DUNN AND HIS SUCCESSORS

THE RECORDS of the Worshipful Company of Founders, in the Guildhall Library, London, date from 1497. They contain much fascinating information and one item of particular interest is the statement that on 3 October 1796, William Dunn, brass founder, was admitted to the Freedom of the Company.[1] I have not found out much about him, but his handbells, like those of the Symondsons, did much to make these instruments popular in the early part of the 19th century. Dunn was born about 1775 in the East End of London. The Founders' Company note his address as 45 Shoe Lane, an area housing many other brass founders at that time. When he joined the College Youths in 1810 he gave his address as Bloomsbury.[2] A set of handbells, size 19 in F, now in the Malmark Museum, has the tenor engraved:

DUNN
2 Castle Street
Bloomsbury.
1822

139   Engraved William Dunn bell at Slapton, Bucks

John W. Taylor senior, in a short article on handbells for *The Bell News* in 1900, mentions that James R. Haworth, a noted London ringer of the 19th century, knew and rang with Dunn.[3] Haworth commented that William Dunn was a tailor by trade, who actually cast and cleverly finished his handbells himself. The London Commercial Directories between 1812 and 1836 are singularly lacking in anyone with the name of William Dunn in the clothing industry. In 1812 a W. Dunn is given as a hat and cap maker at 27 Tichborn Street; the only tailor was R. Dunn of 15 Cirencester Place, Fitzroy Square in 1830.[4] It seems questionable that Dunn, having spent many years learning the craft of a tailor, would suddenly change his trade and become a brass founder. He was a Freeman of the Worshipful Company of Founders in 1796 and in 1808 Richard Osmond, aged 14, was bound to him as an apprentice brass founder for seven years.[5] At that time he was living in Burleigh Street, a road leading off the Strand near Aldwych. Haworth was in his 80s when he gave

140   Crotal by William Dunn

141   Initials of William Dunn

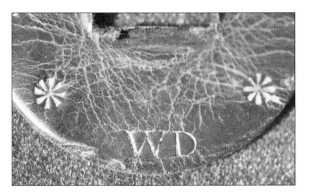

142   Leather stamps used by William Dunn

143   Leather stamp used by Dunn on straps

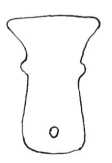

144   Springs used by Dunn

his information to Taylor; either his recollections were faulty, or there was more than one William Dunn.

At that time ringing was at a low ebb in London. Dunn joined the College Youths in 1810, but did not join in their peal ringing activities for some years. He was elected Master in 1827 and then, between the years 1829 and 1847, took part in 10 peals for them.[6] He also became one of the first members of the St James' Society when it was formed in 1824 and, in their 10th anniversary year, he was elected Master. He rang 17 peals for this society, the majority being Grandsire Triples or Caters. On a country trip to St Mary, Staines, in 1830 he rang a peal in which two other London handbell founders took part, Phillip Symondson and James Platt.[7]

Like the Symondsons, he made his bells smaller and lighter than those of his predecessors. The Symondsons, however, had their bells cast for them by Pontifex and Wood; Dunn cast his own bells. It is interesting to speculate that Dunn was a brass founder who was living or working at 45 Shoe Lane when he was admitted to the Founders' Company; Pontifex and Wood's premises were close by in the same road. Was there any connection?

I have four addresses for Dunn. Besides the three already mentioned, he also cast handbells at 23 Suffolk Street West, King's Cross. A set owned by Mr. W. Croft has this address engraved on the tenor with the date 1849.[8] A similar inscription is found on the tenor of a set of eight at Slapton, Buckinghamshire. A photograph of this bell is shown at Figure 139. He also made crotals; one of these is illustrated in Figure 140. Dunn engraved his initials W.D. on the crown of his patterns and these are reproduced on his bells. (Figure 141.) These initials were cut deeply and were rarely removed completely in tuning. This can cause problems in identifying his bells: in some cases the bells are not his but the work of subsequent owners of the patterns. His leather work provides other identifying features. Figure 142 shows one of his caps with his initials and an eight-petalled 'daisy' which he used as an ornament. On some handles he stamped a complete flower, as in Figure 143. He made his clapper shafts thin by modern standards and the staples slight. His springs had small ornamental bulges midway on each side, as in Figure 144.

I have seen many Dunn handbells, but one of the most fascinating sets I have seen was discovered only recently. A West Country ringer was called to Tavistock to inspect a derelict set of bells which had been given to the widow's husband some 30 years earlier. They were in a large, grimy box which had lain neglected in a garage for years. The box contained 48 bells together with seven music stands, a space for music, a conductor's baton and tools for running repairs.[9] The

145   Dunn's initials on a 29C

bells ranged from 04G to 33F, one of the largest bells ever cast. Most of the bells are marked with W D on the crown or on the cap, which is also decorated with the eight-petalled 'daisy'. A photograph of the initials on the crown of the 29C is shown at Figure 145. The 33F, illustrated in Figure 146, is approximately 15 inches in diameter and has no identifying marks on the bell or cap. The two bass octaves have most unusual clapper balls. Instead of the customary ball they have

146   George Francis holding a 33F by William Dunn

a cylinder of solid brass about an inch in depth. This is surrounded by a thick rubber strip tied in place, rather like a solid tyre on a heavy solid wheel. Figure 147 gives a view of this. These clappers have struck the bells so hard that the majority of them are cracked. This is the largest set of Dunn's bells ever discovered; previously known sets have not exceeded three octaves.

Increasing age caused him to give up founding and in about 1852 he passed his patterns and other equipment to George Stockham.[10] He spent his remaining years in St Pancras Workhouse where Phillip Symondson had been committed. The two men often met and, although they had rung together on many occasions, reputedly never spoke to each other.[11] Nothing else is known at present about William Dunn; he probably died in the mid-1850s.

A few handbell founders have been excellent ringers; others have been highly regarded for their personal integrity. By all accounts George Stockham combined both these qualities and was one of the most respected ringers in London in the 19th century. J.W. Taylor records that he was born in London, probably in the last decade of the reign of George III, his father coming from Exeter. The earliest reference to him yet discovered is in the name book of the St James' Society, which he joined in September 1835. His first peal, one of Grandsire Triples, followed later that month and he soon became one of the leading members of the society.[12]

He owed his rapid progress to Thomas Tolladay. Tolladay had learned to ring at Windsor Castle whilst working as a boat builder at Eton College. There was little change ringing at Windsor at that time because the 'scroof', or paid ringers, were only interested in the money they could earn. This was considerable: at the General Election of 1802, 12 ringers shared £110 for ringing three times a day for a week![13] To keep their wages high, they surrounded the band with petty rules and restrictions. One of these prohibited members of the society from ringing with any other band; an irksome restriction for an ambitious ringer. Tolladay decided to leave his native Eton for London for the same reason as William Shipway had left Bath some years earlier; to improve his ringing. He joined the St James' Society and quickly made it the leading company in the country.

Stockham took part in some famous peals, including the 12,096 Grandsire Caters in 7 hours and 50 minutes at Fulham, conducted by Tolladay on 15 May

147 Unusual clapper for 29C by William Dunn

148 George Stockham's signature

1837.[14] He also rang in the 7,325 Grandsire Cinques at St Martin-in-the-Fields on 26 October the same year. The Caters was claimed as the longest length rung by 10 men; the band was not aware of a peal rung at Painswick 20 years earlier which was 216 changes longer, although six minutes shorter in time. Tolladay died in 1844 of tuberculosis and Stockham succeeded him as conductor to the society, calling 61 peals for them.[15] His signature, shown in Figure 148, is taken from a letter he wrote to the ringers at Windsor about one of these peals.[16]

An interesting glimpse of the use of handbells in public houses in the first half of the century is found in some loose papers inserted in James Haworth's peal book.[17] This relates to an attempt for a 'lapped' handbell peal at the *Cock and Bottle*, Bedfordbury, in a street behind St Martin's Lane.[18] There, on the last day of the year 1837, six members of the Westminster Society sat down to ring 6,070 Stedman Cinques. After ringing nearly four hours, 'one member of the party missed giving away', i.e. passing one of his bells to another ringer, and so the peal was lost with just a course to go. George Stockham was one of these ringers, as was James Haworth.

Around 1840 Stockham took the post of steeplekeeper and clockwinder at St Clement Danes, becoming the foreman of the ringers at the same time. During the 42 years he held this post he made St Clement Danes the central meeting point for all the first-class ringers in London. He was always willing to help young ringers to progress, however. He assisted the Richmond Society to ring peals in 1854 and conducted the first peal for the Waterloo Society in 1869.[19] He joined the College Youths in 1838 and during the next 10 years took part in nearly all their peals, conducting many of them. He was also a member of that select band appointed to ring at Westminster Abbey.[20] His last peal for the College Youths was the famous 8,580 Stedman Cinques, rung at St Michael, Cornhill, in 1861. James Dwight, another of the band, composed a song about this which was regularly performed at the annual feast. The seventh of the 14 verses refers to Stockham:

> George Stockham rang the sixth
> A man of wide renown,
> For the many peals he'd rung,
> Both in country and in town:
> He was always willing to call peals
> For any young rising band,
> And for many years was Steeple-Keeper
> At St Clement's in the Strand.[21]

He had a dog that accompanied him everywhere, even into the belfry whilst he was ringing. It would lie quietly in the corner whilst ringing was in progress, but when 'This is all' was called, would bark furiously.[22] Stockham knew William Dunn well and secured his handbell patterns when the latter became too old to work. Some time after 1852 he started casting in Newcastle Court, where the Law Courts now stand. Whilst here he provided shop room for a member of the Oliver family, a worker from the Whitechapel Foundry, who carried out private work repairing clocks.[23] When the Law Courts were built he moved his premises about fifty yards further away to

149   Leather stamps used by George Stockham (1)

150   Leather stamps used by George Stockham (2)

Carey Street, where he cast some of his largest sets. The tenor of one of these is inscribed:

G STOCKHAM
Founder
35 CAREY ST. WC
London
1873

When The Old Steeple, Dundee, was restored in 1872 it was determined to add a ring of bells, similar to those installed the previous year at St Paul's Episcopal Church, Dundee. Mears and Stainbank got the contract to supply both of these rings, but it was Stockham who received the order in 1873 for a set of 56 handbells and not Mears. This may have been through the influence of his College Youths colleagues, who, at a cost of £80, were invited to Dundee to ring the first peal on the bells in May 1873.[24]

Stockham made better fittings than Dunn. He improved his crown staples, making them more substantial, and he made his clappers rectangular in section with bossed staple ends. He discontinued the idea of ornamenting the springs, making them tapered and plain. His leather caps were stamped with his initials, G S, and he mainly used the eight-petalled 'daisy' of his predecessor. (See examples at Figures 149 and 150.) On some of his handbells Dunn's initials are still visible. Towards the end of his life he became infirm and unable either to ring or work, so he sold his plant, patterns and stock to George Welch, of 51 Bankside, London. He died in mid–November 1884, a muffled peal being rung to his memory by the St James' Society on 1 December.[25]

Little is known about George Welch, apart from the fact that he produced some good sets of musical handbells. His workshop was in Southwark, across the river from St Paul's, and here he cast and fitted his bells for 17 years. Where possible he tried to skim the W D off the crown of his bells once they were

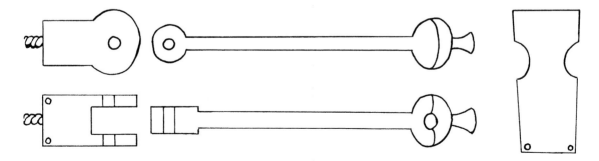

151   Clapper assembly used by George Welch

152 Leather stamps used by George Welch (1)

153 Leather stamps used by George Welch (2)

cast, but he was not always successful. Like Stockham, he finished his bells skilfully, adding a sturdy clapper assembly, as in Figure 151. He used the same set of stamps for his leather caps, adding his initials G W, as may be seen in Figures 152 and 153.

He advertised regularly in *The Bell News*, the first advert appearing in July 1883. He always pointed out that he was George Stockham's successor, no doubt relying on the goodwill this engendered. Unlike his predecessors, he was not a church bell ringer, so he had little actual contact with any of his potential customers. However, he still managed to get quality work. One set of 160 bells was obviously produced for a big northern team to use at the Belle Vue Competition; it consisted of 5½ chromatic octaves with 90 duplicates and triplicates. This set is now in Darley Dale, Derby. In June 1900 he advertised for the last time; shortly after this he retired from handbell work and sold the plant and goodwill to John F. Mallaby.

John Francis Mallaby was born in 1863, the youngest son of Thomas Mallaby of Masham, Yorks. Although the Mallaby family had lived around Masham for many generations they were of French extraction, originally coming from France to work in the mines.[26] Thomas had learned to ring at the early age of nine, an unusual occurrence in the 1840s, and he taught his sons to ring when they too were quite young. Thomas was a bellhanger, and built up a good business in the north of England. His first complete rehanging was at Knaresborough, Yorkshire, in 1865. In an advertisement in one of the Snowdon series he listed 65 churches and cathedrals where he had carried out work, travelling as far south as Soberton, Hampshire.[27] Thomas died on 26 August 1885, aged 52, and a large ornate brass plaque to his memory was placed in St Mary's, Masham.[28]

Thomas' son Peter took over the business. The bellhanging work at Masham could not support all the family, so his brother John left home and found work in Hull. He attached himself to the local band, finding lodgings with Charles Jackson, who at that time was the leading ringer and conductor in the district.[29] He rang several peals with the local band whilst at Hull. In 1887 he took on the job of hanging a new Warner ring of six at Barnby Don. He was attracted to a local girl there and they later married. In the early 1890s he was living with his wife Annie at 105 Rochester Street, Bradford, and working as a church bell hanger for James Shaw. Whilst there he must have gained experience in the casting and furbishing of handbells which stood him in good stead later on. When William Shaw drew up his will on 16 December 1892, John was asked to be one of the witnesses.[30]

In 1894 he moved to Barnby Don where he started up at the Albion Works a bellhanging business of his own.[31] He joined in with the local ringers and helped to build up an expert Minor team, setting very high standards both in striking and method ringing. He composed several peals, including one of Superlative, and also published some Treble Bob Minor methods that had the unusual feature of the tenor as hunt bell. His peal ringing was not restricted to Minor rung cartwheel fashion, for he rang peals of Caters and Royal with some of the famous ringers of the day: Washbrook, Robinson and the Pyes.

His first advertisements for handbells appeared in *The Bell News* for May 1893. These indicated that he would supply musical handbells in diatonic or chromatic scales to any number. It is most unlikely that he cast these himself: they were probably obtained on commission from James Shaw. It is also possible that he obtained them from John Warner for whom he carried out bellhanging work. In May 1896 he changed the name of his firm to J.F. Mallaby and Co., no doubt to gain more capital. When George Welch retired, he bought his plant, tools and patterns and began to cast his own handbells at Barnby Don. He changed his advertisements to reflect this, announcing that he was now a church bell hanger and musical handbell founder. He added a small plaudit to himself at the end, stating that all his handbells had 'excellent tone'!

Dunn's patterns were still being used for casting handbells. Examples of Stockham, Welch and Mallaby's castings have been found with traces of the initials W D on the crown. A miscellaneous set at Bradford Cathedral have 'J F Mallaby Founder Barnby Don' on the strap handle, whilst some of the bells have W D on the crown.[32] Jennings, in his book on handbells, states that Stockham, Welch and Mallaby used Symondson's patterns for their handbells.[33] This is not so; examination of their handbells definitely shows that they used Dunn's patterns and tools. The confusion may have arisen because Mallaby also had a few of Symondson's patterns; five of these are still in the possession of his great grand-daughter.[34]

Advertisements for Mallaby's handbells continued throughout the life of *The Bell News*. When it closed down in December 1915, John Mallaby ceased advertising. No doubt, like other founders, he turned over to war work in 1914 and never resumed handbell founding after hostilities ceased. He worked for Pilkingtons of Doncaster as a pattern maker in the interval between giving up bellhanging and retirement. On 4 July 1950, exactly a year after his wife, he died aged 87, the last of the Yorkshire handbell founders.[35]

Eleven

TAYLORS OF LOUGHBOROUGH

THE NAME 'TAYLORS of Loughborough' is well known to ringers. The firm has cast some magnificent rings of bells and also constructed some excellent carillons. The history of the firm has recently been extensively documented by Trevor Jennings and for a more detailed exposition of the foundry the reader is directed to this volume.[1] Whilst dealing with Taylors I shall concentrate on their small bells and musical handbells as I did with Whitechapel.

According to an 1882 catalogue, the firm claims to be the successors 'to the ancient firm of Watts, Eayre and Arnold, of Leicester & St Neots'.[2] Thomas North describes how in 1717 Joseph and Thomas Eayre were in partnership, with Thomas at Kettering and Joseph at St Neots.[3] When Joseph died in 1772 his nephew Edward Arnold continued the business and around 1780 he took on a young apprentice named Robert Taylor. Robert was born at Riseley, Bedfordshire in 1759, the fifth child and only son of William and Mary Taylor.

154 Taylor lettering Type I

William was a draper, hatter and grocer and it is interesting to speculate why, like most sons of the period, Robert did not follow him into this business. Robert married Elizabeth Fowler, a relative of the local brewer and, in the course of time, they had three sons and three daughters, of whom William and John survived to carry on the foundry.

Robert managed the foundry at St Neots when Edward Arnold moved to Leicester, and by 1786 he owned the business. William was introduced into the firm at an early age. His name appears on a bell at Braybrooke, Northamptonshire, dated 1806, when he was only 11 years old! John, two years his junior, was also taken into the business and from 1821 the firm traded as R. Taylor and Sons. In this year they moved the foundry to Blackfriars Road, Oxford. After working here with his father and brother for four years John moved with his new wife to Buckland Brewer, Devon, to start a branch foundry. Robert died aged 70 in 1830 and was buried in the churchyard of St Ebbe's, Oxford. John continued operating from Buckland Brewer for some years, but in 1839 moved his premises to Packhorse Lane, Loughborough. William continued to keep the bell foundry running at Oxford despite a much greater interest in clockmaking. He died a bachelor in 1854 and the Oxford branch of the family business closed.

155 Rubbing of Type I lettering

Amongst my collection I have an inscribed house bell of 19th-century shape with a very flat crown and a wide lip. On the flat crown are two concentric circles and within these, parallel to the argent, is inscribed 'J T & Co' with '7 oz' opposite. (Figure 162.) Whilst at Buckland Brewer in 1831 John Taylor cast a bell for Eye, Hereford inscribed 'John Taylor and Company'. This house bell may date from this period. It is probable, however, that most small bells, criers' bells, house bells and musical handbells date from the Loughborough foundry of the 1850s. In 1860 a special alloy was derived for musical handbells,[4] consisting of 39 per cent copper, 8½ per cent tin, with the remainder being made up with old handbells. This formula was used for very many years in the firm's production of handbells.

Their first price list for handbells appears in their catalogue for 1867.[5] This advertised peals of four, five, six, eight, 10, 12 or 15 handbells from size 23B to 8C. This suggests that their prime reason for supplying handbells was for ringers to practise change ringing: more than half the table is devoted to fewer than eight bells, surely the minimum number any team would buy for tune ringing. It also gives a clue to the range of bells produced, from 23B to 01C. A copy of a price list quoting the same prices is given in Figure 237; this is taken from their 1882 catalogue and it is interesting to note that the range of bells now extended to 29C. These handbells were made from their first patterns. They had rounded shoulders and crowns, with the letters J.T and the bell number deeply engraved either side of the argent. The letters and numbers all had serifs as may be seen from Figures 154 and 155. I will call this lettering Type I. The serifs provide a useful clue when dating Taylor handbells as later patterns omitted them.

From the start Taylors took note of the problems other founders had encountered with their handbell fittings and tried to overcome them. They made their clapper staples more substantial and screwed them into the bell. The clapper stems were flat in section, tapering from the ball to a square-shaped staple end. An iron pin secured the clapper to the staple. Springs were brass with the felts riveted to them, not attached by sealing wax. (See the diagram at Figure 156.)

John died in 1858 and left the foundry to his only surviving son, John William Taylor. One of John William's first tasks on inheriting the foundry was to find larger accommodation and in 1860 he moved the firm to custom-built premises on the current site in Freehold Street. Amongst the stock he transferred from Packhorse Lane to the new buildings were many sheep and cattle bells and handbells.[6] A woodcut of the works, as illustrated in the 1882 catalogue, is shown at Figure 158.

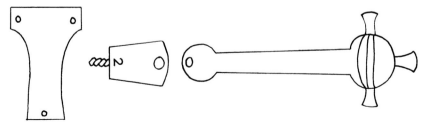

156   Taylor handbell assembly

157 J W Taylor junior

A period of prosperity followed and, with his sons John William junior and Edmund Denison, the firm built up a reputation for fine bells. To cope with some of the additional work that was being obtained the foundry was extended in 1874; this provided separate brass founding facilities for handbells,[7] However, this side of the business received a major setback in 1875 when customers awaiting delivery of their handbells were sent this notice:

> … we are sorry we cannot help you as we have ceased the manufacture of handbells because of the heavy pressure of church bell work.

When other work declined the handbell shop was reopened, but it proved quite difficult to regain the confidence of customers! However, it was steadily recovered and to some extent it helped the firm survive a decade later when less church bell work was forthcoming. Some experimental work was carried out with aluminium handbells in 1883, but they proved very difficult to machine and their tone was markedly inferior.[9]

158 Woodcut of Taylor Foundry about 1882

Disaster struck in 1891. On the evening of 23 June, fire was discovered in the foundry. Because the water pressure was very low, the machine shop and handbell shop were gutted, the handbell patterns were destroyed and stores were reduced to ashes. In addition, they lost 500 finished handbells awaiting delivery and their 10 hundredweight stock of horse and bicycle bells.[10] The premises were greatly under-insured: the estimated loss was £3,500, whilst the insurance settlement was only £1,419. A new handbell department was given top priority, but some time was to elapse before production restarted.

It is extremely likely that the handbells were redesigned after this. The pattern shop was destroyed by the fire together with the old handbell patterns, so the opportunity was taken to reshape them. The patterns they

159   Taylor lettering Type II

160   Rubbing of Type II lettering

produced were now similar to those of James Barwell of Birmingham, with flat crowns and almost right-angled shoulders. On one side of the argent the number was deeply etched, on the other J T was etched, now without a full stop between the letters and printed in letters without serifs. I call this lettering Type II. These are illustrated in Figures 159 and 160.

Bells produced for semitones now had an X added to their number; for instance, 10G sharp now had 10X engraved on the pattern. (Figure 161.) Small bells such as shop, house and horse bells were sold by weight and have their weight on the crown. A slight modification to the handbell clapper assembly was made about this time; probably for cost reasons, the felts on the springs were attached with sealing wax and not riveted on.

Some idea of the volume of business at this time can be seen from the schedule of work for the moulder who worked in the handbell casting department. He was required to complete 32 moulding boxes a day, each containing 12 patterns.[11] He probably had other jobs as well: a regular production of nearly two thousand handbell castings a week would require a considerable number of staff to finish them. Music hall items often included handbell ringing and acts such as Campanologists Royal, or the Walford Family, used massive sets of over 250 bells. One of their concerts in 1893 advertised:

The Grandest Carillon on Earth, containing the Largest and the Smallest Handbells ever cast, in addition to a large peal of Orchestral Cup Bells, all manufactured specially for the Company by Messrs Taylor & Co, of Loughborough.[12]

John William Taylor senior was given the opportunity to buy several firms manufacturing handbells in the period 1885-1903. The first of these was William Blews & Sons. After William Blews died in 1887 the firm virtually closed down, although his wife, Frances, reopened it two years later to try to sell it as a going concern. Some of the plant and bell moulds would have proved a valuable extension to Taylor's business, but he decided against it and Charles Carr bought Blews.[13] In the 19th century James Shaw of Bradford produced more handbells than any other firm in the world, as well as being a major clock and church bell manufacturer. A catastrophic fire in 1901 gutted most of their premises and William Shaw offered the goodwill of the business to Taylors.[14] The firm refused this business also.

Perhaps an even stranger refusal was the opportunity to take over Mears and Stainbank at Whitechapel. J.W. Taylor considered this carefully, even to the

161 Numbering of semitones

extent of visiting them and examining their books, but eventually came down against the involvement.[15] Finally, when Thomas Blackbourn's business was faltering for lack of capital in 1903, John William was offered the concern at a very low price. He considered the asking price too much and it was sold by the Official Receiver at auction.[16]

John William senior died in 1906, aged 79, and two of his sons, John William junior and Edmund Denison, carried on what was now a world-wide business. The former's interest in handbells extended beyond their manufacture, for he had a tune ringing team that took part in the celebrated Belle Vue competitions. A woodcut of him made about 1890 is at Figure 157. Jennings describes how John William Taylor improved clapper design at the beginning of the new century by tapping a small screw into the argent to prevent the clapper staple from working loose.[17] I have not seen any bells with this fitting: I presume it was discontinued owing to the difficulty of removing the clapper assembly without removing the strap.

During the First World War the firm went over to war work, producing components for shells. The return on this work was miserly, barely paying the wages and keeping the plant and buildings operational. Three of John William junior's sons were killed in the war and, when the handbell department reopened afterwards, their expertise in this field was greatly missed. It took some time before the backlog of orders was dispatched.

John William junior died in 1919, aged 66. He passed his interest in the foundry to his surviving sons, Pryce and Paul. Pryce, born in 1891, was 23 years older than his half-brother Paul Lea, who was a child of John William's second marriage. Edmund Denison continued as senior partner and his sales of carillons in the post-war years made 1921 the best year ever for the firm. Whilst on a business trip to Toronto in 1927, Pryce died of peritonitis, aged thirty-six. He had been married only two years and had no family. Edmund Denison ran the foundry on his own until 1935 when Paul Lea joined him as a junior partner.

During the early 1930s Edmund Denison experimented with increasing the tin content of handbells, but didn't find a satisfactory alternative to their 1860 formula.[18] When New Philharmonic Pitch, which made A equal to 440 Hertz, became standard he was quick to advertise that Taylors handbells conformed to this and sent the first set tuned to this pitch to Keswick in 1932. During the Second World War the foundry again went on to war work, this time making aircraft components and tank turrets. Early in the war they received permission to cast 'Great George' for Liverpool Cathedral and this was successfully accomplished in July 1940. This tuned bell,

162 7 oz shop bell of J Taylor & Co

163 Leather stamps by Taylor 1870s

weighing more than 14½ tons, had to wait more than 11 years before it could take its place in the cathedral. Edmund Denison died a bachelor in 1947, aged 83, and Paul Lea now assumed full control of the foundry. His only son died in 1961, aged seven, and in 1977, when approaching retirement, he formed a limited company under the name of John Taylor & Co (Bellfounders), Ltd. A general manager was appointed and following Paul's death in 1981 his wife, Merle, assumed the chairmanship of the board of directors. She continues to take an active interest in the company's affairs, thus continuing the family connection in an unbroken line for over 200 years.

In the immediate post-war flurry of activity, church bell work predominated and no work on handbells was carried out. After 1949 it was organised on a customer service basis; odd bells would be supplied or a strap fitted, but no one member of staff was responsible for handbells. In the 1960s it stopped completely due to a heavy programme of tower bell work and the deaths of several key employees.[19] It was not until 1978 that an employee was again engaged to work specifically on handbells. Since then a gradual increase in orders for handbell work, both in refurbishment of existing bells and provision of new bells either singly or in sets, has resulted in more employees being taken on to deal with the growing order book.

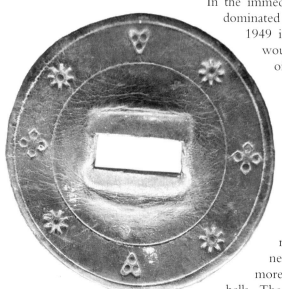

164 Leather stamps by Taylor 1890s

The handbell department at Taylors has now been reorganised on a more cost effective basis. Since 1991 new handbell patterns have been introduced, reverting more to the dome-shaped heads of the first Taylor handbells. The patterns are engraved with TAYLOR on the crown and this is reproduced on the bells. These bells are cast in the traditional way except that the metal is filtered into the moulds. This improves the quality of the castings. They are cast about three tones high and machined down to pitch, the final polishing working through six grades of emery. Currently, the range of handbells manufactured covers the five octaves from 29C to 01C, although bells outside this can be produced to special order.

The ornaments used for the leather caps have altered very little over the last century. Figures 163 to 165 compares those from Victorian times with now. Taylors no longer manufacture their own clapper assemblies; it is more cost-effective to buy in the parts. Nineteen sizes of clapper are used; bells of 24A sharp and below are given split ball clappers. Nylon pegs are used for 4G to 01C; leather pegs for 23B to 5F sharp; leather pegs covered with chamois for 17A to 14D sharp; leather pegs covered with felt for 23B to 18G sharp. Modern adhesives are now used to attach felt to springs instead of the traditional sealing wax, thus bringing the production of their handbells right up to date.

165 Leather stamps by Taylor 1990s

Twelve
CRIPPLEGATE AND CROYDON

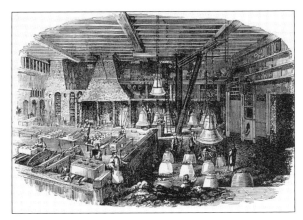

166 John Warner's moulding shop about 1862

167 Advertisement for John Warner's pocket handbells

ABOUT THE YEAR 1739 a Quaker by the name of Jacob Warner established a brass foundry in Wood Street, Cheapside.[1] He married Ruth Tomson of St Albans and they had six sons and one daughter. John was the eldest, born in 1735, and he, together with Tomson, three years his junior, followed Jacob into the business. Jacob died in 1762 and the two boys inherited the foundry, moving it the following year to Jewin Crescent, Cripplegate, where they maintained an uneasy partnership for the next 17 years. In 1780 they parted company and John set up on his own as a bell and brass founder in Fleet Street. He traded under the name of John Warner and Son although no son has been traced. It is interesting to note that this is the first recorded use of a bellfounder including his son in the title of the firm.[2] Being used to founding in brass, he initially used the traditional method of patterns in sand moulds when casting small bells, but around 1788 he began moulding larger bells by the clay model technique. By the time of his death in 1820 he had cast nearly two dozen church bells. After his death in 1820 this foundry closed down.

Meanwhile, Tomson kept the foundry in Jewin Crescent, where he was later joined by his sons, John and Robert, born in 1776 and 1777 respectively. Tomson died in 1816 and the business passed to John and Robert who expanded it, dealing mainly with plumbers' brassware, coppersmiths' ware, pumps, steam fittings, copper baths and handbells.[3] John married twice, the eldest child of his second marriage being Charles Borham Warner, born in 1812. He entered the business and, after Robert's death in 1833, helped his father reorganise it. In 1850 they ventured into church bell founding, a new enterprise for this branch of the firm. It is said that one reason they had for doing this was to use up the large stocks of copper they had in store.

John died in 1852 and Charles took his brother Robert into partnership, together with his own sons,

Henry and Compton. A year later the firm took out a patent for an improved method of casting large bells.[4] It was granted to Frederick Warner, of the firm of John Warner and Sons, together with John Shotton, one of the foremen, and was for the now-familiar method of producing a cope in a cast iron case, independent of the core.

The firm was proud to place the royal coat of arms on its bells, for a royal warrant had appointed them bellfounders to Queen Victoria. Charles tendered for casting the first Big Ben and was pleased when he was awarded the contract, for he knew that casting the largest bell in the country would bring the firm more business. The bell was too large to be cast at Cripplegate, so a relative, William Warner, of the firm Warner, Lucas and Barret, cast it at their works at Stockton-on-Tees. The contract was dogged by difficulties. Miscalculations in the size of the mould made the bell overweight at 16 tons but, more important, it was too large, by three inches, to be hoisted up the central shaft of the clock tower! The necessity for this never arose, however. While they debated back and forth what should be done, the bell was cracked with a 13 hundredweight clapper whilst being tested in the Palace Yard. Much controversy followed. Robert Warner was asked to re-tender, but his estimate for recasting was too high, so the contract went to George Mears. At the end of 1857 a popular rhyme was:

> Poor Mr Warner is put in the corner
> For making a bad Big Ben.
> Good Mr Mears, as it appears,
> Is to make us a new one—when?[5]

Charles died in 1869 and his two sons retired from the business, leaving it solely under Robert's control. For some time the firm had been expanding its production of small bells and handbells. One of their catalogues from the 1860s showed that they kept extensive stocks of 'house bells, house bells turned and lacquered, house bells with springs for shutters, bells for ships, yachts and steamers, horse bells, sheep bells, dog bells, clang bells for cattle, ferret bells, squirrel bells, dinner bells, tea bells, Bellman's bells, self-acting alarm bells and small clock bells'! The catalogue noted that they took old bells in part exchange. A woodcut, showing the moulding shop for small bells about 1862, may be seen in Figure 166.

When the fourth, revised edition of Henry Hubbard's *Elements of Campanalogia* was published in 1876, Warner's placed their usual advertisement in it, but this time they included a complete page on musical handbells. From this it can be gathered that they had recently improved their clappers and modified their pegging system 'which gives a superior tone and facility for ringing'. They went on to add: 'Cheaper bells are supplied by some persons, but the bells by J.W. & Sons are warranted of the best description both in accuracy of note and finish.' The man in charge of the handbell shop and their tuning was Henry W. Haley, a celebrated ringer, composer and conductor of the time. Originally a Spitalfields weaver, he was an expert tune and change ringer on tower and handbells.[6] He started his career as a ringer in 1839 by lapping handbell peals of Grandsire and Stedman in public houses in the east end of London, later ringing Double Norwich Maximus and Tebb's composition of Stedman Triples.[7]

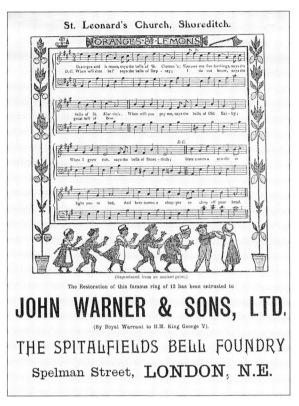

168 Advertisement for John Warner

He was one of the five members of the Society of Cumberland Youths which toured America in 1850 giving handbell concerts with P.T. Barnum's 'Greatest Show on Earth'.[8] Whilst in Philadelphia he collected a band together and conducted the first peal to be rung outside the British Isles.

The manager of the bellfoundry at that time was Samuel B. Goslin, a nephew of Robert Warner.[9] He took out a number of patents for improving the hanging of church bells, which Warner's subsequently used.[10] One of these was for the placing of plain bearings in a special casing on top of the side frame instead of sinking them into the wood and weakening the frame. He also wrote a number of pamphlets on ringing, three concerning handbells. The first of these was *The A B C of Musical Handbell Ringing*, subtitled *The Handbell Ringers Instructor*. This first appeared in print in 1879 and went through several editions. The *Musical Hand-Bell Ringer's Instructor Part II* was first advertised in *Church Bells* in August 1880; various other dates are quoted for reprints. The third booklet was the *Theory and Tunes for Handbells*. Robert Warner published these and details of them were always included in the firm's advertisements for handbells. About 1888 Goslin left Warner's and set up on his own as a founder and bellhanger, working from the Bishopsgate Art Metal Works, Artillery Lane.[11] In general, the casting and bellhanging work done on his own was very poor.[12]

By the mid-1880s the firm of John Warner and Sons was a prosperous concern. The brass foundry at Cripplegate was a large, five-storeyed building with six brass furnaces and one bell metal furnace. A steam engine drove the tuning machine and lathes. Four hundred men were employed there, although the bell foundry had only a foreman and two men, with a foreman-carpenter and three assistants for the bell hanging.[13] Another extensive works making mainly pumping plant had been established at Walton-on-Naze, Essex.

In 1890 Robert Warner was 74 and he decided to retire. He sold the Cripplegate works, giving the goodwill of the bell foundry jointly to his son-in-law, Andrew Marriage, and his nephew, Henry Warner. They were unable to find the capital to run it, so they set up a limited company in which Andrew's relatives were the principal shareholders. They bought out Henry and moved the premises to Spelman Street, Spitalfields. They advertised their handbells often throughout the late Edwardian period. They were progressive in their advertisements, usually taking a whole page and changing it several times a year. For instance, in 1912 they ran a series of full-page advertisements, one of which was for sets of eight pocket handbells for just 50 shillings; another gave the price of sets of handbells in various sizes; a third gave the music for 'Oranges and Lemons' from an old print and a fourth gave the same music written out in number notation for handbells. Others detailed their work on church bells. Examples of two of their advertisements are shown in Figures 167 and 168.

A strong contingent of ringers worked in the foundry and on 13 December 1913, to mark the 150th anniversary of the firm, they rang a peal of Grandsire Caters on the bells they had just rehung at St Leonard's, Shoreditch. *The Ringing World* picked on this footnote and commented that this was the first occasion a foundry band had rung a 10-bell peal.[14] This brought a swift reply from John Taylor, who noted that his foundry had rung one 25 years earlier at Loughborough!

William Haley, who had written several pamphlets on handbell ringing, took over the handbell tuning shop after the death of his father in 1886. Robert Warner printed these booklets and included them in the firm's advertisements instead of Goslin's books. The four titles generally advertised were: *The Bell Hymn Book, Twelve Carols, Twelve Popular Airs* and *The Handbell Tutor*.

Robert Warner died in 1896 and in his will left the Walton-on-Naze firm to Andrew Marriage's son. He took the name Robert Warner under deed poll and soon relinquished this business, which shortly afterwards went into liquidation! He set up a bellfoundry for a short time at Richmond and an iron foundry in Osborne Street. When his father was killed in the First World War he became the sole owner of the Spelman Street foundry.

Most foundries went over to war work in 1914 and the Spelman Street works was no exception. In January 1916 they stopped advertising in *The Ringing World* and for three years did not appear to take any interest in bells. They resumed with a simple quarter-page advertisement at the beginning of January 1919 and maintained it unchanged until 7 July 1922 when the last one appeared. The reason for this is not hard to find. The last Robert Warner was a wealthy man and did not really want the bother of the business. After 1918 he allowed it to run down and finally wound it up in 1924. He died in 1949, leaving over £20,000 to the Founders' Company to establish a fellowship in metallurgical research as applied to bellfounding practice.[15]

During their years of business Warner's produced many sets of handbells. Copies of their catalogues are difficult to acquire and I have only examined a few photocopied pages. Nevertheless, I have inspected many of their bells. These are not marked in any way, having neither numbers nor distinguishing marks. However, they are smaller than those from the other principal handbell suppliers of the time. For instance, note for note, handbells from Whitechapel have considerably greater diameters. If the bells still have their original fittings, their clappers are distinctive. They have rectangular shafts with

169   Warner's clapper assembly

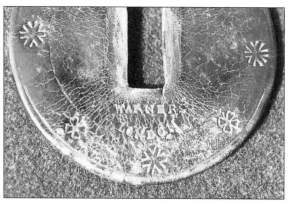

170   Warner's leather stamps

171   William Gillett

172   Arthur A. Johnston

the number of the bell filed on them in Roman numerals. This is sometimes under the ball but more often just above the staple end. (Figure 169.) The flights are small; the staples are sturdy and, on older bells, iron pins were used to fasten the clapper shafts to them. They used tapered brass springs with semi-circular cut-outs. Their caps are stamped with a four-leafed clover and what looks like a crossing point for three tram lines! (Figure 170.) Their straps have the name 'WARNERS' stamped above 'LONDON' at the apex.

Another prominent bell foundry had its origins in Hadlow, Kent, in the reign of William IV. William Gillett, with the patronage of Lord Sackville of Knole, set up as a clock maker. A photograph of him taken later in his life is given at Figure 171. William was an ambitious man and he decided that to improve his prospects he needed to find more customers, so he moved his premises to London. In 1837 he was in Clerkenwell; seven years later he moved to a site on the junction of Whitehorse Road and Union Road, Croydon. In time this was to grow into one of the largest bell foundries in the world.

At that time he made only small clocks. However, he wanted to expand so he took Charles Bland into partnership. Charles had been a manufacturer in the north of England and was, by all accounts, a dynamic salesman. He travelled all over the country seeking orders from church and public buildings and it is said that on more than one occasion he sat on the doorstep of his customer until it was obtained![16] The firm was now known as Gillett and Bland and, in addition to small clocks, also produced turret clocks. Through Charles Bland's salesmanship these were supplied to churches, cathedrals and the new town halls being built in the prosperous north of England. More capital was needed to finance this expansion and it was provided by Arthur Anderson Johnston. (Figure 172.) He entered the business by buying a junior partnership in 1877, the resulting firm being known as Gillett, Bland and Co.

A.A. Johnston was a wealthy man. He had spent his youth with his uncle, Arthur Anderson, the M.P. for Shetland who was the founder of the P & O Line and also the Union Steamship Company.[17] When his uncle died, A.A. Johnston inherited his money. On becoming a partner he soon realised the advantages of adding bellfounding to the firm's activities, to complement the clockmaking, and

173 Cyril F. Johnston

174 Gillett clapper assembly

175 Cap stamped by Gillett & Johnston

this quickly became an important part of their business. Some of their first bells were supplied to Reading Town Hall as part of a chime for their clock.[18] In addition to church bells they decided to include handbells in their products. Some of their first were produced about this time, for advertisements in *The Bell News* between October 1881 and March 1883 indicate that they supplied sets of musical handbells. I have not identified any bells from this period.

Charles Bland died in 1884 and the name of the business was changed to Gillett and Co. In 1887 Johnston became the senior partner and a few years later the sole owner when Gillett is reputed to have emigrated to America. Cyril F. Johnston was born in 1884 and joined his father in the firm in 1902. (Figure 173.)

A 1905 catalogue gives some idea of their range of products. They could supply a variety of sizes of turret and striking and chiming clocks with dials up to 12 feet in diameter. Larger sizes, 16 feet in diameter, as produced for Manchester Town Hall, were available on special order. Drum clocks and stable clocks could be supplied on demand. A range of grandfather clocks, house, office, library and English bracket clocks were kept in stock. They would make cast iron clock towers. Then there was the bell foundry. This not only produced bells of all sizes for their clocks to strike upon, it also made school, factory and church bells, together with carillons. These all included, of course, the mechanism for ringing them, the frames, bearings, chime barrels and so on; in all, a very wide range of goods.

In 1907 Cyril was promoted to junior partner. He regarded the tuning of the bells as his special responsibility and, being interested in the tuning theories of Canon A.B. Simpson, carried out many experiments of his own. By 1909 the volume of work was increasing at such a rate that they rebuilt and enlarged the foundry. During the next 10 years they employed more people than any other bell foundry in the world. Cyril was a competent ringer and rang 32 peals, including one at Edenbridge, Kent, when all those taking part were employees of the foundry. During the war he served as an officer in the Grenadier Guards. Whilst on active service in France in 1916 he received the news of his father's death. He was now the sole owner of the business.

176   Gillett cap with six pointed stars

In the 1920s he took advantage of the post-war boom for bells as war memorials. Carillons proved to be an extremely successful line and he sent over 50 to America alone. He converted the business into a limited company with his mother holding one share whilst he held the remainder.[19] The title of the firm was now the Croydon Bell Foundry, Ltd. and Cyril was the Managing Director. In 1930 he changed the name of the firm to Gillett and Johnston, Ltd. and five years later, in an endeavour to raise more capital, sold some shares to Lord Falmouth and R.C. Graseby, members of the Howard family. Cyril continued as Managing Director until 1948 when he resigned over a policy disagreement and Mr. H. Michael Howard took over.[20] This was his last connection with the firm: he collapsed and died on 30 March 1950 whilst waiting for his wife on Liverpool Street Station.[21]

The bell foundry closed down in 1957, but work really ceased in 1955. A brief item in *The Ringing World* announced that the Croydon site was to be sold and plans for a new foundry were ready.[22] It was never built. The few church bells cast under their name between 1955 and 1957 were made by J. Taylor and Co.[23] A few handbells were produced in the post-war period, but they were never advertised. The handbells have rounded shoulders on the exterior but a flat crown with a sharp shoulder on the interior. They have no identifying marks on the bells. Their fittings are easy to identify. Their clapper stems are flat in section and widen from the ball to the staple end. (Figure 174.) Their leather caps have GILLETT & JOHNSTON, CROYDON, ENGLAND stamped in an annular ring around the argent hole; in some examples I have seen a six-pointed star used as an ornament which is 8mm between points. (Figures 175 and 176.)

The firm was in the hands of the Official Receiver between July 1957 and September 1958, after which the bellfounding side of the business was bought by Cope Allman International. They paid off all the foundry creditors and now trade under the title of Gillett and Johnston Ltd. at Portsmouth.[24]

Thirteen

SPORADIC HANDBELL FOUNDERS OF THE 19TH CENTURY

177 Alfred White

The bell-hanging firm, Whites of Appleton, is well known throughout the home counties. However, the firm might never have come into existence if it had not been for Robert Southby, of Appleton Manor. In 1817 he gave a ring of six bells to St Lawrence, Appleton, and one of the local men who volunteered to learn to ring was Alfred White, illustrated in Figure 177. In 1821 he took part in the first recorded 720 on the bells and he remained a staunch member of the band for the rest of his life.[1]

Alfred was born in 1800 and, after working as a blacksmith, became an innkeeper at the *Greyhound*, Besselsleigh. In 1824 he started business as a bell hanger. He used the yard at the rear of his premises for this, carrying out work on the bells and constructing his oak bell-frames here.[2] As his work became better known, the firm prospered and his sons Frederick, Henry and Noble assisted him, later being taken into partnership. In 1867 they placed this advertisement in a local paper:

A WHITE and SONS Bellhangers were made,
  Because it was their fancy trade;
In hanging bells they take delight
  To make them go with all their might.
They in their brasses don't confine them,
  Or else no man could ever rise them.
In clappering they're quite expert,
  For in the bell they put the work
That makes the clapper to rebound,
  Which brings the true and proper sound.
In tuning they are competent,
  To tuning fork, and instrument.
In ringing bells also they're right,
  For they're a band whose name is WHITE:
They'll ring the bells with any band,
  To Treble Bob, Grandsire, or Stedman;
Hand Bells they make; are skill'd in tuning,
  Can ring some tunes that are amusing;
If you've a peal that's not quite right,
  Just drop a line to ALFRED WHITE,
And with his SONS he will come down,
  Re-hang the bells, and make them sound
The proper note, that's not been heard
  Perhaps for as much as twenty years.
His SONS the clocks and chimes can do,
  Make them play tunes and keep time true.
If you've a job that's worth attention,
  They will do their best to give satisfaction.

A WHITE & SONS, BESSELSLEIGH, NEAR ABINGDON, JULY 1867[3]

178   Leather cap stamped with Alfred White's name

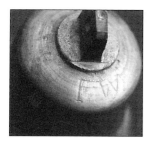

179   Frederick White's initial scratched in mould

180   Frederick White's leather stamps (1)

181   Frederick White's leather stamps (2)

The advertisement might not win many prizes for poetry, but it does summarise the activities of the firm quite accurately. Alfred's three sons were capable ringers: Frederick and Henry rang in Alfred's first peal on 4 March 1855.[4] They rang many peals together, including a long peal of Grandsire Caters in 1871 in which all three sons took part. Altogether, Alfred rang about forty peals.[5] The advertisement also mentions that they produced handbells and rang tunes on them. It was Frederick who cast these first handbells, although some of the earliest had Alfred's name stamped on the caps. (Figure 178.) An early set of Frederick's bells stamped thus may be seen in the tower at Long Crendon, Buckinghamshire.

Alfred died in 1875 and Frederick, then aged 42, inherited the business as the eldest son. During the next 30 years he introduced some contemporary ideas. The firm was well known for its traditional oak frames; in some towers he erected wrought iron ones. Within five years of his father's death he moved from the *Greyhound* at Besselsleigh to the *Three Horse Shoes* at Appleton and built a new workshop in the village.[6]

Most of the handbells produced by the Whites date from this period. The only time they advertised 'musical handbells to order' was in *The Bell News* from August 1897 to July 1898. Although their tone is quite pleasing, Frederick's handbells often have minor imperfections in the castings. Few of his bells are marked; many do not have numbers. When they do the font size of the numbers used does not reflect the size of the bell; some of the smaller bells have bigger figures than those on the larger bells! In a few cases he scratched his initials F W in the moulding sand before casting and these appear on the crown of the bell. (Figure 179.) He usually stamped these initials on his leather caps. (Figures 180 to 182.)

Like his father, Frederick was a fine ringer. He rang about 250 peals, conducting many of his early ones including some of his own compositions. He had a liking for long peals. In 1888 he took part in four at Appleton: 10,080 Double Norwich, 12,041 Stedman Caters, 13,265 Grandsire Caters and, on the last day of the year, 15,041 Stedman Caters, which took 9 hours and 16 minutes.

Frederick had nine sons and four daughters. The eldest son, born in 1863, was F. Stedman White, who also was a very competent ringer. He, too, used the patterns to cast some handbells: some of his work may be found at Hinton Waldrist, Oxfordshire, with F S W on the caps. On smaller bells he used S W. In October 1909 Frederick died and the bell-hanging business passed to a younger son, Richard, although the firm's advertisement in *The Bell News* continued under Frederick's name until 1913. Richard, or Dick as he was universally known, was 31 when he took over. Under him the business prospered and flourished, work being carried out in counties from Devon and

182   Frederick White's leather stamps (3)

Yorkshire. He discontinued the use of hoop gudgeons innovated by Frederick, replacing them with the now common plate gudgeons. In 1926 he also introduced the use of self-aligning ball bearings instead of the plain brass bearings formerly used.

Some handbell work was still carried out. Towards the end of this period the patterns were no longer available, probably having been used as handbells themselves! The firm's policy then was to take a handbell of the correct size and move it slightly in the mould, thus making the resultant bell thicker, which allowed for tuning. A bell in a set given to the Standlake ringers may have been made this way. Inside the bell there is a dabchick and R Cor, but the impression is doubled as though moved in the mould. On the crown of the bell is the size 12. The bell has been turned and the cap has F S W on it. I am sure Stedman White made this bell using a Cor bell as a pattern, adding the size 12 on the crown: the Cors did not use sizes on their bells. The last full set of handbells cast at Appleton was for Great Bedwyn, Wiltshire. This set was later returned and some of the bells incorporated in the family set.[7] In 1925 the furnace was dismantled and the family was no longer able to cast its own bells.

Dick was an accomplished ringer and, following his first peal in 1893, rang a total of about 230, most of them being at Appleton. He rang over 100 on the ninth at Appleton, with his brother Fred ringing the tenor. Included in his peals were a number of long lengths, the most notable of which were 21,363 Stedman Caters in 12 hours and 25 minutes at Appleton in 1922,[8] and 12,663 Stedman Cinques at Christ Church, Oxford in 1946. He was 69 when he rang this peal, ringing the one-ton 11th bell for 8 hours and 48 minutes![9]

Dick took his son Francis A. White (Frank) into partnership in 1945, and the firm traded as Richard White and Son.[10] Dick died in 1956, and Frank continued the business assisted by his nephew, Brian R. White, eventually taking him into partnership and trading as 'Whites of Appleton'. They, too, are excellent ringers, and have followed the family tradition in taking part in long peals. In 1968 a new record was achieved when they both rang in 16,559 Grandsire Caters at Appleton in 9 hours and 10 minutes.[11] They modernised the premises in 1985 by bringing together the carpenter's shop and the blacksmith's shop, formerly situated in different parts of the village. A new workshop was built alongside the carpenter's

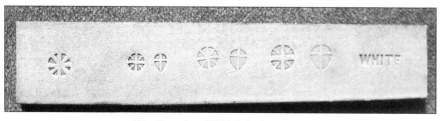

183   Examples of White's leather stamps

184 White's clapper assembly

shop, the construction work being carried out by another member of the White family. The new building now contains the lathes, power saws and drilling machines formerly found in the old black-smith's shop, together with a new forge and a travelling crane. Another workshop is devoted to the tuning and refurbishment of handbells.[12]

Frank officially retired in 1988 and Brian now heads the firm. Some restoration and refurbishment of handbells has been carried out during the last four decades, but no new handbells have been cast at Appleton. When they have supplied new bells, they have been tuned from Whitechapel blanks.

Identifying White handbells can be difficult. In general the bells are not marked and you need to examine the leatherwork and the fittings. The caps often display initials, as mentioned earlier, and each member of the family made his own ornaments. Some of these are illustrated in Figure 183. Their clapper assemblies had fairly small staples, with clapper shanks which were round and tapered to the ball. The staple end of this shank was triangular in shape; at the other end of the clapper the flights were longer than normal. Their springs followed the standard pattern although those on their larger bells were not shaped. An example of one of these may be seen in Figure 184.

Whilst Alfred White was steadily building up his bell-hanging business in Berkshire and the surrounding counties, Henry Bowell was doing the same in East Anglia. He was a native of Great Bromley who moved to Ipswich in 1852 to start a seven-year apprenticeship as a shipwright. After completing this, he worked for some years at his trade, but a slump in the demand for sailing ships forced him to look for other employment. At that time he was a ringer at St Mary-le-Tower, Ipswich and, whilst discussing the poor state of frames and fittings in many bell installations with the ringers one evening, suddenly realised that he had the expertise to set up as a bell hanger.[13] He did this and worked up a good living in the eastern counties. He died in 1911, aged 81.

Henry's son Alfred, born in 1874, joined him in the business when he was thirteen. By the time he was 20 he had become dissatisfied with only hanging other founders' bells and wanted to cast his own. This was a brave step, for not only had he no experience of the trade, he had never been inside a foundry! Through trial and error he succeeded in this formidable task and during his lifetime cast over 400 bells.[14] A photograph of Alfred is at Figure 185. Alfred was very proud of the fact that he had personally poured the metal for every one of his bells. These may be found in 18 counties throughout Britain, although much of his work was for East Anglia. His first ring was in 1897 for Mistley, Essex, where he added five bells to an existing old bell to commemorate Queen Victoria's Jubilee.[15] Probably his best-known work was the recasting and augmenting of the old six bells for Maldon, Essex, in 1922. This is the only triangular tower in England and it is a tribute to his skill that he was able to hang all the bells on one level whilst retaining a good circle of ropes in the ringing chamber.[16]

185 Alfred Bowell

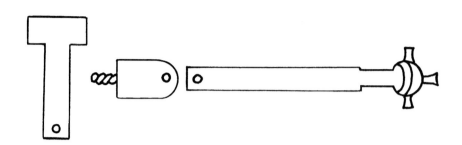

186 Sketch of Bowell's clapper
assembly

He lived in Wykes Bishop Street, Ipswich, and in his early days used the old copper as a forge and the kitchen as a workshop, no doubt without the approval of his wife Rosa, whom he married in 1896.[17] About the turn of the century he obtained the use of a building just across the road. This had been built about 1845 as a day school and had later been converted to a Wesleyan Chapel. First he constructed workshops in the old playground and later in the chapel itself.

Alfred today would be described as a workaholic. He had little interest in anything outside a church tower. If he had a hobby, other than ringing, it was church clocks. He eventually incorporated this into his business, quoting for carrying out clock repairs, alterations and reconstructions whenever he was doing work on the bells. He was an accomplished change ringer on both tower and handbells. His work left him little time for peal ringing and he rang fewer than thirty. His first was Plain Bob Major on handbells in 1893 and he rang several of Maximus in Ipswich and Cambridge. He was also one of the few ringers who could claim to have rung a bell at East Bergholt, Essex, where the bell frame stands on the ground. He could also ring methods on four handbells: with his son Frederick he would demonstrate how to ring Double Norwich Court Bob Major![18]

In his early days he wanted to widen the business by producing sets of handbells, and up to July 1909 advertised these in *The Bell News*. He found that producing them on a small scale was unprofitable, so he gave up this work.[19] All of his sets of handbells probably date from this period. The bells do not have any identifying features; his work is usually identified by the fittings. The clapper stems are flat and fastened to the staple with a steel pin. His springs are T-shaped. A sketch of this assembly is shown at Figure 186. His leather work is stamped with an eight-pointed star; sometimes he used a clover leaf. He also stamped BOWELL, IPSWICH on the top of the leather handle.

187 Frederick Bowell's leather
stamps

He was joined in the business by his only son Frederick, who was born in 1896. During the First World War the foundry stopped making bells and turned to munitions, although they did rehang the heavy eight at Warminster, Wiltshire, in a new steel frame. When they resumed casting bells after the war, Frederick carried out all the tuning,[20] using a tuning machine constructed by his father. Between the wars they worked hard to satisfy the demand for bells and frames, supplying a number of installations to Kent.[21] They cast their last church bell in January 1939 for Doddington, Cambridge, although Frederick may have cast a few handbells after this. I have a handbell cap in my collection which has F BOWELL & SON stamped on it, ornamented with seven-pointed stars. (Figure 187.)

Some months earlier a slum clearance order had been made for the area to make room for a new road. When the war started all the houses round the foundry had been demolished and it was the only building left standing.[22] Although bombs fell all around, it was not extensively damaged. Alfred contracted pneumonia in August 1940 and died two days later, aged sixty-six. The foundry did no more work. I visited it on 25 September 1948, not long before it was finally demolished, and saw the handbell patterns still hanging in the shop. I wonder what happened to them?

The Whites made and supplied handbells for more than half a century. Alfred Bowell offered them for less than 20 years. Thomas Blackbourn and the partnership of Blackbourn and Greenleaf cast them for only a few years. Their association began in 1890, but Thomas Blackbourn was born in 1860 at Holbeach, Lincolnshire, the son of the station master at Fleet.[23] He learned to ring at Spalding, his tutor being J.R. Jerram, a bell hanger and agricultural engineer from Sutton Bridge, some 12 miles away. On 1 January 1878, some time before he was 18, Blackbourn was taken into partnership by Jerram, the business being known as Jerram and Blackbourn, operating from the West End Iron Works at Sutton Bridge. A photograph of Blackbourn taken some years later is at Figure 188.

188 Thomas Blackbourn

Blackbourn's order book from this period contains two references to handbells.[24] One is labelled 'Ibstock Handbells' and gives the prices for sets of eight and 10 handbells in the keys of 15C, 18G and 20E flat. It is not dated, but is opposite a page headed 'Bletchingley, 1880', so may be of a similar date. The other page lists prices for sets of eight and 12 bells in the keys of 15C, 18G and 20E. These prices are lower than for Ibstock, so they may be of an earlier date. They are opposite an undated quote for repairs to the six bells at Fulbourne, Cambridge. I presume these quotes were for handbells bought on commission from one of the other foundries. These pages are illustrated in Figures 189 and 190.

Jerram moved to Salisbury about 1882 and a year later Blackbourn followed. He acquired some premises in an area called The Friary and called it 'The Friary Works'.[25] From here he ran a bell-hanging business with Jerram probably acting as a silent partner, providing financial backing and expertise as required. Blackbourn was an excellent bell hanger and frame maker: he supplied

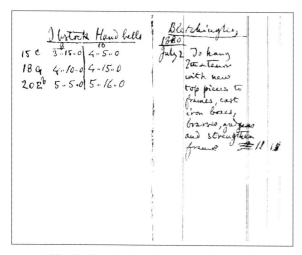

189   Blackbourn's Order Book—Ibstock handbells

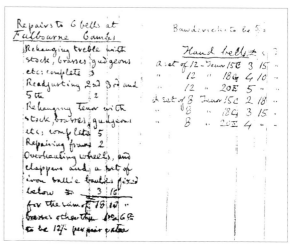

190   Blackbourn's Order Book—prices for handbells

191   William Greenleaf

frames to Canterbury Cathedral and to Wells Cathedral as well as many other places.[26] In March 1890 he formed a partnership with William Greenleaf, the new firm being called:

BLACKBOURN & GREENLEAF
CHURCH BELL HANGERS, TUNERS,
AND HANDBELL FOUNDERS,
No 100, Bedwin Street, Salisbury.[27]

William Greenleaf was born in Bethnal Green on 23 November 1847.[28] A 1903 woodcut of him is illustrated in Figure 191. He learned to ring at Hackney, joined the College Youths in 1868 and served as their Master in 1875 and 1883. A genial, though slightly erratic character, he worked for Mears and Stainbank for 20 years as a bell hanger and tuner. This work took him all over the country; for instance, he retuned the bells of St Martin, Salisbury in October 1883. His association with Blackbourn was not a long one. It was dissolved in August 1893 and Greenleaf left Salisbury and went abroad for a time, visiting Canada, Australia and New Zealand. When he returned he went to live at Hereford, where he set up on his own as a bell hanger and tuner.[29] In 1903 he took a man named Tristam into partnership, a relationship that continued until early 1912. Some time after this he retired to Auckland, New Zealand, where he died on 26 August 1920.[30]

Blackbourn continued on his own at Salisbury, advertising throughout 1893 and 1894 that he would cast handbells. In January 1895 he revised the advert to say he would supply them. This may indicate he had stopped casting them

192   Auction of Friary Works

and was obtaining them from elsewhere at a discount and passing them on. He later stopped advertising this service. He added church bell casting to the bell-hanging business in 1899 when he cast a ring of six for Woodford, Wiltshire.[31] A ring of eight for Farnworth-with-Kearsley, Lancashire followed later that year, and two years later a ring of eight for Hersham, Surrey. He lacked capital, so made the firm a limited company on 5 February 1902. Despite this, and all the work he was doing, the firm was not sound financially. It was offered for sale at a very low price in *The Bell News* for 1903, but still finished up in the hands of the Official Receiver.[32] It was finally offered for auction in April 1904.[33] Figure 192 gives a page from the Auction Catalogue.

Blackbourn rang over 200 peals during his lifetime, including one in 1892 which was the first peal in which a woman took part.[34] He married late in life a much younger woman and had four sons and one daughter. He left Salisbury in 1918 for Luton and finished his career as a bicycle repairer. He joined in the ringing at Luton and was steeplekeeper for some years. He died on 24 January 1933 and is buried in the parish church cemetery.[35]

Fourteen
FOUNDING IN BIRMINGHAM

193 Martineau & Smith house bell

IN THE LATE 18th century Birmingham was the centre of the Industrial Revolution. Men of ideas were attracted to the locality. James Watt, who improved and patented Newcomen's steam engine, resided there together with Matthew Boulton, an engineer of vision who financed Watt and manufactured his engines. Joseph Priestley, the noted chemist who discovered oxygen, lived there, as did John Baskerville, the printer and type-face manufacturer. New methods of production were being pioneered in the metal and engineering trades and the city expanded to accommodate them.

In particular the metal and gun trades prospered and Birmingham became known worldwide as a source of arms and small goods, the latter including jewellery, buttons and brass trinkets. A profusion of one-man businesses appeared, the cry being 'every man his own master'. Plumbers' ware was the most important product of the brass founder, but candlesticks and candle snuffers, thimbles, snuff boxes and inkstands were also produced in great quantities. Some of these small businesses also cast bells, thousands of which were exported to South Africa and South America.[1] It is a little known fact that significant quantities of bronze founding rarely took place in any of the principal brass casting regions.[2] Before I deal with the well-known Birmingham bell foundries, i.e. those casting in bronze, I want to look at some of these smaller businesses who were casting brass bells.

An examination of the Birmingham Trade Directories for the period reveals the names of founders who specialised in producing brass goods including bells. A good example is the firm of Martineau and Smith. In 1860 they were at 65 Hill Street and, although their main business was brass cock founding, they also produced house bells.[3] One of these from my collection has M & S cast in the crown and may be seen in Figure 193. It is not from Mears and Stainbank! Fifteen years later the firm was at Holloway Head and cast office, clock, dinner, house and turret bells. They issued an extensive catalogue of all their wares; one of the pages dealing with bells is illustrated at Figure 194. It is quite possible that some of their house bells have been tuned and included in handbell sets.

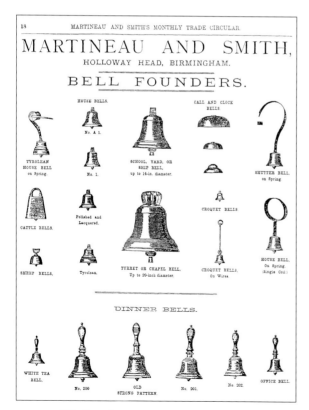

194 Page from Martineau & Smith catalogue

Other Birmingham brass founders were producing bells at this time. One of these was Edwin Barber, whose premises were adjacent to St George's Church in Great Hampton Street. He started his business in about 1854. Four years earlier Thomas Bartleet was casting bells at 126 Great Charles Street; in 1860 he took his sons into partnership and moved to 22 New Hall Street. George Dowler also cast bells and patent corkscrews at 90/91 Great Charles Street, but this was in the years prior to 1850. Round the corner, at 198 Livery Street, was Bernard Harris, another bellfounder.

Whilst John Evans, of 105 Moland Street, described himself in the Directories as a brass and imperial candlestick maker, a snuff box maker, a bellfounder and a charquasilla button maker, John Fullwood said he cast only house bells and brass candlesticks at his premises in 49 New Town Road. John Kelsey set up in 1853 as a bell and brass founder at 60 Ashted Row, taking, as a partner, a man called Millward. He apparently left the business before 1860. Another small manufacturer of bells and brass cocks was Samuel Sheppard. He shared a workshop at 11 James Street with Edwin Lee, a die stamper and tool maker, and Clifford James, a tin plate worker.

Thomas Wootton made bells at 23a Great Hampton Street as an adjunct to his normal trade as a clockmaker; he probably cast hemispherical bells for his own use. William Vale and his sons also ran a clockmaking business and made bells in Bore Street in nearby Lichfield. Samuel Tonks in Church Street, Wolverhampton, described himself as a brass and bellfounder, as did Thomas Hughes Smith, of Stafford Street, Wolverhampton. It is unlikely that any of these men cast musical handbells. However, in some cases what they cast as house bells have been tuned and added to sets of handbells, so the bell historian should be aware of their existence.

William Blews and Sons was the earliest of the Birmingham founders whose sets of handbells are still be found. They claimed they were established as brass founders in 1782. Documentary evidence shows a William Blews junior was at 16 Bartholomew Row in 1830, working as a manufacturer of brass and steel fire irons and brass candlesticks.[4] By 1850 the firm had grown in size and they recorded that they now manufactured brass and imperial metal candlesticks, candle and oil lamps, standard weights, fire brasses, door knockers, plated snuffers, Britannia metal and British plate ware. They also made bells.[5] Their premises were now at 9 New Bartholomew Street, adjacent to the London and North Western Railway. Next door at No.10 was a firm of merchants, Blews and Keep, probably part of the family concern, or maybe owned by William himself.[6] During the next six years the business flourished and the foundry took over these premises and also those of William Keeley, an iron tinned-spoon and pressed-hinge manufacturer at number 11.[7]

Although the firm described itself as 'bellfounders' from 1850, no church bells from that period have been positively identified. It is likely that these early bells were brass rather than bronze, for in 1854 he was advertising 'lamps, bells and scuttles for ships'.[8] Similarly, it is improbable that musical handbells were made during these early years; advertisements for them did not appear till much later. However, in the years subsequent to 1860 the firm established a solid reputation as good, competent church-bell founders. Their castings were of high quality and H.B. Walters, the eminent bell archaeologist, commented favourably on the neat Gothic capitals they used for their inscriptions.[9] In 1869 they cast a ring of eight for Bishop Ryder's church, 'the first eight ever cast in Birmingham'.[10] Henry Bond II was working here in this decade, gaining experience before returning to Burford, Oxon, and becoming a partner in his father's bellfoundry.[11]

It was at this point in the firm's growth that they added musical handbells to their range of products. I have two price lists for their handbells. The first is not dated but must be after 1869 because it advertises that they won the Premier Award at the Amsterdam Exhibition for that year. I infer from this that it was the quality of their handbells that gained them the prize. The second list, printed in Figure 235 and originally published in January 1873, noted 'all other lists are cancelled'. Both lists comment that improved clappers were now being fitted to their handbells. This implies that they had made handbells for some time and that their earlier clapper assemblies had given cause for concern. I suggest that from the above data a debut of 1865 be given for their musical handbells.

Their bells are usually good, clean castings of a pleasing shape. They have a domed crown with a button under the argent and a depression around the crown staple hole. The initials W B & S are incised in Lombardic capitals on the crown of each bell with the number opposite. A rubbing of these initials is at Figure 195. These initials are present on all their bells in all the sets that I have seen, so Blews handbells are not difficult to identify.

Their clapper staples are of standard shape and sturdy construction. Clapper stems are round in section and taper from the staple end up to the clapper ball. The flight lengths vary, but in general they are a little longer than normal. They do differ from other manufacturers by having a bevelled end. The ball of the clapper is tapped to allow the leather pegs to be screwed in. The staple end of the clapper in unusual in shape. The circular shaft is filed on either side to a flat section roughly one third the size of the original stem. This gives it a 'pinched' look and would give rise to more clapper rattle. Early models were fixed to the staple by a steel pin; later models had a wooden or fibre pin. The clapper springs curve gently from the parallel sides fixed to the staple to the head where the felts were attached with sealing wax. Figure 196 illustrates some of these points. Their leather caps were devoid of ornament apart from two annular rings. In some cases W BLEWS & SONS, BIRMINGHAM, is stamped on the top of the strap.

195 Rubbing of William Blews' initials

196 Blews clapper assembly

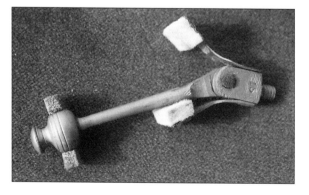

Writing in *The Church Bells of Buckinghamshire* in 1897, A.H. Cocks states that the foundry ceased to exist after 1876, but reopened in 1889.[12] William Blews died, aged 59, on 30 January 1887 after an illness of two months.[13] Among the mourners, and conductor of the half-muffled ringing at Bishop Ryder's church, was his tuner, Thomas Miller. I will discuss him later in this chapter; he became the last of the Birmingham handbell founders. William's wife, Frances, reopened the foundry in 1889, probably to sell it as a going concern. Little work was carried out. Advertisements started in *The Bell News*

197   Cow bell by James Barwell

from 2 March 1889, first with a small display but later with a half page. The first edition of *Grandsire*, published in 1888, carried a half-page advertisement for musical handbells. Frances invited John William Taylor to purchase the bell foundry business, but he refused. Eventually, Henry Bisseker acquired the brass founding and general interests of the firm in July 1891.[14] Charles Carr took over the bellfounding.[15]

Charles Carr moved from the Potteries to Smethwick in about 1863, establishing a brass foundry at the Woodland Works, Grove Lane.[16] He ran it as a family concern, employing his father and two brothers, initially in producing brass ware such as beer engines, but later in casting church bells. He cast mainly single bells until 1887 when he cast a ring of six for Malins Lee, Salop.[17] He decided to expand this side of the business, put his son James in charge of bell founding, and other rings followed. In 1891 they cast a maiden ring of six and this pleased the directors so much that they sent the ring off on a tour to advertise their expertise![18] These bells are now at Pensnett, Dudley, Staffordshire.[19] The phrase, 'Gold Medallists and Founder of Maiden Peals' henceforth appeared in their advertisements.

Charles Carr took his two sons and other members of his family into partnership in 1890. The following year saw the takeover of William Blews. Charles died shortly after and his son James Carr became Managing Director. Amongst the stock purchased from Blews would have been the handbell patterns and James decided that Carrs should produce sets of musical handbells. I have seen no evidence that the firm cast them before this. This side of the business was not publicised extensively: the only advertisements I have found appeared in the short-lived paper *Campanology*, where they stated that they would make 'musical handbells in any size and any number'.[20] Their advertisements for church bells and bell hanging continued weekly in *The Bell News* till the final issue of that paper on Christmas Day 1915, and in copies of *The Ringing World* from the first in 1911 to the 999th in May 1930. After this date they ceased to take an interest in bells, although the firm was still advertising in trade journals up to 1960. I have not identified any handbells by Carr.

Samuel Fiddian was making brass candlesticks and ships' bells in Great Hampton Street from 1784. About 1840 he sold the business as a going concern to James Barwell. Born in 1818, James had started work as a traveller for a japanning firm named Jennings and Betteridge and, when they were declared bankrupt, used his savings to buy out Fiddian. He retitled the firm James Barwell, Ltd, but retained the name of Fiddian for use as a trademark on brass goods. He married Sarah Palmer about the time he took over Fiddian's and they had 12 children, of whom five boys and five girls survived to adulthood.

198   Barwell house bell

199   Rubbing of Barwell's initial

The Post Office Directory for 1854 described him as 'a cock and bell founder' and it is about this time that he started casting small bells. His obituary records that these were cow bells for Australia.[21] One of these bells is illustrated in Figure 197. Many traditionally shaped house or shop bells may be found with square shoulders and very flat crowns. These may be in brass or bronze and they usually have a B cast in relief on the crown with a number opposite, also cast in relief. One is illustrated at Figure 198 with a rubbing of the letter at Figure 199. These bells are usually attributed to James Barwell.

About the year 1870 he cast his first ring of church bells, a ring of six for North Lydbury, Salop.[22] During the next 40 years he cast many more rings together with many single bells for churches, clocks, chimes and schools. He would cast these to any size or note. He emphasised he could recast cracked bells retaining the ancient inscription, reproducing it in facsimile if required. Bell hanging was an important adjunct to this work. In his advertisements in *The Bell News* he stressed that he would send 'a ringer' to report on the condition of the bells, frames and fittings: a sales pitch that would appeal to the readers of that journal.

These advertisements in *The Bell News* ran from April 1886 till the last issue of 1915 and all carried the message 'musical handbells tuned in diatonic and chromatic scales in sets of any number'. After *The Ringing World* started in 1911 the firm took space here to advertise their handbells, but phrased it, 'musical handbells in any size and number, for tune or change ringing, in guaranteed quality'. The last advert appeared in December 1918. They also advertised in the Snowdon series of books; one of their price lists for handbells taken from the 1892 edition of *Standard Methods* is shown in Figure 241.

James died in his 81st year on 29 March 1898, leaving the bell foundry to two of his sons, Edward and Arthur. During the First World War the foundry was set up for war work and retooled as a machine shop, so no bells were produced. Edward died at the close of hostilities and his brother Arthur assumed control. About this time the firm decided they would not resume making church bells or be involved in their hanging, so all bell work at Great Hampton Street ceased. A small factory was acquired for the manufacture of small bells and many thousands were produced, although they were not musical handbells. Edward's son Cecil managed the firm after Arthur's death in the 1930s and was responsible for the many ARP bells the firm produced during the Second World War. Cecil was succeeded by his son Bryan in the 1950s and the firm

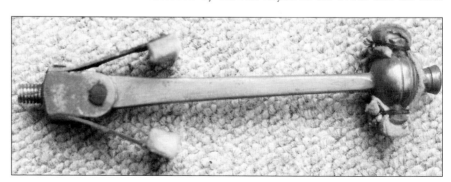

200   Barwell clapper assembly

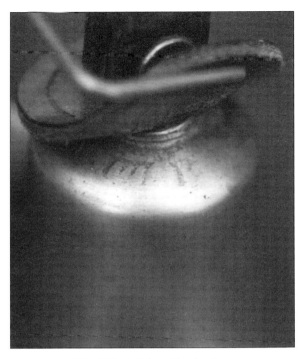

201 Miller bell from Blews' pattern

was taken over by Delta Flow Ltd. in about 1970.[23] Although they made bells till 1960, after 1914 none was larger than 20 inches in diameter.[24]

Barwell's handbells are difficult to identify, for they bear no numbers or marks of any description. Their larger bells, up to 29C, are very straight-sided with little flare at the lip, and consequently are not usually of good tone. On some of these they put boxwood handles instead of straps.[25] Their leather work was plain, their caps bearing a simple annular ring and no ornaments. Their clapper assembly was of reasonable quality for the period, with a fairly substantial staple. The clapper shaft was flat and tapered towards the ball, whilst the clapper flight was a little longer than the Whitechapel equivalent. (Figure 200.) The felts were held to the normal shaped springs with two rivets.

Birmingham's last handbell founder was Thomas Miller. Born in London on 6 July 1858, he was taken to Birmingham as a baby and spent most of his long life there.[26] He learned to ring at St Philip's Church before it became the Cathedral and in his early days rang with William Chattell and his celebrated band. Tom was a Roman Catholic and so naturally gravitated to St Chad's Roman Catholic Cathedral, eventually becoming responsible for looking after the bells and the service ringing. In his early 20s he joined the Guards and during his service in London made a name for himself as a good heavy bell ringer. He took part in many peals throughout the country, including the last peal on the old bells at Coventry Cathedral in 1883. He was an excellent handbell ringer and took part in the first peal of Grandsire Cinques and the second of Stedman Cinques. E.C. Shepherd recalls him in middle age as being a sturdy, lively character, with a whimsical sense of humour, and an impishness that had no trace of malice.[27]

When he left the army he took a job with William Blews and Sons as their tuner. After William's death and the closure of the firm he joined James Barwell and remained with them until they ceased trading in handbells. W.E. Box records that he then set up on his own account as a handbell founder, working at Barwell's foundry premises at 70 Mott Street at the rear of the Great Hampton Street works.[28] I have been unable to find any advertisements for his handbells for these initial years; he may have made them on a contract basis for another supplier.

It has always been assumed that, as he worked from Barwell's premises and had previously been employed by them, he used Barwell's patterns. However, an examination of the profiles of his bells shows that this was not the case; they bear a marked resemblance to Blews' handbells. I am sure he used Blews' patterns and then machined the 'W B & S' from the crown of the bell. On one occasion he did not succeed completely and the bell can be definitely identified as from Blews' pattern.[29] (Figure 201.)

202   Leather work by T. Miller

Like Barwell's handbells, it can be difficult to identify Miller's bells once they have been restored. With the exception quoted above, I have never seen his bells with any identifying marks or numbers. He carried on the Birmingham tradition of inscribing the caps with an annular ring and not using any ornaments. He did, however, place his name on the top of the strap, 'T MILLER'. (Figure 202.) His clapper assemblies closely resemble those of Barwell except that he covered his leather strikers with chamois leather.

He first advertised when he was nearly 70 in *The Ringing World* for 11 May 1928. The advertisement appeared as a two-line notice, giving his address as 6 Windsor Place, St Mark's Street. He repeated similar notices at about six-monthly intervals, specifying one or two peals of 12, tenor 15C, 17A or 18G. He never quoted a price and advertised them for only two or three weeks, obviously making some extra money to help out in his retirement. He gave his address as 70 Mott Street in 1933 and continued trading from here until he was eighty. In 1938 he moved to 21a Smith Street, Hockley, and from here he advertised only a few more rings, the last appearing at Christmas 1940. Increasing age and the Second World War put an end to this business and he went into St Joseph's Home, Edgbaston, where he died on 5 January 1950, aged 91. With his death the long line of Birmingham handbell founders came to a close.

Fifteen
FOUNDING IN THE NORTH

203 Rubbing of James Shaw's initials

IN THE MID-19TH CENTURY the demand for musical handbells in the north of England was considerable. The Yorkshire and Lancashire tune ringing teams were acquiring greater skill, dexterity and precision, and were seeking to upgrade their bells. Longer and better tuned sets were demanded. Handbell founding seemed to be concentrated in the south of England and the way was open for a northern entrepreneur to fill the gap. James Shaw came forward and started the firm which eventually grew into the largest manufacturer of musical handbells in the world.

James said he originated from Low Moor, Bradford. At that time this was a small village or collection of houses about three miles south of Bradford, which provided homes for the mining community. The parish records at Slack Side, Low Moor, show that in 1826 a son James was born to James and Charity Shaw. However, Dennis Greenwood, in his book on Shaw, traces him by his marriage certificate to Headingley, near Leeds, where he was born in 1826, the son of William and Patience Shaw.[1] The 1851 Census records him as a mechanic: an account of the firm written nearly forty years later implies that he had long practical experience as an engineer.[2] The article gives 1848 as the year when he started casting bells. These were only small bells such as sheep or cattle bells, house bells or handbells. It is most unlikely that it was his main occupation; he would have carried out his bell founding during his spare time in the evenings and weekends, gaining experience whilst accumulating some capital. In April 1851 he took a wife, marrying Ann Lightowlers at St Peter, Bradford.[3] Their son William was born later that year and other children followed.

By the time of the 1871 Census, James had established a good reputation for his bells and the census records his occupation as a 'musical bell founder'. The firm expanded over the next few years, taking on workshop premises at 145 Leeds Road with a brass foundry in Mount Street. Sometime before 1875 James took his son, William, into partnership.[4] One of the first acts of the new firm of James Shaw and Son was to expand the production of musical handbells.

Over the next few years the firm continued to grow. Casting of church bells was added in 1879 and a clockmaking firm, Cryer's of Bingley, was purchased about the same time. This expansion demanded new capital and in 1882 a limited company was formed with Thornton Harrison as an additional partner. This was reflected in the name of the firm. The third edition of *Ropesight*, published in 1883, carried an advertisement headed:

JAMES SHAW, SON & CO.
Church & Musical Hand-Bell Founders
Penny Oaks Bell Foundry and Church Clock Works
LEEDS ROAD, BRADFORD, YORKSHIRE

James' second son, Walter, was also taken into the business but, unlike his elder brother, was not made a partner. In addition, two men and two boys were employed. The Shaw handbell industry was prospering; in 1882 they sent over a thousand handbells to all parts of the world.[5] A typical example of their work was a set sent to Frostbury in the United States of America.[6] The local paper there, the *Queen City Courier*, wrote of these bells:

> The above society have just received a splendid set of silver-toned musical handbells, made especially for the band by the renowned firm of bellfounders, Messrs Shaw, Son & Co. of Bradford, England. The bells are pronounced by several judges to be of the purest tone.[7]

The Great Exhibition of 1851 had demonstrated the Victorians' love of craft fairs. Others were spawned throughout the country and, at the 1882 Exhibition held at Bradford Technical School, Shaw's won three medals for their clock and bells. This included a silver medal, the highest award, for a set of their handbells, the jurors making special mention of their great purity of tone. Shaw's sent 15 of this set to the editor of *The Bell News* for his comments and Harvey Reeves asserted that they were the sweetest toned bells he had ever heard. He continued:

> There has been at times various individuals totally unconnected with any trade akin to bell-founding, who claim to be regarded as efficients in the manufacture of handbells, but in most instances the products of such persons have, when weighed in the balance of critical examination, been found wanting.[8]

He concluded it was better to apply to a firm who 'had the proper appliances for their manufacture'; it was a false economy to purchase second-hand sets, especially as the price of new sets of handbells was so low. He predicted an abundance of orders for Messrs Shaw.

Shaw's were also innovators. One of the most irritating faults of late 18th- and early 19th-century handbells was clapper rattle. As large handbell teams began to move towards concert performances instead of public house entertainment, they began to demand better instruments. At that time, most founders used steel pins as pivots for their clappers. The brass clapper staples they used were narrow and unsubstantial, so wear rapidly took place and clapper rattle was inevitable. In 1884 James Shaw introduced clappers with large bossed ends which required very wide staples. When used with leather pins they virtually eliminated clapper rattle, allowing the bells to sound more clearly.[9]

Another example of their innovative work was in extending the range of handbells downwards. Chapter 10 showed how William Dunn had produced a one-off experimental 33F sometime before 1850, but the standard bass bell was 29C. As the music played at the Belle Vue contests became more complex, longer sets were demanded and Shaw produced bells from 29C down to 32G. A set containing these bells was used by Whitefield, who were among the prize winners in the 1887–8 contests.[10] During the 1880s the firm reached its peak of prosperity and moved to larger premises in a two-storeyed building on the corner of Lyndhurst Street and Maud Street. On the upper floor were the offices and the handbell shops; the ground floor contained the workshops for the clocks. The foundry for casting both hand and tower bells was in a separate building in Beck Street.

A subsequent review of the foundry in *The Bell News*, later published as a broad sheet, outlined some of their achievements, including their 'fine ring of eight for St James, Bolton'.[11] It mentioned their range of clocks with dials up to 15 feet in diameter, their workshop where church clocks and bell frames were assembled prior to being dispatched and their large handbell shop, fully equipped with lathes and other machinery. This machinery, according to the article, 'appeared to be new and of excellent character, combining all modern improvements and capable of turning out an immense quantity of work'. The article concludes by giving their scheme for some further new premises, which would bring together under one roof all the various trades and skills.

Perhaps their best ever year was 1887. In this year they won a gold medal for their handbells at the Royal Yorkshire Jubilee Exhibition and they were able to claim they were the largest musical handbell manufacturer in the world. This was all to change over the next few years. Walter, James' younger son, died of typhoid fever in 1886 when he was only 26, leaving a young wife. James was in his early 60s and suffering from indifferent health; he had both heart disease and dropsy. He retired from the day-to-day decisions of the business and left the running of the firm to William and Thornton Harrison. They made one important acquisition in 1890. William Pawson, the Leeds handbell manufacturer, died in this year, and his executors sold his stock and equipment to Shaw.[12]

Most of the Snowdon series of Change Ringing books contained advertisements for the bell founders. In *Standard Methods*, published in 1892, Shaw's advertisement stated that they had made the largest peal of handbells in the world for the Dewsbury Hand-Bell Band. This contained 240 bells. They also listed 36 other bands for whom they had made 'large' peals.[13] They concluded by saying they had made 'hundreds of smaller Peals, of 3 to 4 octaves, including Bells to persons of great musical eminence, and also to the profession.'

On 4 October 1892, James Shaw, the founder of the firm, died aged 66. Although he had started from a poor background, he had built up a worldwide business through hard work and business acumen and he ended his life as a highly respected Bradford business man.[14] He was not wealthy: a brief note at the end of his will shows the gross value of his estate was only £223.[15]

It is difficult after 100 years to be specific, but I gain the impression that from this time onward the firm seemed to lose that vital spark which had earned it universal recognition as the best handbell manufacturer in the world. There was a change of partners. In 1894 the 12-year-old partnership with Thornton Harrison was dissolved. Reginald Adams took his place until 1897, when he too parted company with the firm. William removed his father's name from the title of the firm calling it 'Shaw, Son & Co.' Maybe he had lost interest in the business. He had bought Belmont House at Calverley Moor some miles northeast of Bradford around 1892 and perhaps he wanted to spend more time there. Anyway, by 1901 the firm employed only six workers.

What finally finished the firm was a fire which swept through 50 Lyndhurst Street on 2 August 1901. William was the last to leave the building on this Friday evening and he claimed he left everything secure from any risk of fire. Forty-five minutes after he had left, the fire had gained such a hold that the

204   Photograph of a pre-1884 Shaw clapper

205   Photograph of Shaw's 'new improved clapper system'

206   Photograph of the new clapper assembly post-1884

building was completely gutted. The intense heat melted all their white metal bell patterns, besides doing between £500 and £600 worth of other damage. Fortunately, the majority of this was covered by insurance.[16]

The firm continued to advertise in trade journals until 1909, although how much work was carried out is not clear. At the Cartwright Memorial Hall Exhibition in 1904 an advertisement in the official catalogue gives the firm's title as 'Shaw, Son & Co. Ltd' and indicates that sets of handbells from eight to 240 in number were available.[17] It was about this period that William offered to sell the goodwill of the business to John Taylor, at Loughborough.[18] Taylor was not interested and neither was Arthur Hughes of Mears and Stainbank, Whitechapel, when he was offered it two years later. William Shaw died on 16 March 1910 and, although the firm may have continued for a short while to complete outstanding contracts, it was virtually no more. Their last advertisement appeared in *The Bell News* for 1912, after which the firm of James Shaw, one of the greatest names in the manufacture of musical handbells, faded from sight.[19]

Shaw's handbells are well-finished castings, with the number of the bell and J S cast intaglio in the crown, parallel to the argent. A rubbing of the initials may be found at Figure 203. The smaller bells are a standard shape with the lip swelling from the waist, but as the bells increase in size they tend to be more straight-sided; the 29C has very little flare at the lip. The insides of the castings are smooth and they have no recessed 'button' around the staple hole. All the very large bells I have seen have been tuned with a harmonic of a tenth rather than the normal twelfth; this was probably an intentional characteristic of their larger bells.

Prior to the mid-1880s their clapper staples were wedge-shaped, being slightly narrower at the end adjacent to the bell. The clapper stems were flat with a circular staple end. Sometimes they carried the name J. SHAW. Felts were riveted to the tapered brass springs which had a D cut-out. An example of one of these is illustrated at Figure 204. They later introduced their 'new improved clapper and clapper staple': the round-stemmed clappers were fitted with a large bossed end and the staples

207   Photograph of J. Shaw cap of the early 1870s

208   Photograph of J. Shaw, Son & Co. cap of 1882

209   Photograph of J. Shaw, Son & Co. cap post-1884

210   Photograph of unlabelled Shaw cap post-1884

machined to fit them. (Figures 205 and 206.) Sometimes they appeared to use wooden pins on which to swing the clapper, but more often leather was used.

Initially, James used leather stamps on his caps of eight pointed 'suns'. Two sizes were used, alternating around the cap. On the largest bell of the set he would also stamp his name, J SHAW FOUNDER. A photograph of one of these from the early 1870s is given at Figure 207. Figure 208 shows a cap from *circa* 1882 after taking his son and Thornton Harrison into partnership; the larger 'suns' have now been stamped more heavily, giving them the appearance of gears! After the changeover to the new, improved clappers, the stamps were replaced with a cross, which appears to be made up of four bells with clappers at right angles to each other. (Figures 209 and 210.)

Whilst James Shaw was steadily building up his handbell business at Bradford in the 1850s, William Pawson was trying to establish a similar concern at Leeds 10 miles to the east. A native of Leeds, he was born in 1830 and, when 14 years of age, joined the ringing band at the parish church as a probationer. His love of bells and ringing induced him to take up

211   Photograph of William Pawson cap and stamps

manufacturing handbells and he continued to make these for the rest of his life, although it was never his sole occupation. He was a competent ringer and was present at the founding of the Yorkshire Association in October 1875: he credited 11 peals to them out of his total of twenty. These included the first of Kent Treble Bob Maximus and Oxford Treble Bob Royal for the Association. He was also a capable performer on handbells in both tune and change ringing.

Pawson worked as a mechanic from his home at 10 Plaid Row, Shannon Street and it was also from here that he produced many handbells.[20] These included some long sets. He seemed to advertise exclusively in *The Bell News*, sending out price lists on request.[21] Examination of one of these lists, illustrated in Figure 238, shows that he catered mainly for change ringers with sets of up to 12 bells, but on request would cast sets of any number down to a bass bell of 26F. A set of 4½ chromatic octaves made by him, originally the property of Rev. W.E. Mills, is now at Benington, Hertfordshire and another of 37 bells is at Bishops Waltham, Hampshire. Finally, a set of 23 bells made by him was given by Rev. Erskine Clark to St Mary's, Battersea in the 1870s.[22] He died on 3 February 1890 after ailing for some months, and a band of his friends rang some of his handbells over his grave.[23] After his death his executors sold his plant, fittings and stock in trade to James Shaw, as mentioned earlier.[24]

Some of his handbells have numbers cast on the crown, but have no other distinguishing marks. They are neatly lathe-turned, both inside and out, with a 'button' depression round the staple hole. The screwed-in clapper staples are more substantial than usual for the period and are shaped rather like the upper part of a Yale key. Generally, his clappers had rounded shafts with ends similar in shape to the staples, although some have been found with shafts of rectangular section. His clapper balls were lathe-turned with short flights. The springs he used were of the normal truncated pyramid type with felts attached by sealing wax. His leather caps were deeply punched with a circular stamp 10mm in diameter containing diagonal and upright crosses superimposed, giving a star effect. He stamped his name, W PAWSON, on one side of the argent with LEEDS on the other. Sometimes he stamped this parallel to the argent and on other occasions at right angles to it. Photographs of these are in Figures 211 and 212.

Several other names of handbell founders from the north of England are recorded in print although I have seen no examples of their work. *The Bell News* of 1913 has an article about the famous Wigan team of handbell ringers who were very active in the mid-19th century.[25] They took part in the early Belle Vue contests and in 1859 took fourth prize and also the special prize for playing 'nearest to copy' the fifth figure of Julien's 'Martha Quadrilles'. Most of them were also tower-bell ringers, so when they got back to Wigan at one o'clock in the morning they rang the bells of the parish church, much to the astonishment of the local population, many of whom believed 'that either the town was enveloped in flames or the French had landed'!

The Bell News reported that the majority of their set of 79 bells, now unfortunately replaced, were by a London maker, Charles D'Albert. I have not been able to trace any founders with this name, but it is possible he was the composer, Charles D'Albert. I have seen some sheet music entitled, 'The New Lancers, a quadrille by Charles D'Albert'. Scholes' *Oxford Companion to Music* mentions Eugene Francis Charles D'Albert, a concert pianist, whose father held important London theatrical positions and composed popular quadrilles.[26] It may have been he who supplied bells on commission from one of the London manufacturers.

The article also implies that four or five of Wigan's larger bells were cast by Roger Bolton, a local founder. Roger Bolton & Son, Ltd., was one of Wigan's oldest brass foundries, dating back to the middle of the 18th century. Situated in Standishgate, the foundry turned out beer pumps, steam pipes for collieries, miners' lamps, copper brewing pans and many other goods during its 200-year history.[27] There is no record of the firm casting any more bells; it was probably a 'one-off' for the local team.

Rumbler bells were also made in Wigan in the 18th century. Two men who cast these were John Latham and Gerald Tarleton. Brears searched the Wigan Corporation Freeman's Rolls and discovered a number of residents with these initials, but the only one described as a founder was John Latham. He was elected a burgess in 1759 and was Mayor 20 years later. He probably died about 1782. His rumblers bear the inscription:

I.L. / WIGAN

Gerald Tarleton's rumblers also bear his initials over the name of Wigan, but

he inscribed these on the base of the bell and not the face. He was identified from the Freeman's Rolls as the only bellfounder or brazier with these initials between 1730 and 1800. He was casting for about 14 years before he died in 1753.[28]

Crotals with the initials E S are credited to Edward Sellers or his son from York. Benson discusses the Seller family in his monograph on York Bellfounders.[29] He intimates that the earliest member was William Seller, who from 1662 had his foundry in Jubbergate. He cast a number of church bells for North Lincolnshire, all of which bear his initials. It is certainly possible that he also cast the crotals with W S on them which currently have not been attributed to any founder. From 1683 to 1687 his church bells also bear the initials H W as well as his own. North suggests that these are those of his foreman or an apprentice.[30] If we assume that crotals bearing W S are William Seller's work then it is probable that those with H W are the work of his foreman.

212   Photograph of William Pawson cap and stamps

Benson records that Edward Seller succeeded William; his foundry was also at Jubbergate. He was admitted to the freedom of the city as a brazier in 1678, becoming Sheriff in 1703. He cast bells for several churches in York and also sent two to North Lincolnshire. He was joined in the business by two of his sons, Richard, who was made free in 1713, and Edward, made free in 1723. The elder Edward died a wealthy man in 1724. He left the foundry and all the casting and work tools to Richard and Edward and then divided the rest of his houses and other property between all three sons and two daughters.

Richard survived him by only a few months so the foundry was carried on solely by Edward II.[31] His son, John, joined him in 1733 and they ran the business together until the late 1750s. Edward determined to retire and in 1761 sold off several houses, household and shop goods and the stock in trade in the braziery, coppersmith and founders business. Two years later a further sale was announced in the *York Courant* of 5 July 1763:

> TO BE SOLD at the Warehouse of Mr Edward Seller, in High Jubbergate, York, (by virtue of an Order from His Majesty's Court of Common Pleas at Westminster) THE remainder of the Stock in Trade of the said Mr Edward Seller, consisting of a large assortment of Braziers, Brass and Bell-Founder's Goods, together with a large quantity of Bell Metal, yellow Metal, Pot Brass, Copper Shruff &c. The Sale to begin on Thursday next, and to continue till all was sold. A large Horse Mill and Wheel, very useful for several Branches of Business will be disposed of at the above place.[32]

The 'Bell-Founder's Goods' probably included the moulds for the crotals. It appears that these were obtained by Robert Wells and used to increase his range of rumblers, as I indicated in Chapter Five. Edward Seller died in November 1764. Rumbler bells with the initials E S were cast either by him or his father.

Two founders who advertised in the Yorkshire trade directories appear to have made small bells. Joseph Arthington at the Eagle Brass Foundry, Chapel Street, Huddersfield, described himself as a 'brass, bell and cock founder';[33] Thomas Simpson from 20 Orange Street, Halifax, appeared in the classified section of a number of directories as a brass and bellfounder.[34] It is most unlikely that either of them made handbells; their products were probably cattle bells or servant bells.

Small rumbler bells with the initials A G have been found. The only church bell founder with these initials in the north of England was Andrew Gurney of Hull, whose bells bear dates between 1676 and 1678.[35]

Sixteen
FOUNDING IN THE WEST

213 Rubbing of John Rudhall's initials

IN PREVIOUS CHAPTERS I have discussed the church and handbell work of the major bell foundries of England. The last of these great dynasties left to be described is that of the Rudhalls, based in Gloucester. Bliss illustrates the importance of this bellfounding family by showing that 35 per cent of all the bells still hanging in Gloucestershire towers were cast by them.[1] They sent their bells to nearly all the counties in Great Britain, also exporting them to the colonies—which included America at that time! As I have not traced any handbells by the earlier members of the family I propose only to mention them briefly. For a detailed discussion of their family history and the bells they cast the reader is referred to *The Church Bells of Gloucestershire* by Mary Bliss and Frederick Sharpe.

Abraham Rudhall was the first to be connected with bellfounding. He was a carpenter who, according to an advertisement placed in *The London Postman* for 20 February 1705, started casting bells in 1684.[2] The foundry passed through his son, Abraham Rudhall II, and his grandson, Abel, to his great-grandson, Thomas. On Thomas's death the firm was managed by Thomas's brother, Charles and his step-brother, John. John was probably the only member of the family to produce musical handbells.

Chris Pickford, in a very interesting article published in *The Ringing World*, points out that musical handbells were not mentioned by any of the earlier Rudhalls in their broadsheets or catalogues published in 1705, 1715 or 1751.[3] John Rudhall, in his broadsheet published in 1804, states that besides church bells he also cast:

> … all Sorts of Plantation, Ship, House, and Clock Bells; and Mill-Brasses, on the most reasonable Terms.[4]

But again, handbells are not mentioned. However, when Rev. Dr. Samuel Parr raised money from amongst his friends in 1809 to install a ring of six in his parish church of Hatton, Warwickshire, his parishioners presented him with a set of 12 handbells cast by John Rudhall.[5] The parish paid three guineas for the bells, and a further 2s. 6d. to bring them from Gloucester.

A trade card distributed by John Rudhall about 1825 mentions he would supply tuned sets of hand, horse, sheep and dish bells and his final catalogue issued in 1830 ends with:

> Orders addressed to John Rudhall, Gloucester, will be executed on the lowest terms; who also casts Plantation, Ship, House and Clock Bells; likewise tuned Sets of Hand, Sheep, and Cup Bells.

I would suggest from the above evidence that we can presume a date of about 1808 for his addition of musical handbells to his normal range of goods.

His estimate book for the period 1828 to 1835 has been preserved amongst the Prideaux papers at the City of Bristol Record Office.[6] Amongst his estimates for church bell work he gives a few quotations for sets of handbells. Two of these were to firms in Bristol, Wasbrough Hale & Co. and Peter Llewellin, for hand-bells 'fitted up' ready for resale. He charged different prices to each of them, no doubt because he had not dealt with Peter Llewellin before. The details are:

Wasbrough Hale & Co. 20 December 1830			
8 Tenor less than 5 Inch Diam^r	2	18	0
from 5 to 6½ inch	3	10	0
10 Less than 5 inch	3	15	0
from 5 to 6½	4	5	0
12 less than 5	4	10	0
5½ Inch	4	15	0
to 6½	5	5	0

Ready money 10 pr Ct off to them

Peter Llewellin 26 April 1831			
8 hand Bells Brass spring Clap^r &c			
Tenor under 5 Inch Diam^r	2	15	0
from 5 to 6½	3	5	0
10 Tenor less than 5	3	12	0
from 5 to 6½	4	0	0
12 Tenor less than 5	4	5	0
5½ Inch	4	10	0
6½	5	0	0

5 per Cent money

Sharpe records an advertisement in the *Gloucester Journal* for Monday, 1 May 1826 announcing the opening of a new ring of eight at Chipping Norton, Oxon, and the offer of three money prizes for the best ringing.[7] The estimate book contains a quotation to the Chipping Norton ringers five years later for a set of handbells; the prices were the same as those quoted to Wasbrough Hale & Co. although he offered the Chipping Norton ringers a discount of 10 shillings. John sold the business to Thomas Mears II in 1829, although he continued to produce bells up to his death in February 1835 aged 76. To the best of my knowledge, the only handbell I have seen which I would credit to John Rudhall is in the Sharpe Collection. It has a wide mouth compared with its height, 123mm to 98mm, and has the initials I R inside. (Figure 213.) I think John Rudhall also made some crotals. A photograph of one is shown at Figure 214. Moir suggests that crotals bearing these initials were made by John Read of Aldbourne between 1751 and 1753, the same period as Edward Read.[8] There is, as far as I aware, no documentary evidence for a John Read, so I credit them to Rudhall.

In the 19th century Llewellins and James was a firm of Bristol bellfounders, first appearing under this name in a Bristol trade directory of 1854.[9] The business itself was much older, however, tracing its origins as a brass foundry back to 1740.[10] In 1830 it traded as Emerson and Llewellin, whilst from 1831 to 1853

214 Photograph of a John Rudhall crotal

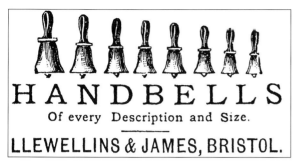

215　Llewellin & James advertisement

216　Llewellin & James handbell

it was under the control of Peter Llewellin and called Llewellin. The foundry was at Castle Green, although their tuning shop was in Cock and Bottle Lane, off Castle Ditch.[11] A leading article in *The Bell News* for 1884 gives some idea of the size of the firm at that time. It had 90 lathes and many radial drills and planing machines, all previously used in the engineering business, but now partly employed in making fittings and for the tuning of bells. An article in the *Victoria County History* for Gloucestershire, published in 1907, states they employed about 180 people in the engineering and bell-founding departments and undertook bellfounding of every class and scale, from musical handbells to complete rings.[12]

Although they are said to have cast church bells from about 1851, it has been shown that most of these earlier bells were cast by the major bell foundries and supplied by Llewellins and James. Christopher Pickford has carried out extensive research on this firm and concludes that their first bells date from about 1862.[13] In common with other Victorian foundries, they displayed their products in the various shows that took place and in the Kimberley Exhibition of 1890 they won a silver medal.[14] Their last bell is probably the one at All Hallows, Easton, Bristol, dated 1940.[15]

It is difficult to know when they first manufactured handbells. They advertised their church bells in *The Bell News* from 25 August 1883, but did not allude to musical handbells. An advertisement in Snowdon's *Grandsire* published in 1888 notes:

> Makers of the L & J Cabinet for the Safe-
> keeping and preservation of Hand Bells

but did not mention that they supplied the handbells. In 1892 they began to advertise them consistently in *The Bell News* (Figure 215), and this continued for the next few years until 1898 when the advert was dropped. They still manufactured them, however. Two other books, *Standard Methods* in 1901 and the 1905 edition of *Grandsire*, carried their illustration containing eight handbells in their adverts. In 1912 they rehung the bells at St James, Trowbridge in a new metal frame, recast the tenor and Simpson tuned the existing bells.[16] They also supplied a set of handbells which are still kept in the church.

Their larger handbells, e.g. size 21D, have square shoulders similar to Taylor's second patterns. Unlike them they have a low domed crown as well. (Figure 216.) They have very little flare at the lip, the bell having almost straight sides

217 Llewellin & James clapper assembly

218 Llewellin & James strap

219 Llewellin & James leather stamps

from crown to lip. The bells are not marked, having neither numbers nor initials. There is a small 'button' under the argent, but none around the staple hole. Although their bells carry no identifying marks, their fittings are characteristic of the firm. Their clapper staples are very substantial for the period and are nicely finished. Their clapper shafts are square, with chamfered edges and a rounded staple end. The clapper ball is drilled and tapped for the leather striking pegs and besides the turned line bisecting the ball at the pegs there are two lines around the flight. An unusual feature is the way the flight curves gracefully from the ball instead of looking like a screwed-in addition. The springs are of normal shape with a single iron rivet and with the lower end bent round the staple to prevent movement. The felts are attached in the usual way with sealing wax. (Figure 217.) Their leather work is conventional. The straps are attached to the argents with copper rivets and the largest bell has LLEWELLINS AND JAMES, BRISTOL marked on the apex, as in Figure 218. The caps are marked with a symbol similar to four seeds or leaves in the form of a cross.

I have notes of a set of smaller bells (largest 18G) with similar characteristics to the above with the exception that the bells have more rounded shoulders and flared lips. The staples and clappers are identical. The leather work differs only by having domed brass washers and rivets for attaching the strap, together with a new leather stamp depicting a shamrock or Ace of Clubs in addition to the earlier mark on the cap. (Figure 219.) All their premises were destroyed by fire in an air raid in November 1940 and the firm moved to Princess Street, Bedminster, Bristol. They continued to trade here as process plant engineers until 1973 when the firm closed.[17]

A man who cast some church bells and handbells in the Bristol area in the first half of the 19th century was William Cary. Walters states that he cast the third bell at Nettleton, Wiltshire in 1830 and adds a footnote that he came from Bristol.[18] I think Struckett is wrong when he suggests that he was founding at Bridgwater between 1830 and 1852, for Ellacombe also gives his base as Bristol when he cast the old treble at Christ Church, Bath.[19] A further reference may be found in R.C. Hope's article, 'English Bellfounders 1150-1893'. He gives a T. Cary of Bristol who died about 1854. I have been unable to trace him in the few Bristol directories I have been able to consult, although I did find a Mary Cary who was a livery stable keeper in 1830.[20] Christopher Dalton notes that Thomas Mears cast church bells for William Cary.[21] As far as I am aware, only one handbell of his has been found. This had engraved on the waist:

W CARY
Bristol

I regret I have no further information.

I have a small house bell with T.W embossed inside in letters seven millimetres high. (Figures 220 and 221.) Thomas Wroth was suggested to me as a possible founder. Ellacombe discusses a founder with this name who cast two bells for Wellington, Somerset, in 1748.[22] Again, in *The Church Bells of Devon*, published in 1866, he mentions 64 bells in that county cast by men with those initials between 1691 and 1774. Although embossing the initials inside the bell was an 18th-century practice, the shape of my bell is more typical of the early 19th century and it may have been cast in Bristol by a member of the Westcott family. In 1815 this firm of church bell founders consisted of Jasper Westcott & Sons.[23] Later, his sons cast bells independently as well as in partnership. For instance, J. & N. Westcott cast a ring of six for Bretforton, Worcestershire in 1823; B. Westcott at Burrington, Somerset in 1828; L. Westcott at Timsbury, Somerset in 1842; and John Westcott, who cast a bell for Holy Trinity, Taunton, also in 1842. Pigot's Commercial Directory of 1830 gives Nathaniel Westcott's premises at 64 Radcliff Street, Bristol. Dalton suggests that these men did not cast their own church bells but obtained them from Gloucester or Whitechapel.[24] A member of this family may have cast this small bell. However, I think the most likely founder is Thomas Wootton, the clockmaker of Great Hampton Street, Birmingham, whom I discussed in Chapter 14.

William Aggett and Sons were a firm of bellhangers who worked from the Church Bell Works, Chagford, Devon. They invented and patented a design of self-aligning and self-lubricating ball bearings which they used on several hundred rings of bells. They advertised as having hung the ring at Buckfast Abbey and claimed to be 'Bell Hangers to His Majesty's Government'. *The Church Bells of Cornwall* records that they cast several rings of bells, the earliest being a six at St Columb Minor in 1882. The following year they appear to have cast six for Ladcock, which they augmented to eight in 1926. It is almost certain that these bells were cast by one of the major bell foundries: the six bells at St Eval are marked above the lip with 'AGGETT BELL HANGER, CHAGFORD, DEVON' although most of them were cast by Mears and Stainbank at various times.[25] When the bells of Chagford were recast and rehung in 1915 Taylors recast them although Aggett rehung them.[26] From 1922 to 1925 they advertised in *The Ringing World* that they would supply handbells. It is most unlikely that they manufactured these themselves; they probably bought blanks from Taylors or

220   Rubbing of T.W mark

221   Photograph of house bell by T W

Whitechapel and furbished these, or merely resold complete handbell sets from the same source.

E(paphrus) Seage, an engineer of Codrington Street and Clifton Road, Exeter, advertised from August 1887 to September 1888 in *The Bell News*. He was publicising his Church Bell Dumb Practice Apparatus, together with his improved clapper stays. The latter fixed the clapper so the bell did not strike and then, by an ingenious system of wires and levers, a stud on the side of the headstock caused a handbell, fixed in the ringing chamber, to sound. When fixed to all the bells this enabled ringers to practise without annoying the general public. He did not cast his own handbells, but obtained them chiefly from Taylor's.[27] They valued this work, often sending regular quantities of 50 sets to his Exeter workshops. He did undertake repairs to handbells, however, for he also advertised: 'HANDBELLS re-clappered with Seage's silent Hinge clapper'. I have not seen any of these.

Thomas Doble and his sons were church bellhangers at Taunton, Somerset. From 1915 to 1921 they advertised in *The Ringing World*, stating that they sold handbells in either chromatic or diatonic sets. It is unlikely that they cast these themselves; their probable source of supply was either Whitechapel or Loughborough.

Seventeen
A FINAL MISCELLANY

222 Henry Bastable

IN THIS FINAL chapter I propose to discuss documentary references to handbell manufacturers whose bells have not yet been identified and then consider inscribed bells by founders whose names are not known. I will also review one or two suppliers of handbells who retailed other founders' products and deal with items I omitted from earlier chapters. Finally, I will report on initials found on crotals by unidentified founders.

In the Central Council Library Collection of Manuscripts is a scrap book which previously belonged to John E. Acland-Troyte, of Huntsham Court, Devon. Amongst the miscellaneous press cuttings are two handbell price lists from William Blews of Birmingham. One is dated 1872; the other from the prices is probably a couple of years earlier. On the top of the latter is a brief note in Troyte's handwriting:

> The very best Bells that are made in Birmingham made by <u>John Banister</u> - William's brother

This suggests that John Banister worked at Blews making handbells. The Banisters were a famous ringing family from Woolwich, Kent. John's father, Henry Banister, was born in 1781 and was a contemporary of Henry Symondson with whom he rang a few peals. One of these was the first peal on the bells at St Mary's, Woolwich, one of Grandsire Triples rung for the Eastern Scholars on 13 November 1821.[1]

Henry had six sons who became ringers and on 29 March 1852, with the help of a tenor man, they all rang together in a peal of Grandsire Triples at Woolwich.[2] The records show that they rang in age order with James, the youngest, ringing the treble and Francis, the eldest son, ringing the sixth. Henry conducted the peal from the seventh. William, who rang the fourth, was born in 1824 and was a very talented ringer. He was only 19 when he composed and conducted the second peal of London Surprise Major which was rung at Woolwich with the local band! This band went from strength to strength through William's ability and the cohesion provided by the six brothers. However, the band broke up in 1854 at the outbreak of the

Crimean War because of their involvement in the war effort, for they all worked at Woolwich Arsenal.

William moved to Devonport early in 1865 and his expertise in all matters connected with bells and ringing was put to good use by men like Rev. H.T. Ellacombe, Col. C.A.W. Troyte and his brother Capt. J.E. Troyte.[3] He retired from government service in 1879 and spent many of his remaining years in public works as a councillor and J.P. He died in 1917 at Fulham, aged 94.

John was the fourth of the brothers. He was born in 1826 and probably had a talent for music. He too was a capable ringer and was for six years a tutor to the Lewisham ringers.[4] In William's obituary the following statement is made: 'Mr. Banister excelled in tune ringing on handbells. He and his brothers had a magnificent set of over 70 bells which they themselves manufactured, and with which they delighted many audiences and benefited the funds of many a worthy cause.'[5] In view of John's employment by Blews and the comment by John Ackland-Troyte I should think he was the likely instigator and founder of this large set of handbells. It would be interesting to know what happened to them. John moved to Birmingham whilst at Blews and took part in a number of peals for the St Martin's Guild. He also rang some in Devon, obviously when visiting his brother William and it would have been there that John Ackland-Troyte got to know him. He died in Birmingham on 10 August 1880 aged 54.

Although not a handbell founder, Henry Bastable, illustrated in Figure 222, was involved in tuning and supplying sets in the last quarter of the 19th century. Born in Pensnett, near Dudley, Worcestershire, on 30 December 1848, he moved to Handsworth, Birmingham, while still a young boy.[6] His introduction to bells was chiming for service when he was 12 and he learned to ring four years later when a new band was set up after a dispute with the existing ringers. He quickly became a skilful tower and handbell ringer and conductor, proving very popular with his contemporaries, who knew him as 'Henry Bas'. He rang peals with most of the prominent ringers of the period and conducted the first peal of Stedman Caters on handbells outside London and the first of Stedman Cinques on handbells ever rung.

He advertised his services as a handbell tuner and fitter in *Church Bells*, stating he could undertake any repairs, including the mending or replacing of cracked bells.[7] In addition, he would supply handbells in diatonic and chromatic sets and send price lists on request. He probably obtained his blanks for making handbells from William Blews or James Barwell. He gave his address as 45 George Street, Lozells, near Birmingham. He was not a well man; a serious illness in his younger days left him in poor health and this caused his early death on 18 January 1899, aged 50.[8]

Whilst searching for old bells in the late 1980s I came across a large handbell in Petworth Antiques Market. It was a large bronze bell with a rosewood handle, rather like a town crier's bell. It had an overall height of about twelve inches, the bell being six inches in diameter. The initials W H were incised in the crown, with the number 13 opposite. It had a large, heavy, tapered iron clapper with an oval ball and a large flight hooked in to a cast-in iron staple. The initials are shown in Figure 223. The only handbell founder I have encountered with these initials is William Haley.

223 William Haley's initials from a post bell

Haley was born in 1857, the son of Henry W. Haley, a well-known ringer of the 19th century.[9] Like his father, William was blessed with a keen musical ear and he too became a church and handbell tuner. According to his obituary, he worked as tuner to John Warner for over forty years.[10] However, he could not have worked for them continuously, for William Fussell recorded in his diary for December 1884, when he was working for Alfred Lawson, the owner of Mears at that time, that 'W. Haley, our bell-tuner, was married at Hackney on Sunday last'.[11]

Haley received many compliments from well-known musicians on the accuracy of his work, the most notable being from Sir Arthur Sullivan. Haley had tuned a set of bells for a performance of *The Golden Legend* and Sullivan came to inspect them. He commented afterwards that Haley had a better musical ear than he did himself.[12] He was also an author: one of his works, *The Bell Hymn Book*, received a testimonial from Sir George C. Martin, the organist at St Paul's Cathedral.[13]

Warner's business was drawing to a close in 1922, so Haley decided to retire and set up in the handbell business himself. This advertisement appeared in *The Ringing World*:

TO THE CLERGY, RINGERS, AND ALL WHOM IT MAY CONCERN.

Having had over 40 years' experience as Church Bell and Musical Handbell tuner, in succession to my father (Mr. H.W.Haley), I have decided to carry on the handbell business, and, therefore, respectfully beg to solicit your patronage.
I shall be pleased to execute any orders, however small, at reasonable charges, and guarantee satisfaction.
Prices for new bells, repairs, etc., will be furnished on application.

WILLIAM HALEY
Author of the 'Bell Hymn Book,' 'Twelve Popular Airs,' etc. etc.
50 CLARENDON ROAD, HOE STREET,
WALTHAMSTOW, ESSEX.[14]

This advertisement appeared for four months, after which he replaced it with another depicting a row of eight handbells over his name and address and the words, 'Handbell Manufacturer'. (Figure 224.) It added, 'Repairs Executed.

224 William Haley's advertisement

Price List for New Bells on Application.' He changed his address to 16 Granville Road a year later.[15] The advertisements continued until his death in January 1927. I have not identified any of his musical handbells.

225   Rubbing of W★A mark   **226**   'H', an unknown founder

227   Bell cast by 'H', an unknown founder at present

Several firms of bellhangers have advertised that they sold handbells. I discussed the firm of Blackbourn and Greenleaf in Chapter 13 and Thomas Doble and Sons in the last chapter. Webb and Bennett were operating a similar bell-hanging business in Kidlington, Oxfordshire, in the 20 years either side of the turn of the 19th century. They specialised in rehanging bells in frames of their own design and these may be found in many churches in the Oxford Diocese. They probably obtained their handbells from Whitechapel.

From time to time odd handbells appear with the initials W A on either side of a small star. (Figure 225.) These handbells are 18th-century in origin; a letter from W.D. Tinker in *The Bell News* for 1900 indicates that the ringers at Gainsborough had owned a set of eight of these bells for nearly a century.[16] They were all marked WA on the crown and had wooden handles with wooden balls for strikers. Turning to more recent times, I have been informed of two of these bells which constitute part of a miscellaneous set at Stradishall, Suffolk, although I have not been able to inspect them. However, I was fortunate to find another one whilst examining a set of 14 bells from Little Missenden, Buckinghamshire. The Missenden bell has deeply cut file marks around the exterior parallel to the rim, whilst the interior of the bell has been left as cast. The letters W ★ A are at a right angle to the argent with the number 7 opposite. The bell was extensively restored when the other bells in the set were renovated some years ago so no clues remain as to the original fittings.

I have been unable to allocate these handbells to any known founder. The only church bell founder with these initials in the reference books is William Atton, of Buckingham. He was casting in the early 17th century, however, which is much too early. Another name suggested to me was William Aggett, of Chagford, Devon. However, as I showed in the last chapter, he did not cast handbells and, in any case, was working a century too late.

In 1988 a useful list of handbell founders appeared in *Reverberations*, compiled by Robert W. Leavett and Jean Sanderson.[17] Included in this list are the names or initials of several founders whom I have not previously discussed. The first of these is on a bell which has parallel lines on the inside of the bell at the soundbow and the letter 'A' engraved on the waist outside. Without seeing the bell it is difficult to be sure, but I suspect it is an old Thomas Mears II handbell with the owner's initial engraved on it. I have seen a number of Wells' bells of this period engraved thus with the owner's name or initials. Another bell has the initials C A stamped on the leather cap. The only other identifying feature is that the bell size number appears large on the crown. I have not seen any of

228   Photograph of mark of I H

229   Clock bell mark of H F & Co.

230 Photograph of crown of John Evans' bell

231 Leather work of Frank Barnett

232 One of Codnor's leather stamps

these bells but it is possible that they are the work of C. Andrews of London, whom a business card describes as a 'Handbell Maker'. It is suggested that he may have assembled handbells from other founders' blank bells.

Three sets of initials are mentioned in Leavett and Sanderson's list which are not dealt with elsewhere. The first two are G B and I S: no other information is given and I have not seen bells with these initials. The last is T & T, which appears on a bell in the Sharpe Collection. I cannot suggest a founder for this bell either. George Clews of Birmingham appears in the list as a general founder who cast a few bells and handbells. Trevor Jennings associates him with Charles Carr. William Moore was producing handbells at Salisbury from 1900-1930; the list suggests his large bells have rounded shoulders. I have a note, origin unknown, which indicates that he acted as a middle-man for Whitechapel handbells. I have not seen handbells by either of these men.

Before I leave this list I ought to point out that I disagree with three of its statements. First, bells with M & S on the crown are probably from Martineau & Smith and not Mears & Stainbank: for further discussion on this see Chapter 14. Secondly, the list suggests that bells with I T on the crown are an early form of John Taylor's work. I have not seen any of these bells; those I have examined with these initials have had the letters cast in relief inside. I wrote in Chapter 6 that bells and crotals with these initials are usually credited to John Thornton. Finally, the first name of the founder of the Shaw firm was James and not John.

A brass house bell in my collection has three concentric circles on its crown with the name 'W MILLER' in letters 3 mm high curved round between the innermost circle and the central 'button'. I have not traced where this bell was made. Two further house bells have the letter H inscribed on the crown parallel to the argent. The larger of the pair has the number 7 opposite, the smaller has 3. Figure 226 illustrates a rubbing from the former and Figure 227 is a photograph of the smaller. I cannot give a founder for these.

Amongst my photographs I have one of a bell with a circular stamp on the inside lip bearing the initials I H. (Figure 228.) My filing system appears to have broken down in this case and I cannot trace whence it came! I cannot offer a clue to its founder either: too many church bell founders had these initials.

The London Commercial Directory for 1812 indicates that Thomas Smith of 65 Berwick Street, Soho, was a brass and bell founder. He was in continuous

233   Cover page of *The Handbell Tutor* by W Haley

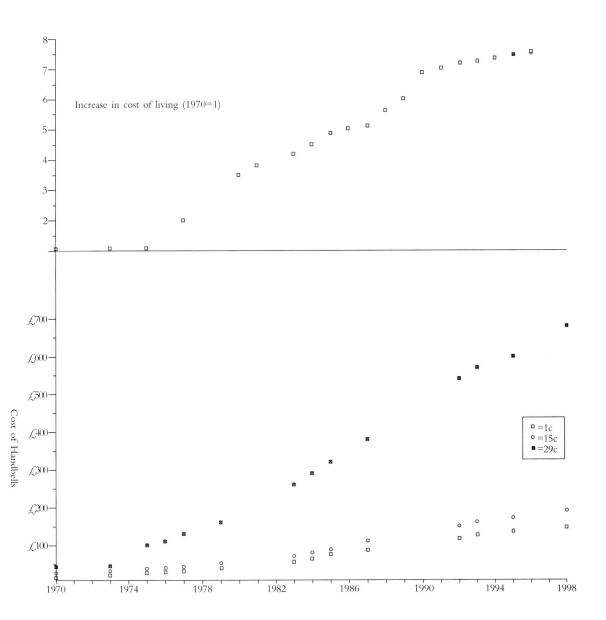

234   Graph comparing handbell prices to cost of living

production from this address until 1830 when he moved to 51 Castle Street, Oxford Market, where he continued for another six years. I have not identified any of his bells.

Some years ago I received a letter from a clock restorer who had a long case clock in for repair. The clock was made by Michael Watson of Newcastle about 1800 and contained a four and a half inch diameter bell with H F & Co cast in the crown. A rubbing is shown at Figure 229. I have no further information on this founder.

Size	Key.	Set of 8.	Set of 10.	Set of 12.	Set of 15.
15	C.	£4 2 6	£4 10 6	£5 7 6	£6 0 0
16	B.	£4 8 6	£4 15 0	£5 14 0	£6 4 6
17	A.	£4 17 0	£5 1 6	£6 0 0	£6 9 6
18	G.	£5 7 6	£5 14 0	£6 6 6	£7 2 6
19	F.	£5 18 0	£6 6 6	£6 13 0	£7 12 0
20	E.	£6 6 6	£6 19 0	£7 5 6	£8 4 6
21	D.	£6 17 0	£7 12 0	£8 8 6	£9 3 6
22	C.	£7 9 6	£8 4 6	£9 3 6	£10 2 6

With Improved Clappers, and in Perfect Tune.
SETS OF SIZE 15, KEPT ALWAYS IN STOCK.

Notice.—All other Lists are Cancelled

JANUARY, 1873.

235 William Blews' price list, 1873

Two other clockmakers have cast bells. John Calcott cast bells for long case clocks about 1806: his address is given as Cotton, but whether this is in Lancashire, Bedfordshire or Suffolk I have no idea. Another name I have found is 'Ainsworth, movement maker and bell founder'. This dates from the middle of the 19th century. Again, I have no further information.

Maurice Davies has a house bell in his collection which has a flat crown similar to house bells by James Barwell of Birmingham. However, this bell has inscribed round the button under the argent 'J EVANS PATENT'. A photograph of this may be seen at Figure 230. This bell is probably by the John Evans of Moland Street, Birmingham, to whom I alluded in Chapter 14.

When The Handbell Ringers of Great Britain was formed in 1967 it gave a great impetus to handbell ringing. Many of the sets found in churches up and down England were in poor condition and needed restoration. As I mentioned in Chapter 7, Whitechapel was deluged with work and had long waiting lists, so a few individuals set up and undertook this work part-time. One of these whose work is often seen was Frank Barnett, of Malvern, who used the characteristic leather stamps illustrated in Figure 231.

Coming right up to date, in the last quarter of the 20th century three men have independently cast

236 John Warner's price list, 1876

PRICES OF HAND BELLS
BY
JOHN TAYLOR & Co.,
Bell Founders,
LOUGHBOROUGH.

No.		Peal of 15 £ s. d.	Peal of 12 £ s. d.	Peal of 10 £ s. d.	Peal of 8 £ s. d.
No. 8	C.	2 15 0	2 6 0	1 19 0	1 12 0
No. 9	B.	2 16 0	2 7 0	2 0 0	1 13 0
No. 10	A.	2 19 0	2 9 9	2 2 0	1 15 0
No. 11	G.	3 2 0	2 12 0	2 5 0	1 18 0
No. 12	F.	3 5 0	2 15 0	2 8 0	2 1 6
No. 13	E.	3 9 0	2 18 0	2 11 0	2 4 0
No. 14	D.	3 13 6	3 2 0	2 15 0	2 7 0
No. 15	C.	3 17 0	3 7 0	2 19 0	2 10 0
No. 16	B.	4 2 0	3 12 0	3 3 0	2 14 0
No. 17	A.	4 6 0	3 17 0	3 8 0	2 18 0
No. 18	G.	4 14 0	4 2 0	3 13 0	3 3 0
No. 19	F.	5 2 0	4 9 0	3 19 0	3 8 0
No. 20	E.	5 10 0	4 17 0	4 6 0	3 14 0
No. 21	D.	6 1 0	5 7 0	4 15 0	4 2 0
No. 22	C.	6 15 0	6 0 0	5 8 0	4 13 0
No. 23	B.	7 15 0	6 18 0	6 5 0	5 9 0
No. 24	A.	8 13 0	7 15 0	7 0 0	6 4 0
No. 25	G.	9 17 0	8 18 0	8 2 0	7 5 0
No. 26	F.	11 6 0	10 5 0	9 9 0	8 10 0
No. 27	E.	13 0 0	11 17 0	11 0 0	10 0 0
No. 28	D.	14 18 0	13 14 0	12 15 0	11 11 0
No. 29	C.	17 0 0	15 15 0	14 14 0	13 6 0

Set of 2 Octaves, each set containing 19 Bells, comprising two extra half tones in each Octave.

No. 15, Tenor Key C.	4 16 6	No. 21, Tenor Key D.	7 9 6
No. 18, " G.	5 17 0	No. 25, " G.	12 0 0

Sets of 2 Octaves, Chromatic, containing 25 Bells.

No. 15, Tenor Key C.	6 14 0	No. 21, Tenor Key D.	10 4 0
No. 18, " G.	8 10 0	No. 25, " G.	16 18 0

Sets of 3 Octaves, Chromatic, containing 37 Bells.

No. 22, Tenor Key C.	14 0 0	No. 26, Tenor Key F.	22 8 0
No. 25, " G.	19 0 0	No. 29, " C.	35 15 0

Prices for other Peals of any size or number will be given on application.

237 John Taylor's price list from 1882 catalogue

WILLIAM PAWSON,
MUSICAL HAND-BELL FOUNDER,
10, Plaid Row, Shannon Street, Marsh Lane, Leeds.

LIST OF PRICES.

CHARGES FOR SINGLE BELLS.
All Bells above C No. 1 Size 4s. 3d. each.

	£ s. d.		£ s. d.
C No. 1 Size	0 4 3	D No. 14 Size	0 7 0
B " 2 "	0 4 6	C " 15 "	0 7 3
A " 3 "	0 4 6	B " 16 "	0 8 0
G " 4 "	0 4 9	G " 18 "	0 9 6
F " 5 "	0 4 9	E " 20 "	0 12 0
E " 6 "	0 5 0	D " 21 "	0 13 9
D " 7 "	0 5 3	C " 22 "	0 15 0
C " 8 "	0 5 6	B " 23 "	0 16 0
B " 9 "	0 5 9	A " 24 "	0 18 0
A " 10 "	0 6 0	F " 26 "	1 4 0
G " 11 "	0 6 3		
F " 12 "	0 6 6		
E " 13 "	0 6 9		

Sets containing 8 Bells for Change Ringing.

	£ s. d.		£ s. d.
C No. 8 Size	1 15 0	D No. 14 Size	2 7 0
B " 9 "	1 16 0	C " 15 "	2 10 0
A " 10 "	1 17 6	B " 16 "	2 13 0
G " 11 "	1 19 0	A " 17 "	2 15 0
F " 12 "	2 2 0	G " 18 "	2 18 0
E " 13 "	2 5 0	F " 19 "	3 2 6

Sets containing 12 Bells for Change Ringing.

	£ s. d.		£ s. d.
C No. 15 Size	3 9 0	F No. 19 Size	4 7 6
B " 16 "	3 14 0	E " 20 "	4 12 0
F " 12 "	3 18 0	D " 21 "	5 2 0
E " 13 "	4 3 0	G " 18 "	4 3 0

Sets containing 15 Bells, arranged to have One Peal of 12, Two of 10, and Three of 8.

	£ s. d.		£ s. d.
C No. 15 Size	4 7 0	F No. 19 Size	5 8 0
B " 16 "	4 12 0	E " 20 "	5 14 6
A " 17 "	4 16 6	D " 21 "	6 2 0
G " 18 "	5 2 6	C " 22 "	6 10 0

Three Octaves on Chromatic Scale, containing 37 Bells.

	£ s. d.		£ s. d.
C No. 15 Size	9 0 0	F No. 19 Size	10 10 0
B " 16 "	9 2 0	E " 20 "	11 5 0
A " 17 "	9 10 0	D " 21 "	12 10 0
G " 18 "	9 18 0	C " 22 "	14 0 0

Four Octaves on Chromatic Scale, containing 49 Bells.

	£ s. d.
C No. 22 Size	15 10 0
A " 24 "	16 12 0

Sets containing 56 Bells, Chromatic Scale.

	£ s. d.		£ s. d.
G No. 25 Size	20 0 0	F No. 26 Size	22 0 0

Any additional information can be obtained on application.

Sets containing 27 Bells, three Octaves in extent, arranged for parties about commencing Tune Ringing in C, 22 size, with three F sharps and two C sharps; also peals in F, 19 size, and A, 17 size, with semitones in proportion to the above.

	£ s. d.
A No. 17 Size	7 5 0
F " 19 "	7 10 0
C " 22 "	9 5 0

ALL ORDERS PROMPTLY EXECUTED.   CARRIAGE FREE TO ANY PART OF ENGLAND.
OLD PEALS REPAIRED OR AUGMENTED ON THE MOST REASONABLE TERMS.

G. BATTYE. "THE PEOPLE'S" COLOUR PRINTER, 17, MEADOW ROAD, HOLBECK.

238 William Pawson's price list, 1885

handbells. Walter Dobbie, of West Peckham, Kent, began about 1974 by casting small aluminium bells and later cast some bronze handbells. I have an 03A of his in my five octave set. It has no distinguishing marks. George Francis, of Warnham, Sussex, has also cast some bronze handbells, but mainly for his own use. On the other hand, Roy Carnall, of Codnor, Derbyshire, has cast many sets. Codnor Handbell Founders, of 86 Heanor Road, Codnor, was established in 1979. This notice appeared in *The Ringing World* for that year and the first advertisement for the firm appeared a few pages later:

> Codnor Handbell Founders has been created for the purpose of manufacturing British handbells. The world-wide demand for these handbells is overwhelming and Codnor Handbells Founders aim to provide this service. Many have expressed a desire for a truly independent concern to attend to the finer points of handbell techniques. Codnor Handbell Founders' existence has been generated by the interest of Mr Roy Carnall, who needs no introduction to the bell world and foundry techniques. An authority on bell tuning, he was employed at the old firm of John Taylor & Co, Loughborough. He has a wide experience in foundry work and artistic skills. Codnor Handbell Founders aim to provide good craftsmanship at all times.[18]

239   George Welch's price list, 1886

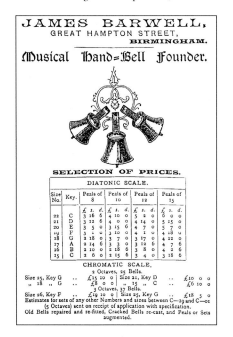

241   James Barwell's price list from 'Standard Methods', 1892

PRICES OF HAND-BELLS
BY
JOHN TAYLOR & CO.,
Church & Hand-Bell Founders,
LOUGHBOROUGH.

Prices of Peals of Hand-Bells in the Diatonic Scale.

Size	Key.	Peal of 8 Bells. £ s. d.	Peal of 10 Bells. £ s. d.	Peal of 12 Bells. £ s. d.
Tenor, No. 8	C	1 15 6	—	—
,, No. 11	G	1 19 0	2 8 0	—
,, No. 12	F	2 1 0	2 10 0	2 18 6
,, No. 14	D	2 6 6	2 15 6	3 4 6
,, No. 15	C	2 10 0	2 19 0	3 8 0
,, No. 18	G	3 2 6	3 13 0	4 2 0
,, No. 19	F	3 7 6	3 19 0	4 8 6
,, No. 21	D	4 1 6	4 15 0	5 6 6
,, No. 22	C	4 12 0	5 6 6	5 19 0

Sets of Two Octaves, *each set containing* 19 *Bells, comprising two extra Half Tones in each Octave.*

Size.	Key.	£ s. d.	Size.	Key.	£ s. d.
Tenor, No. 15	C	5 1 6	Tenor, No. 24	A	10 11 0
,, No. 17	A	5 12 6	,, No. 25	G	12 0 6
,, No. 18	G	5 19 0	,, No. 26	F	13 16 0
,, No. 19	F	6 7 0	,, No. 28	D	18 13 6
,, No. 21	D	7 9 0	,, No. 29	C	20 16 6
,, No. 22	C	8 5 0			

Sets of Two Octaves, Chromatic, *each set containing* 25 *Bells.*

Size.	Key.	£ s. d.	Size.	Key.	£ s. d.
Tenor, No. 15	C	6 17 0	Tenor, No. 22	C	11 10 6
,, No. 18	G	8 1 6	,, No. 25	G	16 18 0

Sets of Three Octaves, Chromatic, *each set containing* 37 *Bells.*

Size.	Key.	£ s. d.	Size.	Key.	£ s. d.
Tenor, No. 22	C	14 4 0	Tenor, No. 25	G	19 16 0

Re-casting and Repairs of all kinds executed promptly and at Moderate Prices.

Illustrated Hand-Bell Catalogue on application.

240   John Taylor's price list from 'Ropesight', 1891

Born in Nottingham, Mr. Carnall was educated in Bradford not far from where James Shaw had his foundry. After taking a foundry apprenticeship and gaining experience with various firms he worked as foundry manager for Paul Taylor at Loughborough. About 1978 he decided to set up as an independent handbell founder. During the next 20 years he built up a solid business manufacturing sets of handbells. He carried out all the work himself, including casting the bells, tuning and polishing them. He fabricated the clapper assemblies and cut and stamped the leather caps and handles. By 1984 his business had increased to such an extent that he had to turn some work away. In January of that year a local paper, the *Derby Evening Telegraph*, carried a full-length feature article on the foundry extolling its success.[19]

MUSICAL HAND-BELLS.

UNED either in the Diatonic or Chromatic Scales; with improved Clappers, which far exceed all others for durability, being also quite free from jingling sounds when ringing. Being the largest manufacturers of Musical Bells in the world, we can guarantee our Bells to be of a pure, distinct tone, and in perfect harmony with each other. Old Sets augmented to any number, repaired, re-clothed, re-pegged, or re-clappered, on our improved principle. Portable Tables, suitable for Hand-Bell Tune Ringers, and Boxes with Trays for any size or number of Bells, in Polished Pitch Pine, Painted Wood, or Oak, made to order. As we are constantly replacing old peals with new, we always have a quantity of Second-hand Bells in stock, at a cheap rate. List forwarded on application.

PRICE LIST FOR MUSICAL HAND-BELLS.

Single Bells required in 5 octaves.

C No. 01	...	£0 4 6	F No. 12	...	£0 7 0
B 02	...	0 4 6	E 13	...	0 7 3
A 03	...	0 4 6	D 14	...	0 7 9
G 04	...	0 4 6	C 15	...	0 8 0
F 05	...	0 4 6	B 16	...	0 8 9
E 06	...	0 4 6	A 17	...	0 9 6
D 07	...	0 4 6	G 18	...	0 10 6
C 1	...	0 4 6	F 19	...	0 12 0
B 2	...	0 4 9	E 20	...	0 13 3
A 3	...	0 5 0	D 21	...	0 15 0
G 4	...	0 5 0	C 22	...	0 17 0
F 5	...	0 5 3	B 23	...	0 19 6
E 6	...	0 5 6	A 24	...	1 2 6
D 7	...	0 5 9	G 25	...	1 5 0
C 8	...	0 6 0	F 26	...	1 8 0
B 9	...	0 6 3	E 27	...	1 11 0
A 10	...	0 6 6	D 28	...	2 2 0
G 11	...	0 6 9	C 29	...	2 10 0

Special Quotations given for all Bells above C 01, and below C 29.

Peal of 6 Bells, for Change Ringing.

Key C 15th Size £2 3 6	Key F 19th Size £2 18 6
,, B 16th ,, 2 7 6	,, E 20th ,, 3 3 0
,, A 17th ,, 2 12 6	,, D 21st ,, 3 10 0
,, G 18th ,, 2 15 6	,, C 22nd ,, 3 15 0

Peal of 8 Bells, for Change Ringing.

Key C 15th Size £2 16 0	Key F 19th Size £3 12 6
,, B 16th ,, 3 0 0	,, E 20th ,, 3 17 6
,, A 17th ,, 3 6 0	,, D 21st ,, 4 6 6
,, G 18th ,, 3 9 6	,, C 22nd ,, 4 12 0

Peal of 12 Bells, for Change Ringing.

Key C 15th Size £3 17 6	Key F 19th Size £4 17 0
,, B 16th ,, 4 2 6	,, E 20th ,, 5 2 6
,, A 17th ,, 4 7 6	,, D 21st ,, 5 14 0
,, G 18th ,, 4 13 0	,, C 22nd ,, 6 3 0

Sets of 15 Bells, arranged to have one Peal of 12, two Peals of 10, and three of 8.

Key C 15th Size £4 16 0	Key F 19th Size £6 0 0
,, B 16th ,, 5 2 0	,, E 20th ,, 6 7 6
,, A 17th ,, 5 7 6	,, D 21st ,, 6 16 0
,, G 18th ,, 5 14 0	,, C 22nd ,, 7 5 0

SETS SPECIALLY ARRANGED FOR PARTIES ABOUT COMMENCING TUNE RINGING.

Set of 17 Bells, arranged with two Accidental Bells.

Key C 15th Size £4 17 0	Key F 19th Size £6 1 0
,, B 16th ,, 5 3 0	,, E 20th ,, 6 8 6
,, A 17th ,, 5 8 6	,, D 21st ,, 6 17 0
,, G 18th ,, 5 15 0	,, C 22nd ,, 7 6 0

Set of 19 Bells, arranged with two Accidental Bells.

Key C 15th Size £5 6 0	Key F 19th Size £6 11 0
,, B 16th ,, 5 12 0	,, E 20th ,, 7 1 0
,, A 17th ,, 5 19 0	,, D 21st ,, 7 9 0
,, G 18th ,, 6 5 0	,, C 22nd ,, 7 19 0

Set of 21 Bells, arranged with four Accidental Bells.

Key C 15th Size £6 3 0	Key F 19th Size £7 12 0
,, B 16th ,, 6 9 0	,, E 20th ,, 8 1 0
,, A 17th ,, 6 17 0	,, D 21st ,, 8 12 0
,, G 18th ,, 7 4 0	,, C 22nd ,, 9 2 0

Set of 26 Bells, three octaves in extent.

Key C 15th Size £7 5 0	Key C 22nd Size £10 0 0
,, G 18th ,, 8 2 6	

Bells on the Chromatic Scale for Tune Playing, 25 Bells, two octaves.

Key C 15th Size £7 12 0	Key F 19th Size £9 10 0
,, B 16th ,, 7 15 0	,, E 20th ,, 9 15 0
,, A 17th ,, 8 8 0	,, D 21st ,, 10 15 0
,, G 18th ,, 8 18 0	,, C 22nd ,, 11 10 0

Three Octaves on Chromatic Scale, containing 37 Bells.

Key C 15th Size £10 0 0	Key F 19th Size £11 0 0
,, B 16th ,, 10 4 0	,, E 20th ,, 12 5 0
,, A 17th ,, 10 15 0	,, D 21st ,, 13 10 0
,, G 18th ,, 11 5 0	,, C 22nd ,, 14 15 0

Four Octaves on Chromatic Scale, containing 49 Bells.

Key C 22nd Size £17 5 0	Key D 28th Size £27 15 0
,, A 24th ,, 18 8 0	,, C 29th ,, 32 0 0
,, G 25th ,, 19 0 0	

Set containing 54 Bells, Chromatic Scale.
Key G 25th Size £20 0 0

Set containing 56 Bells, Chromatic Scale.
Key F 26th Size £22 0 0

ESTIMATES FORWARDED FOR ANY NUMBER OF BELLS NOT ON THIS LIST.
Terms: Cash. Remittances by Cheque, Post Office Order, or Bank Draft.

242 An undated James Shaw price list from between 1887 and 1897

243 John Warner's price list from *The Ringing World*, 1912

About this time the firm published a 32-page booklet containing 42 photographs of the premises and current work. From this and the price lists it can be gathered that his range of bells spanned five chromatic octaves and besides catering for the UK market they were being sent to Africa and Asia. In fact half of Codnor's production was for the overseas market. Mr. Carnall had officially retired by May 1998 although he still carried out occasional work. Codnor handbells do not contain any obvious identifying marks. He used a number of leather stamps depending on the whim of the customer: a simple cross on a circle; a three-legged ornament; a butterfly, etc. One of these is illustrated in Figure 232. He also ink-stamped the name 'CODNOR' on the back of his leather straps.

In sundry places throughout this book I have referred to the crotals cast by the diverse handbell founders. I now need to discuss a range of crotals whose founders are as yet unknown. In some cases their initials are identical to those of known church bell founders, but their dates do not coincide. I intend to list them here for future researchers to identify! Crotals or rumbler bells have been discovered with the initials D S and R E. The latter may be the initials of Richard Eldridge, of Wokingham and Horsham, who was casting church bells in the first quarter of the 17th century. Other initials found on crotals are: H P, W W, S C and W K. Some writers have suggested that the latter may be the work of William Knight, of the very successful Reading Foundry in the 16th century. Another crotal bears the name Joseph Wallis, but when and where it was cast is still not known.

It seems sad to end this book on a negative note. However, as I said in the introduction, the way is now clear for a future historian to build on this work. I hope he or she looks kindly on any errors I may have perpetrated!

Appendix I
IDENTIFYING BELLS, CLAPPERS AND CAPS

For more than three centuries founders have cast small bells which have been used as house bells, horse bells or handbells. Many are easy to identify; for instance, if a bell has MEARS incised in the crown it is reasonable to suppose it was made at the Whitechapel Bell Foundry! What follows may help you to gain experience in identifying these bells.

Names or initials may be incised or cast in relief on the crown, incised or engraved on the waist, or cast in relief inside the bell, either on the lip or on the waist. Care must be taken in interpreting these marks. William Dunn's patterns were still being used half a century after he had died, so bells with W D incised on the crown may be by one of these later founders. Henry Symondson's patterns with H S on the crown were used by his sons Phillip and James as well as by James Platt. The position of the letters may offer a clue as to the age of the bell. In the example given earlier, MEARS incised their name on the pattern at a right angle to the argent in the 19th century; in the 20th century the patterns were re-engraved with the name parallel to the argent.

Many founders cast their bells without any distinguishing marks. Hints must then be gathered from the shape of the bell. Has it a flat or a domed crown; is the lip flared; is there a raised 'button' under the argent or a depression around the crown staple hole? Never forget that a bell may be unmarked simply because the founder forgot to stamp the mould! It may also have lost the marks through later work: for instance, if a COR bell has been tuned on the inside the initials and dabchick would have been removed.

The fittings can point to the founder if you are sure they are contemporary with the bell. The shape, size and fixing of the clapper staple together with the shape, material and size of the springs are often characteristic of the founder. Similarly, the shaft, ball, flight and staple end of the actual clapper can provide a clue. Final evidence may be obtained from the leather work. Some manufacturers stamped their names or initials on the strap or cap; most used individual ornamental stamps for their caps. Some of these were personal to an individual founder whilst others were passed on within the firm from generation to generation.

The following sequence of questions and answers may help you to trace the founder of an unknown bell. Further help can be obtained from individual chapters.

Question 1:
Are there any letters or a name cast in relief **inside** the bell?
Yes: See below.   **No:** Go to Question 2.
Generally, these are 18th- and early 19th-century bells, predominantly from the Aldbourne area. Details of the Cors of Aldbourne may be found in Chapter 3. Information on William Rose of Lambourn, Edward Plumer of Ramsbury, William Gwynn and Edne Witts of Aldbourne is in Chapter 4. Chapter 5 discusses Robert and James Wells of Aldbourne, whilst Chapter 6 deals with Edward Hemins of Bicester, Noah Blomfield of Mendlesham, Robert Romley of London and John Thornton of Sudbury. Thomas Mears II of Whitechapel is in Chapter 7; James Bridgman of Aldbourne is in Chapter 9; Thomas Wootton of Birmingham in Chapter 14 and John Rudhall of Gloucester is in Chapter 16.

Question 2:
Are there any concentric parallel lines engraved **inside** the bell?

Yes: See below.   **No:** Go to Question 3.

The only founder who did this as far as I know was Thomas Mears II of Whitechapel who adopted this style after acquiring the patterns of Robert Wells II in 1825. However, it is possible that some Wells bells have these lines.

Question 3:
Are there any letters or a name cast in relief on the crown of the bell?

Yes: See below.   **No:** Go to Question 4.

James Barwell, dealt with in Chapter 14, used a single letter 'B' in relief on the flat crown of his bells.

Question 4:
Are there any letters or a name engraved on the crown of the bell?

Yes: See below.   **No:** Go to Question 5.

This policy began in the late 18th century and became the general practice by the 19th century. John Kingston (Chapter 6), Thomas Mears I (Chapter 7) and William Dunn (Chapter 10) were amongst the first to do this; later founders engraving their initials on the crown were Henry, Phillip and James Symondson together with James Platt (Chapter 8); Henry Bond (Chapter 9); Mears and Stainbank (Chapter 7); John Taylor (Chapter 11); William Blews (Chapter 14) and James Shaw (Chapter 15). A few minor founders' initials are discussed in Chapter 17.

Question 5:
Has the otherwise uninscribed bell any numbers engraved on the crown?

Yes: See below.   **No:** Go to Question 6.

The Whites of Appleton (Chapter 13); Thomas Miller of Birmingham (Chapter 14); William Pawson of Leeds (Chapter 15); Llewellins and James (Chapter 16).

Question 6:
Has the uninscribed bell been drilled and tapped for a screw-in clapper staple?

Yes: Most of the uninscribed handbells are from the Warner foundry of Cripplegate who produced thousands of sets in the last half of the 19th century. Chapter 12 discusses their work together with that of Gillett and Johnston who also did not identify their bells.

Appendix II
LAPPING

'Lapping' is a method of change ringing on handbells in which the bells physically change positions. In the early part of the 19th century it was practised extensively, mainly in public houses. It is probable that most of the early handbell peals rung were lapped. These days it is either used for fun or to demonstrate to non-ringers the complexities of change ringing.

The ringers sit next to each other in a line, each ringing two bells, going down the scale from right to left. This is known as ringing 'Rounds'. In lapping there are only two operations, called 'crossing' and 'passing'. In the first, each ringer in turn rings his bells right hand, left hand. He* then places both bells in his lap and picks them up in the opposite hands, and rings them right hand, left hand again. This is known as 'crossing'. The other operation is 'passing'. After ringing his bells, each ringer places the bell in his right hand in the lap of the ringer on his right, and the bell in his left hand in the lap of the ringer on his left. At the same time he will receive a bell from the ringers on either side of him. He then picks up these bells and rings them. The ringer at the right hand end passes only the bell in his left hand: the other bell is retained in his right hand. The ringer at the left-hand end operates in a similar manner—only the other way round!

The combination of crossing and passing varies for each method rung, but is generally very simple. The majority of the band need to know nothing of change ringing itself, only to follow the instruction: 'Cross three times and pass' *ad nauseam*. For example, to ring a plain course of Bastow Little Court Bob Maximus you need six ringers. The five ringers sitting second, third, fourth, fifth and sixth carry out the operation 'Cross three times and pass' continually. The ringer with the first two bells follows the pattern, 'Cross, no cross, cross, pass'. In other words, the bells will strike, 1 2; 2 1; 2 1; 1 2. Bell number 2 will then be passed on to the ringer on the left, and a new bell received. I have expressed this diagrammatically on the next page.

* For simplicity in describing these operations I have adopted only the male pronoun: please adjust as required!

Lapping Bastow Little Court Bob Maximus

	Ringer One	Ringer Two	Ringer Three	Ringer Four	Ringer Five	Ringer Six	
Rounds	1 2	3 4	5 6	7 8	9 0	E T	
Cross	2 1	4 3	6 5	8 7	0 9	T E	
Cross	2 1	3 4	5 6	7 8	9 0	E T	'No cross' ringer one
Cross	1 2	4 3	6 5	8 7	0 9	T E	
Pass	1 4	2 6	3 8	5 0	7 T	9 E	
Cross	4 1	6 2	8 3	0 5	T 7	E 9	
Cross	4 1	2 6	3 8	5 0	7 T	9 E	'No cross' ringer one
Cross	1 4	6 2	8 3	0 5	T 7	E 9	
Pass	1 6	4 8	2 0	3 T	5 E	7 9	
Cross	6 1	8 4	0 2	T 3	E 5	9 7	
Cross	6 1	4 8	2 0	3 T	5 E	7 9	'No cross' ringer one
Cross	1 6	8 4	0 2	T 3	E 5	9 7	
Pass	1 8	6 0	4 T	2 E	3 9	5 7	
Cross	8 1	0 6	T 4	E 2	9 3	7 5	
Cross	8 1	6 0	4 T	2 E	3 9	5 7	'No cross' ringer one
Cross	1 8	0 6	T 4	E 2	9 3	7 5	
Pass	1 0	8 T	6 E	4 9	2 7	3 5	
Cross	0 1	T 8	E 6	9 4	7 2	5 3	
Cross	0 1	8 T	6 E	4 9	2 7	3 5	'No cross' ringer one
Cross	1 0	T 8	E 6	9 4	7 2	5 3	
Pass	1 T	0 E	8 9	6 7	4 5	2 3	
Cross	T 1	E 0	9 8	7 6	5 4	3 2	
Cross	T 1	0 E	8 9	6 7	4 5	2 3	'No cross' ringer one
Cross	1 T	E 0	9 8	7 6	5 4	3 2	
Pass	1 E	T 9	0 7	8 5	6 3	4 2	
Cross	E 1	9 T	7 0	5 8	3 6	2 4	
Cross	E 1	T 9	0 7	8 5	6 3	4 2	'No cross' ringer one
Cross	1 E	9 T	7 0	5 8	3 6	2 4	
Pass	1 9	E 7	T 5	0 3	8 2	6 4	
Cross	9 1	7 E	5 T	3 0	2 8	4 6	
Cross	9 1	E 7	T 5	0 3	8 2	6 4	'No cross' ringer one
Cross	1 9	7 E	5 T	3 0	2 8	4 6	
Pass	1 7	9 5	E 3	T 2	0 4	8 6	
Cross	7 1	5 9	3 E	2 T	4 0	6 8	
Cross	7 1	9 5	E 3	T 2	0 4	8 6	'No cross' ringer one
Cross	1 7	5 9	3 E	2 T	4 0	6 8	
Pass	1 5	7 3	9 2	E 4	T 6	0 8	
Cross	5 1	3 7	2 9	4 E	6 T	8 0	
Cross	5 1	7 3	9 2	E 4	T 6	0 8	'No cross' ringer one
Cross	1 5	3 7	2 9	4 E	6 T	8 0	
Pass	1 3	5 2	7 4	9 6	E 8	T 0	
Cross	3 1	2 5	4 7	6 9	8 E	0 T	
Cross	3 1	5 2	7 4	9 6	E 8	T 0	'No cross' ringer one
Cross	1 3	2 5	4 7	6 9	8 E	0 T	
Pass	1 2	3 4	5 6	7 8	9 0	E T	

THE WILL OF WILLIAM CORR 1668

In the name of God Amen I William Corre of Alborne in the County of Wilts GunSmith being sick and weake in body but of sound and pfect minde and memory thanks be given to Allmighty God doe make and ordeyne this my last will and testament in manner and forme following (that is to say) ffirst and principally I comend my Soule into the hands of Allmighty God hopeing and assuredly beleeveing through the previous Death and merritts of my Lord and Saviour Jesus Christ to have full and free pardon and forgivenes of all my Sins and to inherit everlasting life and my body I comitt to the earth to be decently buryed at the discretion of my Executors hereafter named And as touching the disposition of such temporall estate as it hath pleased Allmighty God to bestow upon me I give and dispose thereof as ffolloweth ffirst I will that my debts and funerall expenses shalbee payed—Item I give and bequeath unto my Son Robert Corre three pounds Item I give and bequeath to my Son William Corre three pounds Item I give and bequeath unto my Son John Corre ffouer pounds Item I give and begueath to Margerett Lember of Alborne and her Children three shillings Item I give and bequeath unto Bridgett Lawrance ~~of All~~ also of Alborne and her Children three shillings Item I give unto the Sextone of Aldborne for digging my grave and mending the way two shillings Item I give and bequeath to William Lawrance the elder two shillings Item I give and bequeath to my Kinswoman Elizabeth Corre of the Citty of Glocester ffive shillings Item I give unto William Wedge of Aldborn one shilling—Item I give and bequeath unto my son Johns wife and Children twenty shillings Item I give and bequeath to my son Oliver Corre wife and children twenty shillings—All these Legacyes above mentioned I doe order and Appoynte that it shall bee payed by my Son Oliver Corre out of the Sum of twenty ffoure pounds which is now due to me from him—And I likewise will order and Appoynte that my Sayed Son Oliver Corre shall pay or cause to be payed the Sayed three pounds to my Sayd Son William Corre and the Sayd foure pounds to my sayd John Corre within six months next after my decease All the rest of the afoursayd legasyes I order shall be payed within ~~six mon~~ twelve months by my sayd son Oliver Corre after my decease My will is also that if my son William doe not come to demand his legasy as aforesayed that then I order it to be equally devided amongst his brothers—And for the Remainder of the twenty ffoure pounds which is due to me from my Son Oliver which I have not before bequeathed I give and bequeath to my Sayed Son Oliver Corre—Item I give unto my Son Oliver Corre a paire of new fordge bellowes A cast iron Anvill that is now in my shop And a greate vice that is at my son Robets shop A pistoll belonging to A taf gun And also all the things that are in A coffer standing neare my bed where I now lodge except the melting potts therein and the Coffer—Also I give my Sayd Son the red wascote I have now upon my back after my decease—I give unto my Son Robert Corre also my Birkhorn and one Sledge halfe A flitch of Bacon the grinder stone and spindle by the wood Pile And also what money he owes mee—I give unto my Son John all my wearing Cloathes unbequeathed—All the rest of my goods and Chuttles of what sort soever I give and bequeath to Mary my deare wife and Allen my Son whom I make and appoynte Joynte Executors of this my last will and testament desireing and earnestly entreateing them and the rest of my Children that every thing herein my will may be pformed according to this my will—In Wittnesse whereof that this is my last will and testament of the Sayed William Corre the testator have here unto set my hand and Seale the three and twentieth day of ffebbruary Ano dom one thousand Six hundred sixty and eight

Sealed Signed and declared by the testator William Corre to be hls last will and testament in the presence of

John Adee   Roger Mottenger

The marke of

William Corre

Appendix IV

The Will of John Corr 1714

(Original in the Wiltshire Record Office, Trowbridge)

In the name of God amen   I John Corr of Alborne in the County of Wiltes Bellfounder doe make this my last will & Testament in manner following that is to say Imprimis I give & devise unto my Lovlng wlfe the use of the goods in the best Chamber halfe the Aples that shall grow in my orchard the whole profitt of my bees for & dureing the tearm of her naturall life Item I give to my Daughter Mary the use of Turtons House dureing the tearm of her naturall life except my sonn Will Corr & shee do live to gather in this case I give my Exect the House Immeadiately Item I give unto my Granddaughter Mary Drew five shillings I give unto my Granddaughter Hanna Drew tenn shillings Item I give unto my Daughter Hanna Taylor tenn shillings Item I give unto my Grandsonn John Taylor tenn shillings I give unto my Grandsonns Will and Zacheriah Taylor five shillings each Item I give unto my daughter Joan Woodum fiveteenn pounds to be pd within twelve months after the Decease of my loving wlfe Item I give unto my Grand sonns Will: John and Tho: Woodum five shillings each Item I give to my Granddaughter Grace Bond tenn shillings I give unto her sonn Dyer tenn shillings Item I give to my Granddaughter Mary Corr tenn shillings Item I order all those legaceyes to be pd withthin twelve months after my decease except the fiveteenn pounds wch I order to be pd as above sd Item I do hearby give & bequeath unto my only sonn William Corr all my pesonall Esstate whatsoever subject as aford sd & I do hereby make constitute & appoint him the sd William sole & whole Execr of this my last will & Testament & I do order & appont my Execr to keep & maintaine my Loving wife dureing the tearm of her naturall life In wittness wheareof I the sd John Corr have hereunto Sett my Hand & Seale & doe publish this to be my last will & Testament this nineteenth day of October in the year of Our Lord one Thousand Seaven hundred & fouerteen <u>1714</u>

Signed Sealed & published
by the sd John Corr as his
last will & Testament in
the presence of   the mark of

    Robt Corr   John   Corr
    William Lawrance
    Thomas Smart
                                                        25 May 1715
                                                        Jud Extor od

THE WILL OF WILLIAM CORR 1719

(Original in the Wiltshire Record Office, Trowbridge)

In the Name of God Amen I William Corr of Alborne in the County of wilts Bellfounder being weak in Body but of a Sound and perfect mind and memory praise be therefore given to Almighty God for the Same do make and ordaine this to be my present Last will and testamt in manner following, lmprimis I will that all my Debts and funerall expenses be paid and discharged—Item I give and devise unto my Two Daughters Grace Bond and Mary Corr All my freehold houseing and Lands and all other my freehold Estate of what nature or kind soever in AIdborne aforesed To be equally divided betwixt them Share & Share alike To hold to them my Said Daughters & to their heirs and Assigns for Ever. My will is that my said Daughters do and shall Maintaine and provide for their Grandmother my Dear and Loving Mother Joan Corr all Such provisions and necessaries as are meet for her (in Such a manner as she has been by me maintained) for and dureing the terme of her Natureall Life, And if my Said Daughters or either of them Shall neglect or refuse to maintaine and provide for my sd Dear Mother in Manner aforesd Then my Will is that my sd mother Shall have Ten pounds a year paid her Quarterly for her maintainance dureing the terme of her Natureall life and if my Said Daughters or either of them neglect or refuse the payment of Ten pounds a year in manner aforesd Then it Shall and may be lawfull to and for my Said Dear—mother to charge my Said freehold Estate with the paymt thereof and to enter therein and to dispose thereof untill the sd Ten pounds be paid or such part thereof as shall be to her Due at the time—that she shall be denied the paymt thereof, Item I give—unto my Grandson William Bond ffive pounds Item I give unto my other Grandson Dyer—Bond Twenty Shillings Item I give unto my Two Kinswomen Mary Drew and Hannah Drew ffive Shillings a peice All the rest and residue of my goods Chatles working Tooles ready money debts to mee owing and all other things w'soever to me belonging of what nature and kind Soever not herein before given and bequeathed

I do hereby give devise and bequeath by equall Shares unto my Said Two Daughters Grace Bond & Mary Corr whome I do hereby nominate make and Appoint sole Executrixes of this my present last will and Testamt revokeing disawilling and makeing void all other & former wills by me heretofore made and do declare this to be my present last will and Testamt, In witness whereof I have hereunto Sett my hand and Seal the Third day of August in Sixth year of the reigne of our Sovraigne Lord George by the Grace of God of great Brittaine france & Ireland King defender of the ffaith Anno Dom 1719

Signed Sealed & Published
in the presence of us   Will Corr

    Jos Pizzie
    Mary Austen
    Anna Taylor

Appendix VI
PRICES OF HANDBELLS

It is interesting to note how the cost of handbells has varied over the last 200 years. The earliest price I have recorded is from a 1788 invoice sent by William Mears of Whitechapel to Ashdon, Essex for a ring of six handbells. He charged £1 1s. 6d. for these bells, adding a further 1-2d. for a box to contain them.

John Rudhall of Gloucester wanted £4 10s. 0d. in 1830 to supply a ring of 12 handbells to a Bristol firm of church bell suppliers, Wasbrough Hale & Co. In 1836 William Mears' grandson, Thomas Mears II, charged the Eling, Hampshire, ringers the same price for a similar set, adding an additional charge of 1-6d. for a box. Eighteen years later, his son George increased the price by only 1-0d. for the set.

During the next 18 years prices increased by about twenty per cent. In 1873 William Blews of Birmingham was charging £5 7s. 6d. for 12 handbells, the largest bell being 15C. Taking this set as a yardstick, Warner's price for it three years later was £4 10s. 0d. Prices fell over the next few years: Taylor's wanted £3 7s. 0d. in 1882, William Pawson of Leeds requested £3 9s. 0d. in 1885 and George Welch of Bankside priced the set of 12 at £3 7s. 0d. in his 1886 catalogue. In his 1891 list, John Taylor quoted £3 8s. 0d. for it whilst James Barwell's list for 1892 asked for 3s. less. An undated Shaw price list from between 1887 and 1897 seems to be the odd one out by demanding £3 17s. 6d.

A Mears & Stainbank catalogue of 1919 asked £10 9s. 0d. for this set. They also required 13s. for a 1C, £15 for a 15C and £6 1s. 0d. for a 29C. In 1973 these prices had risen to £9 7s. 0d., £13 12s. 0d. and £44 6s. 0d. respectively. Ten years later, in 1983, they were £51, £73 and £263. Another decade to 1993 and the prices became £111, £155 and £562. In 1998 they were £135, £189 and £677. What might they be in 2003?

The graph in Figure 234, compiled from Whitechapel price lists, shows how the prices of these three handbells, 1C, 15C and 29C, have increased over the last 30 years compared with the purchasing power of the pound. The steep increase in the cost of the 29C is due to Whitechapel introducing a new price structure to reflect the true cost of manufacturing all the larger bells.

Appendix VII
A Chronological List of Handbell Founders

I have tried to include in this list all the founders of small bells that have been discovered. The list therefore contains founders whose names appear in print although their bells have not been identified. Similarly, some bells are marked with initials which cannot be allocated to any known founder. Besides musical handbells the list also includes other types of small bells such as servants' bells, house bells, shop bells, etc., many of which may be found in old sets of handbells. I have also included known and suspected founders of crotals.

Where possible, I have suggested the dates when I consider each founder first began to cast handbells or small bells. In the case of a few founders, this is significantly earlier than hitherto supposed. Most previous writers have dated a founder's production of handbells from the casting of his first known church bell. The casting of a church bell is a far more costly and difficult undertaking than the casting of a handbell and I consider it more than probable that small bells were tackled first. However, some documentary evidence indicates that specific church bell founders cast handbells later in their career and so I have taken this into consideration.

Letters have been used to indicate the type of evidence used for inclusion in this list. The key is:

> D = Documentary evidence only
> H = Musical handbell identified
> S = Shop, house, clock or servant bell known
> C = Crotal, or rumbler bell
> R = Retailer of other founders' bells

The final column indicates the chapter in which I have discussed the work of this founder and where more detailed information may be found.

17th Century

1670	COR, John I	Aldbourne, Wilts	D	3
1675	COR, Oliver I	Aldbourne, Wilts	D	3
1675	SELLER, William	York	C	15
1676	GURNEY, Andrew	Hull, Yorks	C	15
1680	COR, William	Aldbourne, Wilts	HC	3
1683	H W	York	C	15
1685	SELLER, Edward	York	C	15
1685	COR, Oliver II	Aldbourne, Wilts	D	3
1690	COR, Robert I	Aldbourne, Wilts	HC	3

18th Century

1710	ROSE, William	Lambourn, Berks	H	4
1712	COR, Joan	Aldbourne, Wilts	D	3
1715	W C/I L	Aldbourne, Wilts	H	3
1715	SELLER, Richard	York	C	15
1720	COR, Robert II	Aldbourne, Wilts	H	3

1722	COR, Oliver III	Aldbourne, Wilts	H	3
1725	HEMINS, Edward	Bicester, Oxon	H	5
1730	COR, John II	Aldbourne, Wilts	HC	3
1740	COR, Robert III	Aldbourne, Wilts	H	3
1740	LESTER, Thomas	Whitechapel	HS	7
1740	TARLETON, Gerald	Wigan, Lancs	C	15
1743	STARES, John	Aldbourne, Wilts	C	4
1750	PLUMER, E	Ramsbury, Wilts	H	4
1751	READ, Edward	Aldbourne, Wilts	C	4
1755	WELLS, Robert I	Aldbourne, Wilts	HCS	5
1760	WITTS, Edne	Aldbourne, Wilts	HC	4
1760	LATHAM, John	Wigan, Lancs	C	15
1765	BLOOMFIELD, Noah	Mendlesham, Suffolk	HD	6
1770	GWYNN, William	Aldbourne, Wilts	HCS	4
1775	WELLS, Robert II	Aldbourne, Wilts	HCS	5
1780	ROMLEY, Robert	London	S	6
1788	MEARS, William	Whitechapel	D	7
1790	WELLS, James	Aldbourne, Wilts	H	5
1790	MEARS, Thomas I	Whitechapel	HDS	7
1790	JARRETT, John	Worcester	H	6
1790	KINGSTON, John	Bridgwater, Som	HS	6
1796	OSBORN, Thomas	Downham Market, Suffolk	D	6

19th Century

1800	DUNN, William	Bloomsbury, London	HC	10
1800	H F & Co		S	17
1805	CALCOTT, John	Cotton	D	17
1805	MEARS, Thomas II	Whitechapel	HCS	7
1808	RUDHALL, John	Gloucester	HC	16
1812	SMITH, Thomas	Soho, London	D	17
1814	SYMONDSON, Henry	London	H	8
1821	BRIANT, John	Hertford	D	8
1828	BRIDGMAN, James	Aldbourne, Wilts	HCS	9
1830	WASBROUGH HALE & Co	Bristol	R	16
1830	SYMONDSON, Phillip	London	H	8
1831	LLEWELLIN, Peter	Bristol	R	16
1840	CARY, William	Bristol	H	16
1840	SYMONDSON, James	London	H	8
1844	MEARS, Charles & George	Whitechapel	HCS	7
1845	DOWLER, George	Birmingham	D	14
1845	PLATT, James	London	H	7
1848	SHAW, James	Bradford, Yorks	HS	15
1850	AINSWORTH		D	17
1850	SMITH, Thomas H	Wolverhampton	D	14
1850	WARNER, J & Sons	Cripplegate, London	HS	12
1850	D'ALBERT, Charles	London	D	15
1850	BOLTON, Roger	Wigan, Lancs	D	15

1850	EVANS, John	Birmingham	DS	14
1850	FULLWOOD, John	Birmingham	D	14
1850	BARTLEET, Thomas	Birmingham	D	14
1850	HARRIS, Bernard	Birmingham	D	14
1852	STOCKHAM, George	London	H	10
1855	BOND, Henry I	Burford, Oxon	HS	9
1855	SHEPHERD, Samuel	Birmingham	D	14
1855	TAYLOR, John	Loughborough	HS	11
1855	WOOTTON, Thomas	Birmingham	DS	14
1855	BARBER, Edwin	Birmingham	D	14
1855	KELSEY, John	Birmingham	D	14
1855	TONKS, Samuel	Wolverhampton	D	14
1858	TAYLOR, John William	Loughborough	HS	11
1860	MARTINEAU & SMITH	Birmingham	S	14
1860	VALE, William	Lichfield	D	14
1860	WHITE, Frederick	Appleton, Berks	H	13
1860	PAWSON, William	Leeds, Yorks	H	15
1860	BLEWS, William	Birmingham	HS	14
1866	ARTHINGTON, Joseph	Huddersfield, Yorks	D	15
1870	BARWELL, James	Birmingham	HS	14
1875	BOND, Henry II	Burford, Oxon	HS	9
1875	MEARS & STAINBANK	Whitechapel	HCS	7
1880	BASTABLE, Henry	Birmingham	R	17
1880	BLACKBOURN, Thomas	Salisbury, Wilts	DR	13
1883	GILLETT & JOHNSTON	Croydon, Surrey	H	12
1883	WELCH, George	Southwark, London	H	10
1884	BANNISTER, John	Woolwich, London	D	17
1885	WHITE, Stedman	Appleton, Berks	H	13
1888	SEAGE, Epaphrus	Exeter, Devon	R	16
1889	SIMPSON, Thomas	Halifax, Yorks	D	15
1890	WEBB & BENNETT	Kidlington, Oxon	R	17
1890	ANDREWS, C	London	D	17
1890	GREENLEAF, William	Salisbury, Wilts	DR	13
1890	CLEWS, George	Birmingham	H	17
1891	CARR, Charles	Birmingham	D	14
1892	SHAW, William	Bradford, Yorks	H	15
1892	LLEWELLINS & JAMES	Bristol	H	16
1895	BOWELL, Alfred	Ipswich, Suffolk	H	13

20th Century

1900	MOORE, William	Salisbury, Wilts	R	17
1900	BOND, Thomas	Burford, Oxon	HS	9
1900	MALLABY, James F	Barnby Don, Yorks	H	10
1904	HUGHES, Arthur	Whitechapel	HSC	7
1906	TAYLOR, John W, Jnr	Loughborough	HS	11
1906	TAYLOR, Edward Denison	Loughborough	HS	11
1909	WHITE, Richard	Appleton, Berks	H	13

1913	DOBLE, Thomas	Taunton, Somerset	R	16
1916	HUGHES, Albert A	Whitechapel	HSC	7
1919	TAYLOR, Pryce	Loughborough	HS	11
1920	BOWELL, Frederick	Ipswich, Suffolk	H	9
1922	HALEY, William	Walthamstow, Essex	HS	17
1922	AGGETT, William	Chagford, Devon	R	16
1928	MILLER, Thomas	Birmingham	H	14
1935	TAYLOR, Paul Lea	Loughborough	HS	11
1945	HUGHES, William	Whitechapel	HSC	7
1950	HUGHES, Douglas	Whitechapel	HSC	7
1972	HUGHES, Alan	Whitechapel	HSC	7
1974	DOBBIE, Walter	West Peckham, Kent	H	17
1977	TAYLOR, John, & Co.	Loughborough	HS	11
1979	CARNALL, Roy	Codnor, Derbys	H	17
1980	FRANCIS, George	Warnham, Sussex	H	17

Not Yet Dated/Identified

A			H	17
C A			H	17
D S			C	17
G B			S	17
H			S	17
H P			C	6
H H			H	6
I C			S	6
I H			S	17
I G/S K			S	6
I S			H	17
I T			H	17
MILLER, W			S	17
R E			C	17
S C			C	17
T & T			H	17
W★A			H	17
WALLIS, Joseph			C	17
W K			SC	17
W W			C	17

NON-ENGLISH HANDBELL FOUNDERS

The list of 'foreign' musical handbell founders is not large or ancient. With the exception of Aarle-Rixtel from the Netherlands they are all from the United States of America.

As far as I am aware, only two lists have ever been published previously, one in 1957 by Parry and the other in 1988 by Leavett and Sanderson. Mr. Markey of Malmark, Inc. has researched the American founders extensively and has sent me his list which I judge to be the most accurate. The list which follows is his with notes to indicate how the earlier lists differ.

References

1. Scott B. Parry, *The Story of Handbells*, 1957
2. R.W. Leavett and J. Sanderson, *List of Handbell Founders* (*Reverberations*, Vol.21, No.1, Spring, 1988)
3. List by courtesy of Willard Markey, Malmark Inc., May 1997

Name	Dates	Location	References
Mayland, Rowland	1866-1942	Brooklyn, NY	1 2 3
Street, Edward	1880-1920	Hartford, CT	1 2 3 a
Deagan, J.C. & Co.	1890-1920	Chicago, IL	1 2 3 b
Workman, David	1954-1963	Kansas City, MO	1 2 3 c
Petit & Fritson	1955-	Aarle-Rixtel, Holland	1 2 3
Mason, Bernard (Tru-Sonic)	1960-1964	South California	3
Schulmerich Carillons	1962-	Sellersville, PA	2 3 d
Roper, Del (Golden Bells)	1964-1967	California	3
Malmark, Inc	1974-	Doylestown, New Britain & Plumsteadville, PA	2 3
Maas-Rowe Carillons	1986-1996	Escondido, CA	2 3 e

Notes
a. Ref 1 gives dates as 1888-c1920
b. Ref 1 & 2 gives dates as c1880-1915
c. Ref 1 & 2 give no finishing date
d. Ref 2 gives starting date as 1964
e. Ref 2 gives no finishing date (of course!)

In its early years Malmark, Inc. also made handbells with the Verdin label and the Broadman label. It only produces Malmark bells now.

References

1. The Development of the Modern Handbell

1. For a scholarly and detailed account of bells of this type the reader is referred to N. Spear Jr., *A Treasury of Archaeological Bells*, 1978.
2. *Larousse Encyclopedia of Music*, G. Hindley (ed.), English edition, 1977, p.90.
3. A.L.J Gossett, *Shepherds of Britain*, 1911, p.265.
4. Rev. H.T. Ellacombe, *Bells of the Church*, 1872, p.316.
5. Gossett, *op. cit.*, p.268.
6. *Victoria County History of Wiltshire*, Vol.X, p.47.
7. *Ibid.*, Vol.IV, p.253.
8. A. Ingram, *Shepherding Tools and Customs*, 1977, p.6.
9. Gossett, *op. cit.*, 1911, p.270.
10. N. Spear Jr, *op cit*, 1978.
11. Exodus, 28, v33.
12. *Encyclopaedia Britannica*, Vol.14, p.59.
13. *The Countryman*, Summer 1970, reprinted in R. Hawthorne, *Horse Bells*, 1988, p.12.
14. E. Morris, *Tintinnabula*, 1959, p.142.
15. Gossett, *op. cit.*, 1911, p.271.
16. Ellacombe, *op. cit.*, 1872, p.453.
17. Morris, *op. cit.*, 1959, p.141.
18. Zachariah, 14, v20.
19. Ellacombe, *op. cit.*, 1872, p.384.
20. Morris, *op. cit.*, 1959, p.144.
21. Thomas Hardy, *The Woodlanders*, New Wessex edition.

2. The First Handbells

1. Book 3 of Theophilus *De Diversis Artibus* (translated by R. Hendrie, 1847).
2. Dr. J.J. Raven, *The Church Bells of Suffolk*, 1890, p.5.
3. H.B. Walters, *Church Bells of England*, 1912, p.11.
4. *The Bell News*, 4 August 1900, p.157.
5. *The Bell News*, 8 September, 1888, p.302.
6. T.A. Burns (ed.), *Foundryman's Handbook*, 9th edition, 1986, p.74.
7. *The Bradford Observer*, 3 August 1901.
8. A bell that has not been tuned is termed a 'maiden' bell.
9. T.S. Jennings, *Handbells*, 1989, p.14.
10. G. Elphick, *The Craft of the Bellfounder*, 1988, p.79.
11. H.F. Taylor *et al*, *Foundry Engineering*, 1959, p.231.
12. E.J.A. Armarego, *The Machining of Metals*, 1969, p.5.
13. *Encyclopedia Britannica*, Vol.11, p.260.
14. A full explanation of the English numbering system for handbells is given in Chapter 5.
15. E. Blom, *Everyman's Dictionary of Music*, 1975, p.719.
16. *The Ringing World*, 11 September 1970, p.714.
17. Blom, *op cit*, 1975, p.516.
18. *The Ringing World*, 10 December 1948, p.533.
19. Elphick, *op. cit.*, 1988, p.35.
20. See Chapter 13.

3. The Cor Foundry

1. William Cor's will (1668) is printed in Appendix III.

2. John Cor's will is printed in Appendix IV.
3. 12 Geo II cap 26. The author has a copy of this.
4. Rev. W.C. Lukis, *An Account of Church Bells*, 1857, p.118.
5. A photocopy of this is in the author's possession.
6. *Ibid*.
7. *Wiltshire Notes and Queries*, Vol.2, p.449.
8. Treble bell at St Nicholas, Berwick Bassett, Wiltshire.
9. Fourth bell at St Mary, Devizes, Wiltshire.
10. Rev. W.E. Colchester, *Hampshire Church Bells*, 1920, p.79.
11. A.G. Keen, *The Aldbourne Bell Foundry*, Swindon Branch Newsletter, Vol.5, No.3, 1982.
12. William Cor's will (1719) is printed in Appendix V.
13. M.A. Crane, *The Aldbourne Chronicle*, 1974, p.35.
14. In 1727 a pound would buy four pounds of beef, four pounds of butter, 12 loaves and 114 gallons of beer!
15. Written on the unused bottom half of a page about 1686 in the churchwardens' accounts of St Mary Bourne is:
    'Michael Hodges and
    Robert Longman was
    Churchwardens when
    the Bells was cast at
    St Mary Bourne in the
    year 1699: and they was
    Cast by Mr Robert Corr
    of Alborne'
    Michael Hodges and Robert Longman were churchwardens on a number of other occasions, including the previous year.
16. W. Moir, 'The Aldbourne Foundry and Cast Rumbler Bells', *Antique Metalware Society Journal*, Vol.4, June 1996. His source of information was 'Schedule of the Property and Movables of the Corr Family, 1735' in the Wiltshire Records Office, 23/82.
17. Keen, *op. cit*.
18. *Wiltshire Notes and Queries*, Vol.2, p.452; Vol.4, p.410.
19. *Wilts Arch Mag*, Vol.42, p.580.
20. F. Sharpe, *Church Bells of Berkshire*, 1971, p.63.
21. Colchester, *op. cit.*, p.78.
22. H.B. Walters, *Church Bells of Wiltshire*, 1969, p.310.
23. *Wiltshire Notes and Queries*, Vol.2, p.450.
24. Crane, *op. cit.*, 1974, p.35.
25. *The Bell News*, 1900, p.280; *The Ringing World*, 1942, p.9; *The Ringing World*, 1948, pp.300, 320.
26. Ida Gandy, *The Heart of a Village*, 1991, p.16.
27. *Antique Collecting*, Vol.15, No.5, October 1980.
28. Allan Keen, one of the ringers at Aldbourne, is a local historian and has done a great deal of research on the Aldbourne Foundry. I should like to thank him for all the assistance he has given me in the preparation of this chapter.
29. *The Ringing World*, 1948, p.300.
30. *The Bell News*, 1900, p.280.
31. *The Ringing World*, 1948, p.300.
32. *The Ringing World*, 1990, p.670.

4. Successors to the Cors

1. Sketchley & Adams, *The Tradesman's True Guide*, 1770; The Birmingham Directories for 1770, 1786 and 1797.
2. Information from the late Mr. H. Marcon, Devon.
3. Lambourn parish registers.
4. See Appendix III.
5. A.G. Keen, *The Aldbourne Bell Foundry*, Swindon Branch Newsletter, Vol.6, No.2, 1983.
6. *The Searcher*, June 1989, p.52.
7. Keen, *op. cit*.
8. *Ibid*.
9. Information from Mr. R. Newbury, Devon.
10. M.A. Crane, *The Aldbourne Chronicle*, 1974, p.32.

11. *The Searcher*, June 1989, p.52.
12. Keen, *op. cit.*
13. F. Sharpe, *The Church Bells of Oxfordshire*, 1953, p.111.
14. *The Bell News*, 3 Sept 1910, p.362.

5. The Wells

1. H.B. Walters, 'Church Bells of Wiltshire', *Wilts. Arch. Mag.*, No. CLI, December 1929, p.313.
2. Allan G. Keen, *The Aldbourne Bell Foundry*, Swindon Branch Newsletter, Vol.6, No.3, 1983.
3. *Ibid.*
4. *Ibid.*
5. Walters, *op. cit.*, p.314.
6. Rev. H.T. Ellacombe, *Church Bells of Somerset*, 1874, p.137.
7. F. Sharpe, *Church Bells of Berkshire*, Kingsmead Reprint, 1970, p.100.
8. *Ibid.*
9. Walters, *op. cit.*, p.314.
10. *Victoria County History of Wiltshire*, Vol. IV, p.253.
11. M.A. Crane, *The Aldbourne Chronicle*, 1974 p.35.
12. *Pigot & Co.'s National Commercial Directory*, 1830.
13. Rev. W.C. Lukis, *An Account of Church Bells*, 1857, p.10.
14. Ex inform Mr. C. Wratten, Charlton Kings.
15. *Ibid.*
16. Ida Gandy, *The Heart of a Village*, 1991, p.73.
17. Keen, *op. cit.*
18. Gandy, *op. cit.*, p.74.
19. The inscription given by Sharpe in *The Church Bells of Berkshire* is: ROBT WELLS. &. SON. ALDBOURN FECIT : . MDCCLXXXI.
20. H.B. Walters, *Church Bells of Wiltshire*, Kingsmead Reprint, 1969, p.197.
21. THE GIFT OF ROBERT WELLS BELL FOUNDER 1787.
22. Gandy, *op. cit.*, p.37.
23. Crane, *op. cit.*
24. Crane, *ibid.*, p.36.
25. F.E. Dukes, *Campanology in Ireland*, 1994, p.247.
26. *Victoria County History of Wiltshire*, Vol. IV, p.253.
27. J.R. Ellis, 'The Parliamentary Enclosures of Aldbourne', *Wiltshire Arch. Mag.* Vol.68, p.99.
28. *Victoria County History of Wiltshire*, Vol. IV, p.253.
29. Rev. W.E. Colchester, *Hampshire Church Bells*, 1920, p.77.
30. Lieut-Col. W.L. Julyan, 'Robert Wells of Aldbourne', *The Field*, 1 August 1942, p.131.
31. Keen, *op. cit.* Vol. 8, No. 4, 1985.
32. *Pigot & Co.'s National Commercial Directory*, 1830.
33. Becky Mayer, *A Potpourri of Serendipity*, June 1980.
34. Information from Mr. E. First, New York.
35. P.C.D. Brears, *Horse Brasses*, 1981, p.116.

6. Other 18th-Century Founders

1. *The Bicester Advertiser & Mid Oxon Chronicle*, 11 May 1951.
2. His last bell is often quoted as the second at Culworth, the date of which Thomas North gives in *The Church Bells of Northamptonshire* as 1747. His information was incorrect, however; the date on the bell is actually 1741.
3. A.H. Cocks, *The Church Bells of Buckinghamshire*, 1897, p.257.
4. The site of the foundry is reputed to have been in Bell Street.
5. Quoted in C.F.C. Beeson, *Clockmaking in Oxfordshire 1400-1850*, 1962, p.112.
6. Wiltshire Record Society, xvii p.4; Wiltshire Record Office, deed 130/58B.
7. H.B. Walters, *The Church Bells of Wiltshire*, Kingsmead reprint, 1969, p.315.
8. A. Ingram, *Shepherding Tools and Customs*, 1977, p.6.
9. *The Searcher*, June 1989, p.52.
10. Wilts Cuttings v 151 (Wilts. Arch. Soc. Library, Devizes).
11. D.W. Struckett, *A Dictionary of Campanology*, 1985, p.86.

12. The Sharpe Collection was gathered together by the eminent campanologist, Frederick Sharpe, and forms part of the Sharpe Trust. It is housed in the Pitt Rivers Museum, South Parks Road, Oxford, OX1 3PP; F. Sharpe, *The Church Bells of Guernsey, Alderney and Sark*, 1964, p.18.

13. *Ipswich Journal*, 29 November 1766. I am indebted to Mr. Mark Ockelton of The University of Leeds for drawing this and the other references in the *Ipswich Journal* to my attention.

14. *Ipswich Journal*, 19 December 1778.

15. Information from the late Mr. F. Barnett, Worcester.

16. *Reverberations*, April 1976, p.10.

17. *The Searcher*, June 1989, p.52.

18. Dr. J.J. Raven, *The Church Bells of Suffolk*, 1890 p.141.

19. Deedes & Walters, *The Church Bells of Essex*, 1909, p.123.

20. J. L'Estrange, *The Church Bells of Norfolk*, 1874, p.48.

21. Quoted in *The Ringing World*, 26 January 1996, p.87.

22. *Ipswich Journal*, 10 June 1780.

23. *Ipswich Journal*, 30 December 1797.

24. *The Ringing World*, 30 July 1976, p.649.

25. *Ibid*.

26. See Chapter 8 for more details of this contest.

27. *The Ringing World*, 31 January 1986, p.94.

28. *The Church Bells of Norfolk*, 1874, p.49.

7. Handbells from Whitechapel

1. G. Elphick, *Sussex Bells and Belfries*, 1970, p.117.

2. An extract from his will is given in Dr. A.D. Tyssen, *The Church Bells of Sussex*, 1864, p.39.

3. *Ibid*., p.40.

4. For those interested in church bell founding in London during the period 1770-1800 see the article by C. Pickford in *The Ringing World*, 11 December 1992, p.1199.

5. Information from Mr. C. Pickford. The bill is in the Essex Record Office ref: D/P 18/6/2.

6. Elphick, *op. cit.*, p.143.

7. H.C. Andrews, *John Briant, Bellfounder and Clockmaker*, 1930, p.12.

8. See Chapter 9.

9. *The Ringing World*, 24 August 1979, p.714.

10. A.H. Cocks, *The Church Bells of Buckinghamshire*, 1897, p.117; T. North, *Church Bells of Bedfordshire*, 1883, p.83.

11. F. Sharpe, *The Church Bells of Herefordshire*, 1976, p.753.

12. 'A History of Bells and Description of their Manufacture as Practised at the Bell Foundry, Whitechapel' (anon n.d. *c*.1875) p.14.

13. *The Ringing World*, 11 August 1916, p.59.

14. 'Church Bells', Mears & Stainbank Catalogue, 1885.

15. *Strike Note*, Issue 2 Spring 1986, p.4.

16. 'Church Bells', Mears & Stainbank Catalogue, 1911, p.5.

17. *The Ringing World*, 11 August 1916, p.59.

18. Elphick, *op. cit.*, p.152.

19. 'English Handbell Casting at the Whitechapel Bell Foundry' (A.A. Hughes n.d., *c*.1962).

20. *The Ringing World*, 21 August 1964, p.558.

21. *The Ringing World*, 26 November 1993, p.1159.

8. The Symondsons

1. *The Ringing World*, 3 August 1928, p.489; H.C. Andrews, *John Briant, Bellfounder and Clockmaker*, 1930, p.1.

2. Andrews, *op. cit.*, p.2.

3. *Hertfordshire Mercury*, 7 March 1829 (quoted in Andrews).

4. *The Ringing World*, 19 September 1930, p.606.

5. T. North, *The Church Bells of Northamptonshire*, 1878, p.103.

6. *The Ringing World*, 24 May 1985, p.454.

7. *The Ringing World*, 23 January 1953, p.49.

8. Andrews, *op. cit.*, p.3.

9. *The Ringing World*, 31 December 1937, p.866.

10. H.C. Stacey, *The Saffron Walden Society of Change Ringers*, 1976, p.15.
11. Andrews, *op. cit.*, p.48.
12. Dr. A.D. Tyssen, *The Church Bells of Sussex*, 1864, p.42.
13. Andrews, *op. cit.*, p.13.
14. *The Bell News*, 13 October 1900, p.281.
15. *The Bell News*, 1 September 1900, p.209.
16. Information from Mrs. V.M. Payne, Northolt, Middlesex. Mrs. Payne is descended from Henry Symondson's daughter Hannah, and has gathered considerable evidence on the family from parish registers and other sources.
17. Census returns 1841.
18. T.S. Jennings, *Handbells*, 1989, p.25.
19. See Chapter 12.
20. Andrews, *op. cit.*, p.21.
21. S.B. Parry, *The Story of Handbells*, 1957, p.17.
22. Andrews, *op. cit.*, p.22.
23. Owned by Dr. A. Collings, Bisley.
24. Information from Mrs. V.M. Payne.
25. Information from Mr. J. Partington, Rochdale.
26. *The Bell News*, 13 July 1895, p.76.
27. Information from Mr. C. Wratten, Cheltenham.
28. *The Bell News*, 1 September 1900, p.208.
29. *The Ringing World*, 16 April 1943, p.168.
30. *The Bell News*, 13 June 1885, p.81.
31. W. Shipway, *Campanalogia, or, The Art of Ringing*, Part 3, 1816, p.160.
32. Rev. C.D.P Davies, *Stedman*, 1903, p.142.
33. Barthold and Buckton, *The Story of the Piano*, 1975, p.40.
34. *The Ringing World*, 29 December 1933, p.827.
35. 'Transactions of the Thoroton Society', vol.35, 1931, pp.52-3.
36. *The Bell News*, 11 August 1900, p.173.
37. *The Ringing World*, 14 April 1967, p.250. This bell is also mentioned in the *Bedfordshire Magazine*, Vol.13, No.97, Summer 1971, p.9.
38. *The Bell News*, 29 September 1900, p.253.
39. *Hertford and Bedford Reformer*, 12 May 1838 (Information from Mr. C. Wratten).
40. North & Stahlschmidt, *The Church Bells of Hertfordshire*, 1886, p.209.
41. Parry, *op. cit.*, p.18.
42. Post Office Directory, 1846.
43. *The Bell News*, 29 September 1900, p.253.
44. Information from Mr. N. Bullen, Bedford.
45. *The Ringing World*, 14 April 1967, p.250.
46. Census returns 1851.
47. One can be found in the Launton, Oxon, set of handbells.
48. St James Society peal book.
49. *Bell's Life in London*, Sunday 27 October 1850 (information from Mr. C. Wratten).
50. *Bell's Life in London*, Sunday 5 June 1853; Sunday 27 March 1853; Sunday 25 December 1853 (information from Mr. C. Wratten).
51. Information from Mr. M. Goodman, Honingham, Norwich.
52. Some time after writing this chapter I walked past 1 Tottenham Court Road, near St Giles' Circus, and found that the birthplace of some of the best 19th-century handbells is now a Burger King Restaurant!

9. An Aldbourne Diversion

1. 1851 Census returns.
2. *The Bell News*, 30 March 1889, p.650.
3. 'The Whitechapel Bellfoundry', Quatercentennial booklet, 1970.
4. *Victoria County History of Wilts*, vol.IV, p.81.
5. *The Ringing World*, 28 July 1972, p.606.
6. Peal boards, St Michael, Aldbourne.
7. A.G. Keen, *St Michael, Aldbourne, Wiltshire, a Short History of its Tower and Bells* (n.d., c.1977), p.5.

8. H.B. Walters, *Church Bells of Wiltshire*, Kingsmead reprint, 1969, p.187.
9. *The Ringing World*, 30 June 1972, p.518.
10. *The Bell News*, 29 September 1900, p.253.
11. M.A. Crane, *The Aldbourne Chronicle*, 1974, p.36.
12. 1851 Census returns.
13. This and other references to the Bond family details, were extracted from the parish records by Mr. C. Pickford, to whom I extend my thanks.
14. M. Bliss and F. Sharpe, *Church Bells of Gloucestershire*, 1986, p.25.
15. Information from Mr. C. Pickford, Kent.
16. F. Sharpe, *Church Bells of Oxfordshire*, 1953, p.66.
17. List of members, Oxford Diocesan Guild Report, 1885.
18. *The Ringing World*, 24 December 1971, p.1096.
19. F. Sharpe, *Church Bells of Herefordshire*, 1976, p.744.
20. G. Elphick, *Sussex Bells and Belfries*, 1970, p.183.
21. *The Ringing World*, 28 July 1972, p.606.
22. F. Sharpe, *Church Bells of Oxfordshire*, 1953, pp.469, 471, 473, 477, 481 and 483.

10. William Dunn and his Successors

1. Information from Mrs. V.M. Payne, Northolt.
2. Information from the late Mr. W.T. Cook, Sidcup.
3. *The Bell News*, 29 September 1900, p.253.
4. 'London Commercial Directory', 1830.
5. Parish of St Pancras—Register of Apprentices—Film No.X30/31. Information from Mrs. V.M. Payne, Northolt.
6. College Youths Peal Book.
7. St James' Society Peal Book.
8. Information from the late Mr. K. Croft, Southampton.
9. *Reverberations*, Spring 1993, p.48.
10. Trevor S. Jennings states on page 26 of *Handbells* (Shire Publications, 1989) that Stockham used Symondson's patterns. This is incorrect: he used Dunn's patterns.
11. *The Bell News*, 29 September 1900, p.253.
12. Information from Mr. H.W. Rogers, Isleworth.
13. W. Butler, unpublished MSS on the 'Ringers of New Windsor'.
14. J.W. Snowdon, *Grandsire*, 1888, p.143.
15. J.A. Trollope, *The College Youths*, 1937, p.83.
16. Butler, *op. cit.*
17. His peal book is in the College Youth library. A series of extracts was published in 'The Ringing World', 6 November 1970, p.883 *et seq.*
18. 'Lapping' is a method of ringing handbells in which the bells physically change positions. For a detailed explanation see Appendix I.
19. E Morris, *History and Art of Change Ringing*, 1931, p.115.
20. Information from the late Mr. W.T. Cook, Sidcup.
21. E.A. Young, *James Robert Haworth*, 1952, p.9.
22. *The Bell News*, 24 March 1888, p.11.
23. *Ibid.*, 29 September 1900, p.253.
24. *Ibid.*, 27 January 1883, p.342.
25. *Ibid.*, 6 December 1884, p.426.
26. *The Ringing World*, 23 March 1990, p.293.
27. Advertisement in J.W. Snowdon, *Double Norwich Court Bob Major*, 1884.
28. *The Bell News*, 5 September 1885, p.179; *The Ringing World*, 23 March 1990, p.293.
29. Yorkshire Association Reports 1888-92. I am indebted to Mr. J.M. Thorley for extracting this information.
30. D. Greenwood, *James Shaw, Son & Co*, 1996, p.15.
31. Yorkshire Association Report, 1893.
32. Information from Mr. F.A. Munday, Pudsey.
33. T.S. Jennings, *Handbells*, 1989, p.26.
34. Information from Mr. D.I. Johnson, Masham.
35. *The Ringing World*, 14 July 1950, p.446.

11. Taylors of Loughborough

1. T.S. Jennings, *Master of My Art*, 1987.
2. 'Bell Catalogue', John Taylor & Co., 1882.
3. T. North, *Church Bells of Leicestershire*, 1876, p.94.
4. Jennings, *op. cit.*, p.86.
5. *Ibid.*, p.38.
6. *Ibid.*, p.41.
7. *Ibid.*, p.47.
8. *Ibid.*, p.61.
9. *Ibid.*, p.110.
10. *Ibid.*, pp.53, 76.
11. T.S. Jennings, *Handbells*, 1989, p.14.
12. T.S. Jennings, *Master of My Art*, p.76.
13. See Chapter 14.
14. See Chapter 16.
15. Jennings, *op. cit.*, p.71.
16. See Chapter 13.
17. T.S. Jennings, *Handbells*, 1989, p.21.
18. T.S. Jennings, *Master of My Art*, p.86.
19. Information from the late Mr. H. Marcom.

12. Cripplegate and Croydon

1. F Sharpe, *Church Bells of Herefordshire*, 1976, p.733.
2. Deedes and Walters, *Church Bells of Essex*, 1909, p.141.
3. G.F. Elphick, *Sussex Bells and Belfries*, 1970, p.163.
4. *The Ringing World*, 28 February 1964, p.140.
5. P. Ferriday, *Lord Grimthorpe*, 1957, p.45.
6. *The Bell News*, 13 February 1909, p.591.
7. *The Bell News*, 16 January 1909, p.545.
8. E. Morris, *History and Art of Change Ringing*, 1931, p.312; on page 728 of *The Ringing World* for 8 September 1972 is an interesting snippet of information referring to the time Henry was Master of the Cumberland Youths. A note by him is appended in the membership book, dated 23 March 1852: 'John William Kitson (late of Birmingham) Ejected by vote for stealing the Societie's [*sic*] Hand Bells'.
9. *The Ringing World*, 31 October 1997, p.1095.
10. *The Bell News*, 29 November 1884, p.412.
11. *The Ringing World*, 18 May 1973, p.390.
12. *The Ringing World*, 1 June 1973, p.434.
13. Elphick, *op. cit.*, p.167.
14. *The Ringing World*, 19 December 1913, p.407.
15. *Ibid.*, 2 September 1949, p.414.
16. *Ibid.*, 21 January 1944, p.28.
17. *Ibid.*, 10 November 1916, p.190.
18. F. Sharpe, *The Church Bells of Berkshire*, 1970, p.232.
19. Elphick, *op. cit.*, p.170.
20. *The Ringing World*, 17 December 1948, p.553.
21. *Ibid.*, 7 April 1950, p.217.
22. *Ibid.*, 7 June 1957, p.368.
23. *Ibid.*, 5 July 1957, p.436.
24. Elphick, *op. cit.*, p.175.

13. Sporadic Handbell Founders of the 19th Century

1. *The Ringing World*, 24 March 1933, p.185.
2. Oxfordshire Women's Institutes, *Oxfordshire within Living Memory*, 1994, p.162.
3. Quoted in F. Sharpe, *The Church Bells of Berkshire*, 1970, p.17.
4. Peal board, Appleton.
5. *The Ringing World*, 24 March 1933, p.188.

6. *Oxfordshire within Living Memory*, p.162.
7. Information from Mr. B.R. White, Appleton.
8. *The Ringing World*, 28 April 1922, p.258.
9. *The Ringing World*, 6 September 1946, p.414.
10. M. Bliss and F. Sharpe, *The Church Bells of Gloucestershire*, 1986, p.96.
11. *The Ringing World*, 8 March 1968, p.189.
12. *Ibid.*, 3 January 1986, p.2.
13. *Ibid.*, 6 November 1987, p.972.
14. *Ibid.*, 3 April 1964, p.222.
15. Deedes and Walters, *The Church Bells of Essex*, 1909, p.341.
16. *The Ringing World*, 20 September 1940, p.453.
17. G. Elphick, *Sussex Bells and Belfries*, 1970, p.183.
18. *The Ringing World*, 14 July 1989, p.644.
19. T.A. Bevis, *The Ipswich Bellfounders* (n.d. *c.*1965), p.4.
20. *The Ringing World*, 13 July 1962, p.460.
21. *Ibid.*, 7 September 1962, p.590.
22. *Ibid.*, 17 August 1962, p.541.
23. Elphick, *op. cit.*, p.179.
24. In the possession of Mr. N. Skelton, Salisbury.
25. *The Ringing World*, 9 April 1976, p.320.
26. Rev. F.E. Robinson, *Among the Bells* (n.d. *c.*1910), p.177.
27. *The Bell News*, 8 March 1890, p.578.
28. *The Bell News*, 1 August 1903, p.218.
29. *The Ringing World*, 16 November 1984, p.975.
30. *The Ringing World*, 12 November 1920, p.555.
31. H.B. Walters, *The Church Bells of Wiltshire*, Kingsmead reprint, 1969, p.240.
32. *The Bell News*, 12 December 1903, p.449.
33. Auction catalogue in the possession of Mr. N. Skelton, Salisbury.
34. On 24 March 1892, at 49 Clifton Street, Brighton, a peal of Grandsire Triples was rung on handbells by Mrs. George Williams 1-2, Thomas Blackbourn 3-4, George Williams 5-6, Alfred P. Goddard 7-8. The peal, which was conducted by George Williams, was umpired by E.C. Merritt. This was the first handbell peal in Sussex, and the first peal in which a woman had taken part. It aroused great interest in the Exercise. *The Bell News*, 2 April 1892, p.7.
35. *The Ringing World*, 17 February 1933, p.106.

14. Founding in Birmingham

1. A.L.J. Gossett, *Shepherds of Britain*, 1911, p.271.
2. Gentle and Field, *English Domestic Brasses*, p.51.
3. Birmingham Trade Directory, 1860; a 'cock' is another name for a tap.
4. Commercial Directory, 1830, quoted by C.J. Pickford in *The Ringing World*, 9 October 1981, p.900.
5. *Ibid*.
6. Post Office Directory, 1854.
7. Post Office Directory, 1860.
8. Post Office Directory, 1854.
9. H.B. Walters, *Arts of the Church: Church Bells*, 1908, p.50.
10. *The Bell News*, 19 February 1887, p.383.
11. A.H. Cocks, *Church Bells of Buckinghamshire*, 1897, p.263.
12. *Ibid*.
13. *The Bell News*, 19 February 1887, p.383.
14. *The Ringing World*, 21 March 1997, p.285.
15. *The Bell News*, 11 July 1891, p.182.
16. *The Ringing World*, 11 January 1980, p.26.
17. *The Ringing World*, 16 November 1979, p.974.
18. A maiden ring is a set of bells that did not require tuning.
19. *The Ringing World*, 19 December 1958, p.827.
20. *Campanology*, No.1, 16 September 1896.

21. *The Bell News*, 2 April 1898, p.589.
22. Tilley and Walters, *Church Bells of Warwickshire*, 1910, p85.
23. *The Ringing World*, 23 October 1981, p.942.
24. F. Sharpe, *Church Bells of Herefordshire*, 1976, p.631.
25. Set owned by Mr. G. Lane of Kingsbury, Warwickshire.
26. *The Ringing World*, 24 February 1950, p.125.
27. *Ibid.*, 3 March 1978, p.182.
28. *Ibid.*, 23 October 1981, p.942.
29. One of a set of Miller bells owned by the late Mr. R. Arnott, Thame.

15. Founding in the North

1. D. Greenwood, *James Shaw, Son & Co*, 1996, p.2.
2. *The Bell News*, 21 March 1885, p.607. This is an account of the firm, later published as a broadsheet. It suggests James combined a long practical experience as an engineer with a genuine enthusiasm for campanology.
3. Greenwood, *op. cit.*, p.2.
4. Post Office Guide, 1875.
5. *The Bell News*, 23 December 1882, p.304.
6. *The Bell News* gives this as the name of the town; I think they either misread or misprinted it and it should be Frostburg, Pa.
7. Quoted in *The Bell News*, 10 November 1883, p.377.
8. *The Bell News*, 30 December 1882, p.310.
9. *The Bell News*, 21 February 1885, p.560.
10. *Reverberations*, Vol.10, No.2, p.89.
11. *The Bell News*, 21 March 1885, p.607.
12. An account of William Pawson's handbell business is given later in this chapter; *The Bell News*, 1 March 1890, p.572.
13. 'Also Makers of the large Peals for Batley, Barnsley, Bowdon, Bradford, Bolton, Crigglestone, Chorley, Denton, Darlington, Doncaster, Exeter, Frossiburg (sic), USA; Halifax, Headingley, Horbury, Honley, Keighley, Liversedge, Middleton, Mirfield, Middleham, Norwich, Newport, Oldham, Penzance, Penistone, Philadelphia, America; Pudsey, Rawmarsh, Sowerby Bridge, Stafford, Shipley, Shields, Southport, Scarboro', Wheatley Mills, &c, &c.'
14. *The Bell News*, 22 October 1892, p.363.
15. Greenwood, *op. cit.*, p.15.
16. *The Bradford Observer*, 3 August 1901.
17. Greenwood, *op. cit.*, p.19.
18. See Chapter 11.
19. *The Bell News*, 16 March 1912.
20. Information from Leeds Central Library.
21. A one-inch display advertisement appeared regularly in *The Bell News* commencing with Vol.III, 7 April 1883.
22. Information from Miss B.J. Harris, St Peter, Benington; Information from Mr. R.J. Cooles, St Mary's, Battersea.
23. *The Bell News*, 15 February 1890, p.538.
24. *Ibid.*, 1 March 1890, p.572.
25. *Ibid.*, 6 September 1913, p.313.
26. P. Scholes, *The Oxford Companion to Music*, 1947, p.246.
27. *Lancashire Evening Post*, 22 June 1962.
28. P.C.D Brears, *Horse Brasses*, 1981, pp.116-17.
29. G. Benson, *York Bellfounders*, 1898, p.15.
30. T. North, *The Church Bells of Lincolnshire*, 1882, p.137.
31. Brears, *op. cit.*, p.112.
32. Quoted in Brears, *op. cit.*, p.114.
33. Slater's Directory, 1861, White's Directory, 1866.
34. Slater's Directory 1861, West Riding Trade Directory 1889, 1893, 1897.
35. H.B. Walters, *Church Bells of England*, 1912, p.255.

16. Founding in the West

1. M. Bliss and F. Sharpe, *The Church Bells of Gloucestershire*, 1986, p.57.
2. Quoted in Bliss and Sharpe, *op. cit.*, p.59.
3. *The Ringing World*, 13 January 1989, p.33.

4. F. Sharpe, *The Church Bells of Herefordshire*, 1975, p.705.
5. *The Ringing World* 13 January 1989, p.33.
6. City of Bristol Record Office, MSS 20535 (335). Quoted by Chris Pickford in his article on the Rudhall Handbells, see reference 5. I am indebted to him for his help and permission to publish these extracts.
7. Quoted in F. Sharpe, *The Church Bells of Oxfordshire*, 1953, p.91. 'On Monday next will be opened in the newly-erected tower of Chipping Norton Church, Oxon, a peal of eight bells, cast [*sic*] Mr Rudhall, of this city; on which occasion the Churchwardens will give prizes of 5*l*. 3*l*. and 2*l*. for the best three peals of changes that shall be rung.'
8. W Moir, 'The Aldbourne Foundry and Cast Rumbler Bells', *Antique Metalware Society Journal*, Vol.4, June 1996.
9. Bliss and Sharpe, *op. cit.*, p.42.
10. *The Bell News*, 13 September 1884, p.291.
11. Information from J. Slater.
12. Quoted in Bliss and Sharpe, *op. cit.*, p.43.
13. *The Ringing World*, 1 May 1987, p.396.
14. *The Bell News*, 24 December 1892, p.467.
15. *The Ringing World*, 3 April 1987, p.305.
16. *The Bell News*, 23 March 1912, p.23.
17. *The Ringing World*, 13 December 1974, p.1018.
18. H.B. Walters, *The Church Bells of Wiltshire*, Kingsmead Reprint, 1969, p.143.
19. D.W. Struckett, *Dictionary of Campanology*, 1985, p.82; Rev. H.T. Ellacombe, *The Church Bells of Somerset*, 1874, p.109.
20. 'Pigot & Cox's National Commercial Directory 1830', Facsimile edition 1994, p.16.
21. *The Ringing World*, 1 May 1987, p.396.
22. Ellacombe, *op. cit.*, p.86.
23. A. Wright, *The Church Bells of Monmouthshire*, 1942, p.46.
24. *The Ringing World*, 1 May 1987, p.396.
25. A.C. Cannon, *The Church Bells of Cornwall*, 1979, pp.13, 18, 29.
26. *The Bell News*, 13 February 1915, p.495.
27. T.S. Jennings, *Master of my Art*, 1987, p.69.

17. A Final Miscellany

1. E Morris, *History and Art of Change Ringing*, 1931, p.107.
2. Morris, *ibid.*, p.465. This account gives the names of both the third and fifth ringers as George. This is a misprint. The ringer of the third was, according to his age, John.
3. *The Bell News*, 8 September 1894, p.181.
4. *Church Bells*, 4 September 1880, p.643.
5. *The Ringing World*, 16 February 1917, p.53.
6. *The Bell News*, 29 June 1889, p.141.
7. *Church Bells*, 27 November 1880, pp.826, 866.
8. *The Bell News*, 28 January 1899, p.401.
9. Chapter 11 gives more details on Henry W. Haley.
10. *The Ringing World*, 4 February 1927, p.72.
11. *Ibid.*, 16 March 1951, p.170.
12. *Ibid.*, 4 February 1927, p.72.
13. His books are listed in Chapter 11.
14. *The Ringing World*, 8 December 1922, p.783.
15. *Ibid.*, 7 March 1924, p.158.
16. *The Bell News*, 13 October 1900, p.280.
17. *Reverberations*, Vol.21, No.1, Spring 1988, p.20.
18. *The Ringing World*, 6 July 1979, p.566.
19. Quoted in *The Ringing World*, 20 January 1984, p.45.

BIBLIOGRAPHY OF BOOKS ON HANDBELLS

This list of books and booklets on handbell ringing differs from those previously published, e.g. Nancy Poore Tufts' bibliography in *The Art of Handbell Ringing*, in that it deals exclusively with tune ringing. Music for handbells published in the 20th century and books and pamphlets referring to change ringing are not included. This list is not exhaustive, although I believe it is accurate up to 2000 for books published in Great Britain.

Allured, Donald E., *Handbell Composing and Arranging* (National Music Publishers, Tustin, California, USA, 1985)

Allured, Donald E., *Joyfully Ring*, Nashville (Broadman Press, Tennesse, USA, 1974), Revised edition published *c*.1990.

Allured, Donald E., *Mastering Musicianship in Handbells* (Broadman Press, Nashville, Tennesse, USA, 1992)

Allured, Donald E., *Musical Excellence in Handbells*, (Broadman Press, Nashville, Tennesse, USA, 1982)

Anderson, Christine D. and Kramlich, Daniel, *Songs for the Solo Ringer* (Agape, Carol Stream, Illinois, USA, 1987)

Barrett, Rosemary and Bullen, Nigel, *Handbell People* (Mayola Music, Clapham Village, Beds, 1983)

Bedford, Philip, *An Introduction to English Handbell Tune Ringing* (Handbell Ringers of Great Britain, Chelmsford, Essex, 1974)

Bradford, Elizabeth, *The First Quarter Century. A History of the American Guild of English Handbell Ringers, Inc.* (American Guild of English Handbell Ringers Inc., Wilmington, Delaware, USA, 1979)

Calkins, Debra, *A Musical Handbook for Ensemble Ringing* (National Music Publishers, 1984)

Carnall, R., *Codnor Handbell Founders* (R. Carnall, Codnor, Derbys, n.d. [*c*.1980])

Couper, Alinda B., *Rhythmic Exercises for Handbell Ringing* (Harold Flammer Inc., Delaware, Pennsylvania, USA, 1966)

Crabtree, A.J., *Music for Handbells and Church Bells* (A.J. Crabtree, Beeston, Notts, 1979)

De Salis, D.M., *William Hartley Achievement Award Handbook* (n.p., Handbell Ringers of Great Britain, 1987)

Fletcher, C.W., *Handbell Ringing* (J. Curwen & Sons, *c*.1888)

Gordon, William, *A Treatise on Musical Hand-Bell Ringing* (W. Gordon, Stockport, 1885). "shewing 'How to Read' and 'How to Ring'."

Gordon, William, *The Handbell Ringers' Journal* (W. Gordon, Stockport, 1882). This consisted of monthly issues of music, 'arranged for medium peals' and costing 12s. per annum.

Gordon, William, *The Handbell Gamut* (W. Gordon, Stockport, 1882). This was an introduction to the art of ringing by music—notation, timing, scales, etc., fully explained and illustrated. It cost nine and a half pence, post free.

Goslin, S[amuel], *The ABC of Musical Handbell Ringing* (J. Warner & Sons, 1879). The alternative title was *The Hand-bell Ringers' Instructor, Part I*. A thousand copies were originally printed, with a second thousand in 1879 and a third in 1887.

Goslin, Samuel B., *The Musical Handbell Ringer's Instructor Part II* (J. Warner & Sons, 1880)

Goslin, Samuel B., *The Musical Handbell Ringers' Instructor* (J. Warner & Sons, 1891). This was an enlarged edition of *The Musical Handbell Ringer's Instructor Part II*.

Goslin, Samuel B., edited by Hannon, James J., *The ABC of Musical Handbell Ringing* (J.J. Hannon, Oxford,

1974). Hannon reprinted Goslin's books of 1879 and 1891 in facsimile in 1974 under the title of *The ABC of Musical Hand-bell Ringing*. Intermixed with Goslin's arrangements, he included six additional pages of tunes arranged by S.M. Bateman.

Griffin, William H. and others, *Handbell Notation and Grading System* (American Guild of English Handbell Ringers Inc., Dayton, Ohio, USA, 1995)

Haley, William, *The Bell Hymn Book* (J. Warner & Sons, 1889). Sub-titled *A Manual for Church Bell & Hand Bell Ringers*.

Haley, William, *Twelve Carols* (J. Warner & Sons, 1891)

Haley, William, *Twelve Popular Airs* (J. Warner & Sons, 1891)

Haley, William, *The Handbell Tutor, With Tunes for 8 or 10 Bells* (J. Warner & Sons, 1899)

Handbell Ringers of Great Britain, *Rainbow Booklet No 1—Handbells: Facts and Information* (Handbell Ringers of Great Britain, n.p., 1987)

Handbell Ringers of Great Britain, *Rainbow Booklet No 2—Starting a Handbell Team* (Handbell Ringers of Great Britain, n.p., 1987)

Handbell Ringers of Great Britain, *Rainbow Booklet no 3—Arranging the Music* (Handbell Ringers of Great Britain, n.p., 1987)

Handbell Ringers of Great Britain, *Rainbow Booklet No 4—Writing Out the Music* (Handbell Ringers of Great Britain, n.p., 1987)

Handbell Ringers of Great Britain, *Rainbow Booklet No 5—We Want More Bells—But Which?* (Handbell Ringers of Great Britain, n.p., 1987)

Handbell Ringers of Great Britain, *Rainbow Booklet No 6—The Performing Handbell Team* (Handbell Ringers of Great Britain, n.p., 1987)

Hughes, Albert A., *English Handbell Casting at the Whitechapel Bell Foundry* (Whitechapel Bell Foundry, n.d., c.1960). A second edition was produced in 1962.

Ivey, Robert, *Handbell Assignment Book* (Agape, Carol Stream, Illinois, USA, 1993)

Ivey, Robert, *Handbell Ringing—Learning, Teaching, Performing* (Agape, Carol Stream, Illinois, USA, 1995)

Jennings, Trevor S., *Handbells* (Shire Publications Ltd., Shire Album 241, Princes Risborough, 1989)

Kastner, Michael and McChesney, Kevin, *Solo Ringing! Musically* (Jeffers Handbell Supply Inc., Irmo, South Carolina, USA, 1994)

Keller, Michael R., *Developing Coordination Skills* (American Guild of English Handbell Ringers, Inc, Dayton, Ohio, USA, n.d.)

Keller, Michael R., *Developing More Advanced Coordination and Technical Skills* (American Guild of English Handbell Ringers, Inc., Dayton, Ohio, USA, 1996)

Lazenby, Christine and Francis, George, *Handbell Tune Ringing—A Beginner's Guide* (Handbell Ringers of Great Britain, n.p., 1981)

Lorenz, Ellen Jane, *Handbell Ringing in Church* (Lorenz Publishing Co., Dayton, Ohio, USA, 1963)

McKechnie, D. Linda, *Ringing for the First Time (Ringer's Edition)* (Harold Flammer Inc., Delaware Water Gap, Pennsylvania, USA, 1987)

McKechnie, D. Linda, *Ringing for the First Time (Director's Supplement)* (Harold Flammer Inc., Delaware Water Gap, Pennsylvania, USA, 1987)

Merrett, Fred A., *The Art of Rapid Ringing* (Jeffers Handbell Supply Inc., Irmo, South Carolina, USA, 1990)

Parry, Scott B., *The Story of Handbells* (Whittemore Associates, Boston, Mass, USA, 1957)

Parry, Scott B., *Handbell Ringing, A Musical Introduction* (Carl Fischer, New York, USA, 1961)

Powell, Nancy, *Impossible Ringing Made Possible* (Agape, Carol Stream, Illinois, USA, 1985)

Ratcliffe, Guy, *The Handbell Book* (Mayola Music, Bedford, 1997)

Ratcliffe, Guy, *The Ringer's Book* (Mayola Music, Bedford, 1997)

Rosene, Paul E., *Making Music with Choirchime Instruments* (Agape, Carol Stream, Illinois, USA, 1984)

Salzwedel, James V., *A Basic Approach to Handbell Ringing* (Hussite Bell Ringers Inc., Winston-Salem, North Carolina, USA, 1974)

Scholefield, Daniel, *The HandBell Ringers Tune Book* (D. Scholefield, Huddersfield, n.d., *c*.1852) This was printed by Daniel Scholefield, the conductor of the Huddersfield Hand Bell band, at his employer's firm. The music is written utilising letters from a to t.

Shaw, Fred [editor], *Handbell Ringers' Musical Journal* (1884?). Fred Shaw was a member of the renowned Shelley Handbell Ringers, who were twice 'medalled off' at the Belle Vue concerts: i.e they won the first prize three years in succession and were barred from taking part the following year. He advertised this monthly issue of classical and light music in December 1883 (*Bell News*, Vol.II, No.91, p.446), but it is unlikely it was ever issued.

Thompson, Martha Lyn, *Bell, Book and Ringer* (Harold Flammer Inc., Delaware Water Gap, Pennsylvania, USA, 1982)

Thompson, Martha Lynn, *Handbell Helper* (Abingdon Press, Nashville, USA, 1996)

Tufts, Nancy Poore, *The Art of Handbell Ringing* (Abingdon Press, New York & Nashville, USA, 1961)

Tufts, Nancy Poore, *The Art of Handbell Ringing* (Herbert Jenkins, London, 1961)

Tufts, Nancy Poore, *The Bell Ringer's Handbook* (Harold Flammer-Shawnee Press, New York, USA, 1965)

Tufts, Nancy Poore, *The Art of Handbell Ringing* (Nashville, Tennesse, USA, Revised edition, 1973)

Turner, John Maurice, *The Art & Science of Hand Bell Ringing* (The Bookshop, Tiverton, Exeter n.d., *c*.1950) Originally published in *The Musical Times*, July 1933

van Valey, Janet and Berry, Susan, *Using Handchimes* (Lorenz Publishing Co., Dayton, Ohio, USA, 1990)

van Valey, Janet and Berry, Susan, *Director's Manual* (Lorenz Publishing Co., Dayton, Ohio, USA, 1988)

Wagner, Douglas E., *Scoring for English Handbells* (Agape, Carol Stream, Illinois, USA, 1985)

Wall, Martha and Petker, Allan Robert, *Handbell Questions and Answers* (Pavane Publishing, n.p., n.d.)

Watson, Doris, *The Handbell Choir* (The H.W. Gray Co. Inc., New York, USA, 1959)

Whitechapel Bell Foundry, Ltd., *The Maintenance of Whitechapel Handbells* (Whitechapel Bell Foundry Ltd., 1996)

Wilson, Lysbeth, *Arranging Handbell Music for Beginners* (Handbell Ringers of Great Britain, n.p., 1983)

Wilson, Wilfred and Jones, Tracy, *The Joy of Belleplates* (CPP/Belwin Inc., Miami, Florida, USA, 1992)

Winter, Sandra, *Belleplate Basics* [Aardvark Music, Croydon, n.d., 1997]

Winter, Sandra, *The Aardvark Starter Kit* [Aardvark Music, Croydon, n.d., 1997]

Index

References which relate to illustrations only are given in **bold**.

NOTES

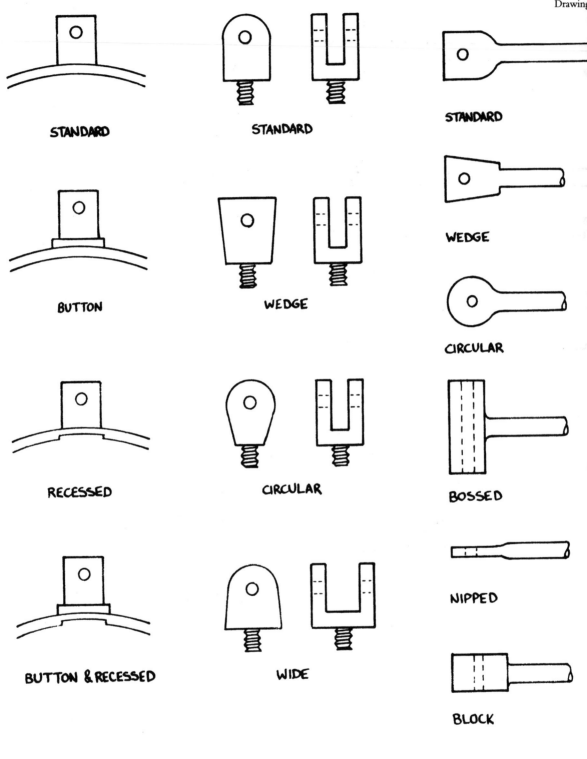

STANDARD

STANDARD

STANDARD

BUTTON

WEDGE

WEDGE

RECESSED

CIRCULAR

CIRCULAR

BOSSED

BUTTON & RECESSED

WIDE

NIPPED

BLOCK

BELL CROWNS

STAPLES

STAPLE ENDS